# STAN
## THE MAN

*The Life and Times
of Stan Musial*

Wayne Stewart

## TRIUMPH
BOOKS

Triumph Books and colophon are registered trademarks of Random House, Inc.

Library of Congress Cataloging-in-Publication Data

Stewart, Wayne.
  Stan the Man : the life and times of Stan Musial / Wayne stewart.
     p. cm.
  Includes bibliographical references.
  ISBN-13: 978-1-60078-322-7
  ISBN-10: 1-60078-322-8
  1. Musial, Stan, 1920– 2. Baseball players—United States—Biography.
  3. St. Louis Cardinals (Baseball team)—History. I. Title.
  GV865.M8S74 2010
  796.357092—dc22
  [B]
                              2010004003

This book is available in quantity at special discounts for your group or organization. For further information, contact:

**Triumph Books**
542 South Dearborn Street
Suite 750
Chicago, Illinois 60605
(312) 939-3330
Fax (312) 663-3557
www.triumphbooks.com

Printed in U.S.A.
ISBN: 978-1-60078-322-7
Design by Patricia Frey

*To Nancy, Scott, Sean, Rachel, and Nathan. Also to the memory of my father, O.J. (who taught me to love words) and his brother Dale, who, along with my dad, chased Stan off a sandlot, saying he wasn't good enough to play ball with the big boys. And to my mother, Margaret (Jones) Stewart, who taught me to love books, and to my uncle Bobby Jones, a big Musial fan.*

# Contents

# Acknowledgments

Thanks to the Donora Public Library, especially Beth Vaccaro, Dennis Lomax, Judy Thomas, and Donnis Headley, and to the library staff of Lorain, Ohio, particularly Julie Marchand and Sandee Ruth. Likewise, a big thanks to Brian Charlton and the Donora Historical Society.

Much of the new, fresh material on Musial came from people I interviewed over the past three years, so a huge thank you goes out to those who cooperated. Thanks are also due to several people who contributed their thoughts and memories but, due to space limitations, did not get quoted in the book.

Here, then, in no particular order, is the list of the people I have interviewed and/or those who have helped on this project:

Hank Aaron, Carl Erskine, Joe Cunningham, Dick Groat, Ray Bradley, Carl Warwick, Ed Musial, Steve Russell, Monte Labash, Angela Labash, Nancy Rumora, Joe Barbao Jr., Ken Barbao, Bobby Del Greco, Dale Stewart, Laurel Grimes, Betty Hendrickson, Stan Isaacs, Dr. Louis Ferretti, Ernie Harwell, Emil Badzik, Jeff Francoeur, Art Galiffa, Minor Hawk, Ignatius Hokaj Jr., Dorothy Kovacik, Stu Miller, Charlie Manuel, Solly Hemus, Joe Kostolansky Jr., Emma Jene Lelik, Charlie James, John Lignelli, Earl Gipin, Ted Musial, George Shuba, Bill Virdon, Ross Farmer, Rose Cousino, Paul Zolak, Don DeVore, Bob Skinner, Joe Patch, Larry Ludwig, Marty Marion, Hugh Forsyth, Jean Morton, Paul Barna, Hal Smith, Mark Gorsak, Loretta Manus, Chet Suski, Abe Barczuk, Roy McHugh, Bimbo Cecconi, Richard Bucchianeri, Vance Bunardzya, Frances Delsandro, Helen and Robert Jones, Todd Ririe, Bill and Goldie Rank, Ron Nagy, Bob Friend, Elroy Face, Helen McCulloch, Greg Oslowski, Ed Pado, Dave Sarkus, Ron

Necciai, Chuck Smith, Joe Ravasio, Martha Muniz, Alex Grammas, Dr. Charles Stacey, Mark Weinstein, Vernon Law, Jean Pansino, Speer Ruey, Wallace Zielinski, Bill Polachek, Michael E. Kelley, Michael J. Kelley, John Benyo Jr., Bill Oslowski, Chris Ercius Elliott, Jim O'Brien, Bobby Bragan, John Kuenster, Bobby Cox, Wally Westlake, Rudy Andabaker, Linda Ruth Tosetti, Casey Blake, Ken Griffey Jr., George F. Will, Dick Pole, Susan Naylor, Jimy Williams, Don Miller, Ulice Payne, Ed P. Sukel, Sally O'Leary, Adam Motin, Tom Bast, Jim Collins, and two sources who wish to remain anonymous.

Finally, a big thanks to my wife, Nancy, for proofreading, deftly catching some errors, and making suggestions concerning my manuscript.

# Introduction

Stan Musial may be the most well-liked, respected, and venerated superstar in the annals of the game. In 1998 *The Sporting News* ranked Musial the 10th-greatest baseball player ever, but the men who topped him statistically trail him in the categories of class and character.

For example, Babe Ruth—No. 1 on the list—was far from being the most moral of men. Willie Mays (No. 2), Ty Cobb (No. 3), Ted Williams (No. 8), and Rogers Hornsby (No. 9) were capable, in varying degrees, of surliness and incivility. Cobb, the self-proclaimed "snarling wildcat," was guilty of bellicose behavior bordering on the sociopathic.

Musial lacked the volatility and egotism of many superstars. From childhood, he exuded a *joie de vivre* even while growing up during the Depression. He has maintained that buoyant attitude all through his life.

Musial's blend of prowess and personality was such that even Cobb graciously stated, "No man has ever been a perfect ballplayer. Stan Musial, however, is the closest thing to perfection in the game today." He glaringly stood out, looming high above the vast majority of his peers—a klieg light among 40- and 60-watt bulbs.

Sportswriters arranged for Carl Mose to sculpt a bronze statue of Musial, a man endorsed universally as a great guy. Upon the pedestal was the following inscription, penned by former sportswriter and baseball commissioner Ford Frick:

HERE STANDS BASEBALL'S PERFECT WARRIOR.
HERE STANDS BASEBALL'S PERFECT KNIGHT.

This man, who came from a modest background, the son of immigrants, rose to become the type of ballplayer and man who not only mingled with presidents but was in demand everywhere. Common men and CEOs alike clamored to meet Musial and shake his hand. Musial's office was festooned with pictures of famous men such as Bob Hope, John F. Kennedy, and Lyndon B. Johnson.

Even as he became more urbane, Musial's mannerisms remained homey and without affectation. When he spoke, his enthusiasm would bubble over, and he would pepper his responses to others' comments with "yeah, yeah, yeah." Mon Valley resident Steve Russell noted, "Those hands would always be going; he's very animated, and he's always smiling. In every picture of him, he always has a smile on, always has a smile. He even said it, 'When that camera's going, I smile.'"

The durable Musial began his baseball career as a pitcher and went on to incredible success as a hitter despite utilizing one of the game's most unorthodox stances ever. In his book, *The Sporting News Selects Baseball's Greatest Players*, Ron Smith states: "He had the menacing look of a cobra—crouched at the hips, legs close together in the back of the box with right heel elevated, bat cocked straight up, eyes peering over the right shoulder in a hypnotic search for a moving target."

Probably the most famous observation about his stance came from White Sox pitcher Ted Lyons, who commented famously, "Musial's batting stance looks like a small boy looking around a corner to see if the cops are coming."

Musial was far from being one-dimensional, though, hitting for average and power. Smith also commented, "Musial was not a Ruthian-type power hitter, but careless pitchers usually paid for their mistakes."

Longtime Dodgers broadcaster Vin Scully succinctly summed up the Musial magic. He said, "How good was Stan Musial? He was good enough to take your breath away."

Despite the litany of praise for his prowess, it's been said that his "greatest legacy might have been the goodwill he brought to a city and the game in general. His love for baseball was genuine; his rapport with the fans was enduring. Musial was living proof that an unyielding, take-no-prisoners intensity is not necessarily a prerequisite for success." As Stan Isaacs put it, "You didn't have to be foaming at the mouth to be a great competitor."

Musial had virtually no ego or any sense of self-importance, rare among the elite in any field. If, as Mark Twain wrote, "Work consists of whatever a body is obliged to do. Play consists of whatever a body is not obliged to do," then Musial never felt the onus of *working* at the big-league level.

Writers Lawrence Ritter and Donald Honig assert that "He went about his business, day in and day out, drilling line drives, winning ball games, never complaining, always smiling."

George F. Will visited Donora from time to time to see his grandfather, a Lutheran minister in town for some time. Will called Musial "an extraordinarily affable man. It was like he was Everyman, except, and this is what you have to keep in mind, no one gets to be that good in athletics by being a normal man. That is, beneath that preternatural affability, and beneath that genuine affection for the fans, there was a…flame burning."

Most people tend to agree with Marty Marion, who stated, "Stan was just a good ol' country boy…No, if you didn't like Stan, you didn't like anybody."

Once, when asked why he was so congenial, why a smile perpetually adorned his face, Musial replied, "Well, if you were me, wouldn't you be smiling?" And smile he did, from his days living in the shadows of United States Steel's smokestacks in Donora, Pennsylvania, to his glory days in St. Louis, Missouri, and eventually all the way to his enshrinement in Cooperstown, New York.

# *Prologue*

May 12, 1958. It is a time that has been portrayed as Panglossian. Envision it as a Rockwell painting, one done in broad, beautiful strokes from his Technicolor palette. It is a world where no real harm can come to the Theodore Cleavers of America.

Delve deeper and it is an environment capable of nurturing much darker deeds. Now we're talking a novel packed with Orwellian despair and ugliness. Five months prior, *Time* magazine exposed the horrific story of serial killer Ed Gein and disclosed how he would, among other atrocities, skin his victims in his "house of horrors." Author Robert Bloch and film director Alfred Hitchcock later developed this tale into the film *Psycho*.

The color barrier in baseball was broken 11 years earlier, but it was not shattered, and some vicious vestiges of racism in the national pastime go unabated. Still, baseball somehow manages to shove aside most of the world's tawdriness. In Chicago, Stan "the Man" Musial and his wife, Lil, having just taken the midnight train from St. Louis, settle in for a two-game set.

Stan doubles in the first contest and then turns to Terry Moore, a St. Louis coach, and says that, while he hopes for a victory in the series finale, being on the threshold of the 3,000-hit plateau, he also hopes to draw a walk every trip to the plate the next day. His desire is to "save the big one for St. Louis."

Moore informs St. Louis manager Fred Hutchinson of Musial's comment, and Hutchinson decides he will keep his star on the bench the following day. He telephones Stan with the news, adding that there is a possibility Musial will be called upon to pinch-hit, but only in a clutch spot.

* * *

May 13, 1958. Morning.

Stan does not go to bed until almost 3:00 AM. He ordinarily requires at least eight hours of sleep. Today, a bit groggy, he showers and shaves and then, as he dresses, he grins, remembering he has the day off.

Stan and Lil leave their 11th-floor corner suite in the Knickerbocker Hotel. As usual, he is nattily attired, now in an immaculate black imported silk suit. Lil wears her gray suit, carries her mink stole, and glances approvingly at her man.

The hotel's doorman flags a taxi. Stan tells the cabbie he's headed to "the old apple orchard." Sensing confusion in the driver, Musial smiles and translates, "The old ball yard. Wrigley Field," and it's off to the game.

At the park, Musial disrobes and heads for the trainer's room for the usual rubdown of his legs. Shortly after suiting up, the affable Musial nods his okay to the photographers and he is engulfed by the media, time for the typical staged shots and a string of mundane questions.

Some fans avoid the game (fewer than 6,000 will show up), disappointed at having heard that Musial is sitting out the getaway-day contest. Hutchinson reiterates that he will try not to use Musial.

* * *

May 13, 1958. Afternoon.

Prior to the start of the game, Musial makes his way to the bullpen and is interrupted by a bevy of autograph seekers. That task complete, it is finally time to relax and soak up some of the sun's rays, which gently illuminate beautiful Wrigley Field.

* * *

May 13, 1958. Late afternoon, under clear skies.

The Cardinals are down 3–1 with one out in the sixth. Now, with light-hitting pitcher Sam Jones due to bat, Hutchinson feels he has to go to his bench and use his star in this spot.

He signals to the bullpen. Boots Hollingsworth, a Cardinals coach, spots his manager's sign, turns to Musial, and says, "Hey, Stan. Hutch wants you." Musial walks toward the dugout to select his bat, while the meager crowd stares in anticipation, their applause beginning to soar.

The PA announcer speaks slowly and distinctly. "Attention. No. 6. Stan Musial. Batting for Sam Jones." Not yet sporting his normal deep-bronze tan, Musial strolls into the batter's box with an air of easy confidence but with no trace of swagger. His 2,999 career hits, many of which left vapor trails in their wake, bolster his calm demeanor.

Now Musial's eyes gaze intently out at pitcher Moe Drabowsky. He assumes his famous, albeit odd, stance. A breeze rustles the ivy on the outfield wall. Gene Green, who doubled moments ago, hedges off second base.

The time is 3:06 PM. Drabowsky comes to the belt. The two-ball, two-strike pitch comes in—a curve. The ball is above-the-belt high and just a bit outside, tantalizingly so for a man with superb bat control. Musial, though briefly fooled, adjusts almost instantly. His bat, an extension of those skilled, thickly calloused hands, flicks. The ball sails past the third-base line and rolls deep into Wrigley Field's left-field corner. Musial cruises into second with a stand-up double. A broad grin adorns his face. In the broadcasters' booth Harry Caray intones, "Holy cow, he came through!"

Third-base umpire Frank Dascoli becomes a fan and chugs across the field to present Musial with the ball.

Hutchinson charges onto the field with all the zeal of a defensive end, eight photographers in his wake. Hutch congratulates Musial and then apologizes, "I know you wanted to do it in St. Louis, but I needed you today." A brief ceremony ensues, and the game resumes with pinch-runner Frank Barnes, normally a pitcher, trotting out to replace the Man.

Stan ambles off the field, bat in hand; stops to kiss Lil, who is sitting in the box seats near the visitors' dugout; then disappears from view. He makes his way up the wooden steps to the clubhouse and addresses the media once again. A writer asks if he knows the woman he has just kissed. "I'd better." He flashes a smile. Then, with Henny Youngman-like timing, he adds, "That's my wife."

Then, even with some meaningful baseball history to discuss, Stan can't help indulging in a touch of baseball irreverence. He tosses out a typically understated Musial line. "You wouldn't think that a little bat and a little ball could make such a commotion," he beams.

It is a defining moment, yet another italicized line for the illustrious curriculum vitae of Stan "the Man" Musial.

* * *

It is a world devoid of the Internet and years removed from the era of instant news coverage. ESPN is an inconceivable enterprise. Still, many hometown friends quickly learn about Stan's 3,000[th] hit on KDKA radio via the 6:00 news or from colorful Pirates announcer Bob Prince. However, a few acquaintances back home wait nearly 24 hours to learn of Musial's milestone because life really is, or certainly seems, slower, more leisurely than today's world; the need to know everything instantly is not imperative. It is okay to wait patiently for the newspaper boy to deliver the *Herald-American* or the *Pittsburgh Press* to the doorstep.

The townsfolk of Donora, Pennsylvania, relish the exploits of their "Man." The vicarious joy of knowing "our guy" has done it again is palpable. Sure, he already had seven batting titles under his 32-inch belt, but now it is official, almost if the Pope himself has stamped his imprimatur on the subject. This boy from a small steel mill town has joined the Honus Wagners and Paul Waners of the game. Membership to the 3,000-hit club accomplished, the Hall of Fame begins to beckon for the Man.

Life is good.

# CHAPTER ONE

# Stan "the Boy" Musial

Long before he was Stan the Man, he was Stanislaus Frank Musial, the boy. To use a steel metaphor, which is fitting since he was born in a steel town, he was a blast-furnace product composed of a mixture of three ingredients: environment, heredity, and his times.

Musial's hometown of Donora, nestled in the Monongahela Valley in western Pennsylvania, is a very rugged Rust Belt town populated by equally rugged men. The town sits in Washington County, named after the man who surveyed it, George Washington.

By the time Musial was born, there were 350 coal mines and more than 30 steel mills in the Pittsburgh vicinity. Donora hosted a coal mine and the thriving United States Steel's American Steel and Wire Company, which perched near the Monongahela River. The Monongahela curls around Donora on its way to rendezvous with the Allegheny River.

From the river's horseshoe curve, the streets of town sloped upward, and many of the houses squatted at precipitous angles to those streets. In icy and snowy weather, cars strained and groaned up the myriad steep hills, desperately seeking a toehold. Meanwhile, children streaked down the same streets, almost sans friction, in a sled rider's paradise. Longjohns were de rigueur, sometimes for sleepwear, and even women and children became adept at banking their coal furnaces at night.

Nicknamed "the Home of Champions," the town has always loved sports and been a veritable hotbed of athleticism. Donora has also been home to a variety of nationalities. In the past, each ethnic group was steadfastly proud of its accolades—its Polish toughness or its Italian grit or its Slovenian strength.

Stan's Polish heritage was indeed a point of pride. "Very much so," agreed Donora native Ted Musial (unrelated to Stan). "He liked to be called 'Stash.' In Polish, that's *Stanley*."

Donoran Wallace Zielinski said, "All of the ethnic groups that came at the turn of the century more or less stuck with themselves—they went to their own churches, they went to their own clubs. They went there and they spoke their language. The churches had their priests that came from the same country and would speak their sermons in their language. When I was an altar boy, the priests would speak the sermon in Polish and in English—we would be there forever."

John Benyo Jr. of Donora said his grandfather, John Danek, whose native tongue was Polish, worked in the mill, where he gained the nickname "Manzanas," (meaning *apples*) from his Spanish coworkers because he always packed an apple in his lunch pail. "I can remember walking uptown with him and hearing, 'Hey, Manzanas, como esta?' My grandfather could actually speak better Spanish than he could English. Those guys worked together in the mill—they spoke Polish, they spoke Spanish, they spoke a little bit of Italian. Enough just to get by, so you could understand each other. And what got me was black people speaking Polish."

Joe Barbao Jr., whose father once coached Musial, stated, "You had so many different dialects in Donora and you got to understand different languages just listening to [fellow natives]. The first thing you know, you start talking like them, emulating them a little bit.

"If you went down to the Sons of Italy, you heard nothing but Italian; if you went to the Spanish Club, you heard nothing but Spanish; you went to the Polish Club, it was the same thing. It was a big melting pot there." Even into the 1960s, polka music was still standard Sunday fare on local radio stations, and some programming was carried out entirely in a foreign language, such as Polish.

Western Pennsylvania dialect, or "Pittsburghese," was quite distinctive anyway. Speech pathologist Speer Ruey said it entails an "unusual manner of speech, a manifestation of all the different ethnic dialects intermixed. If you listen to Dan Marino [of the Pittsburgh area] talk, it's almost like street talk. Instead of saying, 'that's,' it becomes ''ats' [clipped off]; 'this and that' becomes ''is anat,' and sometimes it's like a little bit of a drawl. It's a unique dialect." Further, said Ruey, the Mon Valley's dialect differs from others partly due to the many ethnic groups that settled there.

Once, when Ruey was tending bar part-time in Donora, Musial dropped by, speaking in his distinctive manner. "He comes up to the bar, shakes my hand, and he goes, 'Whaddya' say, whaddya' say? How-ya-doing, how-ya-doing? Stan Musial. Whaddya' say?' It sounded like, 'Come-on-babe, come-on-babe,' just like when we were chattering as kids on a baseball field."

Although the population of Donora topped out at around 15,000, it was often closer to 10,000. Today, that number continues to dwindle and is down to roughly 5,000 inhabitants. Still, the small town churned out an inordinate amount of great athletes with assembly-line precision and regularity. Yes, the hillsides were barren due to the mill's pollutants, but the town itself was fruitful, producing enough athletes to stuff a cornucopia to capacity.

Their 1945 football team was selected as the greatest in the history of Western Pennsylvania in a poll of coaches and sportswriters. They posted a perfect 10–0 record and outscored their opposition 297–13. The '45 team featured "Deacon" Dan Towler, who went on to lead the National Football League in rushing in 1952 as a member of the Los Angeles Rams.

In his senior year in Ringgold High School, Donoran Ulice Payne's basketball team made it to the state tournament semifinals with him leading the squad in scoring, despite the presence of a very talented teammate, Monongahela product Joe Montana. Payne was later a member of the 1977 NCAA champion Marquette Warriors team under Coach Al McGuire. In 2002 he became baseball's first African American president of a big-league team, the Brewers.

The list of local stars goes on. Three of them were bona fide baseball stars in the majors: Musial, Ken Griffey Sr., and Ken Griffey Jr. That trio had, through 2009, combined for 1,257 big-league homers. Another Donoran, Steve Filipowicz, also enjoyed a brief stint in the majors.

Donora was such a sports factory that Griffey Sr., once among the fastest players in the majors, stated that there were probably three or four athletes at Donora High circa the late 1960s who were faster than him.

One time Musial made it a point to meet with and tease Griffey Jr., telling him he was "the second-best left-handed-hitting, left-handed-throwing outfielder ever born in Donora, Pennsylvania, on November 21."

Baseball writer and analyst Bill James summed up what he perceived to be an Achilles-like phenomenon, stating, "My son is a ballplayer; I'm thinking of taking him to be washed in the waters of Donora."

Musial's nephew, Ron Nagy, said he couldn't pick Musial as the best athlete to come out of Donora High. "He'd rank up in the top five. I'm not going to say he's the greatest, only because there were guys who played three or four sports." Griffey Sr. was one such player, and he still holds school records for the most points in a single basketball game (40) and for a career (925) as well as the most rebounds for a game (27) and for a season (307).

In addition to environment—being from Donora, a place seemingly gifted with a magical athleticism—heredity came into play for Stan Musial, beginning with his father, Lukasz. He came from Galicia, a province of what was then known as Austria-Hungary but is now simply called Poland. While Austria is officially listed as Lukasz's place of birth in the United States census, his descent is clearly Polish. He was one of a slew of Poles who endured hardship, came to the United States in a wave of Polish immigrants some 1.5 million strong, and settled in the new country to raise a family. In 1902 there were just 139 Polish residents in Donora; that number bulged to 722 by 1910.

Most Poles found work in American mines, steel mills, and slaughter-houses, taking jobs where they could make money quickly. This often meant taking odious, perilous work. Although most of the immigrants had been farmers, accustomed to rural areas, in the United States they gravitated to towns and cities, hungry for work in this country that was in the midst of the industrial age.

One Polish immigrant commented, "I came to America because I heard the streets were paved with gold. When I got here, I found out three things: First, the streets weren't paved with gold. Second, they weren't paved at all. Third, I was expected to pave them."

The year was 1910. Oceanographer Jacques Cousteau was born; author Mark Twain died. The town of Monessen, Pennsylvania, which sits across the Monongahela River from Donora, at a distance of about five strong throws from a big-league outfielder, established a new speed limit for auto-mobiles in town, 12 miles per hour. The population of Donora was growing rapidly, reaching a total of 8,174 residents.

Across a vast ocean, the young, blond-haired Lukasz Musial began his bold venture. After saying farewell to family and friends, he made his way to Hamburg, Germany; located the waterfront; and, before long, found his ship and hiked up its long gangplank. The first and shortest leg of his trip was over. He was aboard the *President Grant*, heading for the United States.

From the ports of Germany, mighty steamships carried travelers and cargo via the North Sea, through the English Channel, and then across the Northern Atlantic Ocean. The journey had been known to last as long as three weeks for some, but by the time Lukasz made the voyage, he sailed for just six days.

Passengers such as Lukasz, who could afford only the cheapest ticket, were still charged what seemed like a small fortune to them, approximately $25. Such voyagers traveled in third class, if lucky, or in steerage at the bottom of the ship, where they were forced to listen to the incessant pounding of the ship's steering machinery.

Typically, the shipping companies, eager to milk as much profit as they could from each trip, crammed many more passengers into those areas than they had room for. It was not uncommon for travelers to sleep four to a bunk in quarters that were, as one passenger put it, "dark, dank, [and] odor-filled." It mattered little to the companies that housing people in such a fashion violated laws. Furthermore, the human cargo was given inadequate food and had to stave off diseases, seasickness, and dehydration while coping with insubstantial bathroom facilities.

The final destination, Ellis Island in New York Harbor, was a glorious sight for Lukasz. Still, because some—about two percent—of the new arrivals were turned back, Ellis Island was known by a not-so-pleasant nickname, "the Island of Tears."

Emerging from the depths of the ship, Lukasz stared in wonder at the imposing New York skyline. His cool, gray eyes took in the drab January sky, but he felt no sense of gloom. This would be his gateway to a marvelous new country.

Lukasz, just 19 years old, had made his way on what newspaper cartoons called "the European garbage ships" and, after being examined for diseases such as trachoma, he made his way to the Great Hall (aka the Registry Room) on the second floor. There, in the cavernous room, filled with the noise of dozens of voices speaking myriad languages, the inspectors allowed this rather timorous, slight man to pass. No tears for Lukasz, just relief.

Lukasz's stay in New York was brief, so he had little time to be in awe of the behemoth of a city. He had to hop a train headed for Pennsylvania right away, drawn to the Mon Valley by plentiful jobs. Lukasz settled in Donora, the town where he would soon meet his future wife, Mary Lancos.

Mary was born in 1896 in a New York coal-mining town, to a family with Czeckoslovakian roots. Her parents, immigrants from Austria, raised a family of nine children, moving to Donora when Mary was a child.

Mary had been helping her family earn money since she was eight, working then as a house cleaner. She said of her impoverished youth, "Even when I was real little, I picked coal on the railroad tracks to keep us warm."

Unafraid of work, each morning Mary walked with her father down to the shores of the Monongahela and rowed her father to the other side. There, he would trudge four miles to his workplace, the Ella coal mine, where he worked a 12-hour shift beneath the earth for seven and a half cents an hour. Mary would row home, and the process would be repeated when her father got off work each evening.

Mary grew up to become tall (around 5'8"), strong, and spry, and wound up taking a job in the steel mill while still in her teens. There she first saw her husband-to-be. "I went to work sorting nails in the nail mill. I was a big girl, and nobody asked me how old I was. By the time I was 16, I was forelady of the nail room, and we worked long hours, believe me."

Stan would not only come to share his mother's good humor, but, said Joe Kostolansky Jr., the son of a Musial neighbor, "He had much of her mannerisms, and from the facial appearance you could tell that he was her son—they were look-alikes there."

As a 14-year-old, Mary attended a dance in town, and it was there that she met Lukasz. While her native language was English, he had yet to learn the language. That didn't matter. They were attracted to each other. Plus, Mary had picked up enough of his language from Polish girls she worked with to get by.

The small—slightly over five feet and 150 pounds—but muscular Lukasz, six years her elder, was already a veteran of the steel mills. His job, one of many he held, required him to hoist products, such as 100-pound bundles of wire, and load them onto freight cars, straining away day after day in the shipping department of the American Steel and Wire Company. For his toil he earned $44 per month (and he would never gross more than $4 per day).

On April 14, 1913, Lukasz, almost 23 years old, and Mary, just 16 years of age, were married in Donora. She apparently lied to officials about her age, listed on the wedding certificate as 21. Their first child came later that year, and Lukasz, his English steadily improving, became a naturalized United States citizen the following year. Still, being more comfortable with his native tongue, he would communicate with his children in Polish, and he could still neither read nor write in English. Ed Pado stated, "In those days, ethnic families would speak their [native tongue] at home" even though some spoke English quite well.

On November 21, 1920, Lukasz's firstborn son came along. His given name was Stanislaus, but Lukasz came to call him by the nickname Stashu, which was shortened to Stash, the name all of his friends growing up came to use.

He was born on Sixth Street and spent his early years at 465 Sixth St. Four girls preceded Stan in the family—Ida, Victoria, Helen, and Rose—but Lukasz had always wanted a son. Another boy, Ed, better known as "Honey," followed Stan in 1922.

Mon Valley resident Richard Bucchianeri said Honey and Stan "looked very much alike." Barbao Jr. added, "Honey was fun-loving and always laughing. Like Stan, he had an infectious laugh."

Honey has also been described as somewhat shy and diffident. Donoran Art Galiffa said Honey "didn't hang around with those guys [Stan's athletic friends]. It seemed like he was always by himself."

Former Pirates pitcher and Mon Valley resident Ron Necciai said, "Eddie didn't have the ability and couldn't play as good as Stan Musial. There's no question about it. He wasn't as big, wasn't as tall, he couldn't hit the ball as good. He was a pretty fair country player, but he wasn't of that caliber, [just] a pretty fair amateur. He [was] a pretty good minor-league ballplayer, but I don't think he was in anywhere near Stan's class. Not many people [were] in his class."

Ray Bradley, who graduated with Stan, critiqued Honey, saying, "He was a good ballplayer but not exceptional. I don't think he was that great a hitter. Somebody told me he couldn't hit a curve ball [well]." Galiffa said, "He tried real hard, but it seemed like he didn't mature [as a player]. He didn't make it."

In many ways, Honey *did* make it. In high school, he starred in both baseball and football. He was, according to his son Ed, "probably a better baseball player than a lot of people realize."

He was talented enough to play professional baseball and hit as high as .334 in Fayetteville in 1946. He finished in 1950 after he hit .283 for three teams in Class B and D. Overall, in 449 minor-league contests, he hit .304. He passed away in 2003 at the age of 81 after suffering from lung cancer.

Necciai called Honey a "very amicable, good, friendly guy. Nice guy." Necciai did not believe Honey felt he was constantly in his brother's shadow. Necciai said, "I don't feel, from my time playing ball with him, that he had any animosity. I always thought he was vastly proud of his brother and happy." Dr. Louis Ferretti of Donora concurred, saying, "He used to come down to our beer garden and [brag about], 'My boy, Stanley.'"

In any case, by the time Stan was born, Lukasz was a porter at a public hotel. He earned about $5.50 per week, so Mary continued working to help their family get by and held several jobs over the years, including one as a cook in a local restaurant. That work ethic would carry over to her children and would stick with her all of her days. In her late sixties, she woke up daily at 6:00 AM to begin her chores, which included baking and canning. At the age of 67, she was described in a *Pittsburgh Press* article as having "deeply tanned skin, snow-white hair, sharp brown eyes, and a quick laugh."

Stan was born in a year that was rife with baseball activity, including Ray Chapman's death the day after Carl Mays had beaned him in Major League Baseball's only fatality linked directly to play on the field.

The 17th World Series, packed with remarkable plays and events, had been completed not long before Musial's birth. Cleveland's second baseman, Bill Wambsganss, turned in the only unassisted triple play in World Series history and Elmer Smith hit the first grand slam in Series play. 1920 was also the year in which the floundering Cardinals were finally on their way to becoming a great franchise. It would be another 18 years, though, before the Cardinals would acquire Musial's talents.

The hardware it takes to hit a baseball at the game's highest level had been pretty much hardwired into Stan's brain from the cradle. Both of his parents had physical attributes that contributed to his athleticism, though he certainly didn't get his size from his father. Dr. Ferretti said, "Stash, physically, in size and mentally, was like his mother; she was husky. His father was a little runty."

When Stan was around eight years old, his family moved to his Grandma Lancos' frame house on Marelda Avenue, near Eleventh Street. This area was informally known as Polish Hill due, naturally, to the Polish neighborhood located there, a pocket of hard-working, God-fearing people. It was in his backyard that he first picked up a ball and bat. The Musials packed three adults and six children into a tiny five-room house, much like submariners, utilizing every square inch of their living quarters, which overlooked the mill's smokestacks. Back then, Stan had no inkling that the dark puffs of smoke he saw daily foreshadowed death in the family.

While they lived there, the Great Depression came on with a malevolent, omnipresent, suffocating force that put some 15 million people out of work and led to Hoovervilles—poverty-infested shantytowns for the homeless—springing up all over the country. On October 29, 1929, a day known as Black Tuesday, some 16 million shares of stocks were traded on Wall Street. Powerhouse company General Motors would, in just a few years, find its share price had dropped to a microscopic 8 percent of its value prior to the massive, juggernaut-like crash. When the stock market finally crashed with a resounding thud, Stan was approaching his ninth birthday. Earlier that year, the one-millionth Ford had rolled off the Detroit assembly line, but the already impoverished Musials got around on foot.

The year 1929 also featured *Amos and Andy* beginning its long radio run and Hollywood selecting *Wings* as the first film to cop an Oscar as the year's best movie. However, with money being tight, Stan didn't exactly while away his afternoons inside the town's Princess Theater. This was a time when many people's hourly wages—those fortunate enough to have money coming in—were measured in pennies, not dimes or dollars.

Many poor families saved by repairing their shoes, making rugs out of rags, and, in general, wasting very little. Many of them never owned a car but might splurge on a $10 one-tube Crosley radio set (or fashion their own crude ones).

Today there are more than 10,500 broadcast radio stations in the United States, but when Musial was a child, there were only 30. Luckily, he could listen to Pittsburgh's KDKA, a powerful station that was responsible for the first broadcast of a Major League Baseball game.

The Depression spawned popular songs, such as the somber-themed "Brother Can You Spare a Dime," which featured the gloomy lyrics, "Once I built a tower, up to the sun, brick and rivet, and lime; Once I built a tower, now it's done. Brother, can you spare a dime?" The composers of the era also poured out songs with lyrics whose function was that of amelioration, words meant to soothe the public, as exemplified by "Life Is Just a Bowl of Cherries" and the overly optimistic 1933 tune, "We're in the Money."

Growing up in Donora during the Depression was a mixed bag, said Joe Barbao Jr., who was born in 1929. "Life was good. There wasn't a lot of money. We thought we were okay. If you had a couple of nickels in your pocket you could buy a lot of candy. I think growing up there was great. Now, Little League teams have better fields than we had."

Dorothy Kovacik, a neighbor of the Musials, said she and many of the children her age were blithely oblivious to just how deleterious the Depression was to the economy and their lives. Families somehow provided the children with enough to eat. "We didn't have the best of everything, but my mother, for example, made a lot of soup and pasta. We got along. You make do."

Many Donora residents who were living a life of indigence, including the Musials, were able to "make do" only by accepting varying degrees of charity. Organizations such as the Red Cross helped matters by distributing items such as flour and other staples.

Mary stretched every cent the family possessed. She assigned her daughters the task of hauling coal into the house from a backyard pit, and she worked hard at various jobs to bring in a few extra dollars. For example, she was considered to be the best wallpaper-hanger in town.

Ray Bradley, a high school basketball teammate of Stan's, remembered that somehow, "He seemed to always dress fairly well because a lot of friends and teachers took care of him, made sure his family had things, because he was always a good kid. They didn't have a lot, but people made sure that he had food. Their house, up on the hill from the Zinc Works, was always clean. You would never know his family was so poor."

The Donora boosters group would pick up the tab several times a year for a meal for the basketball squad, and Musial ate heartily. A local Pole stated the meals he would eat at home "were extremely traditional. Many Polish families consumed a great deal of food such as cabbage and vinegar, radishes, potatoes, [and] pigs' feet." Children of the Depression did not tend to be fussy eaters.

Ray Bradley continued, "Anything [such as clothing and sports equipment] that [Stan] ever had looked good. I always thought he looked good. I don't know exactly where everything came from, but the Musials seemed to get along even though they didn't have that much money coming in."

Religion was also very important to Stan. "He was a good Catholic," said Ed Pado. "If he's still married, he must be a good Catholic," he laughed, acknowledging Stan's long marriage. Unlike many athletes who marry young due to insecurity or loneliness and then regret their rash move and go on to find a trophy wife, Stan has remained with Lil since the 1930s.

When Musial was young, there were four dioceses spread over western Pennsylvania with some 81 Roman Catholic churches. Many years later, when Musial would return to his hometown as a married man, he would sometimes attend St. Michael's, his wife's Byzantine Catholic church. Lil proudly showed off her famous husband to the congregation.

As an adult, he remained true to his faith, finding and attending a morning Mass even when in Cooperstown for induction weekends. Steve Russell, whose father played in the majors, said that Musial "never wore his religion on his sleeve. They were very religious, but you would never know it because they kept it very private."

When Stan was young, the Musials attended the Holy Name of the Blessed Virgin Mary Church, known to most as St. Mary's. It was founded in 1902 and moved in 1904 to Second Street, where it still stands, high on a hill peering down on the former site of the steel mill. Stan was baptized there and attended Polish and history classes there as well.

Abe Barczuk stated, "They used to teach Polish in the church school. He and I went to catechism together, and since most of the people in our church were Polish they used to have their schooling in Polish. Stan and I never learned Polish that good, so we used to go to the parish home, and Father Radzinski would teach certain guys in our [situation] about Catholicism [in English]."

For many Poles, Christmas customs were adhered to. As darkness set in on Christmas Eve a child was sent to look for the first visible star in the sky, an homage to the Star of Bethlehem." That done, the *Wigilia*, the most important meal of the year, could begin. The table, covered with straw or hay and then with a white tablecloth, was piled high with a bountiful, though meatless, array of foods.

Ed Stanley Musial, Stan's nephew, said that every year Mary Musial made "beautiful Easter eggs. She took [that talent] to the grave with her. They were paisley. She mixed food coloring with vegetable oil, and it made it real shiny. I don't even *know* that she made them because nobody actually saw her make them. You just kind of went up to the house, and they were there."

As a youngster, Stan attended public schools in town, including Castner Elementary School, Donora Junior High, and then Donora High School. Dr. Ferretti remembers seeing Musial, a natural lefty, being forced by a conformity-bent elementary teacher to write right-handed. Such "educational" constructs were rather commonly employed by teachers of that era despite ramifications— Musial said that into adulthood he would stammer when excited.

As a boy, Musial was active in the Polish Falcons of Nest 247. The Falcons subscribed to the maxim, "*W zdrowym ciele zdrowy duch*," or "Within a sound mind in a sound body." During Stan's youth, that organization was very big on sports in an era where neither pro football nor basketball captivated children as they do today. Professional football was so relatively insignificant that in 1925 the New York Giants franchise sold for a paltry $500.

Along with baseball, club sports such as soccer, gymnastics, and track and field held sway. One local commented, "The ethnic groups had their own clubs—the Germans had the Turners, the Slovaks and Italians had their clubs, the Poles had the Falcons, and on and on and on. The Falcons used to barnstorm all over the Northeast doing track and field and gymnastics."

Stan said he was encouraged by his father, who himself had been involved in "gymnastics and balancing on chairs," to participate in activities with the Polish Falcons. As early as the age of 10, Stan was a Junior Falcon and participated for about four years, excelling mostly in gymnastics. That involvement was, in fact, his first organized sporting experience. Through 2004 he was still a dues-paying member of the Donora Polish Falcons.

Musial said his time spent with the Falcons helped prepare him for baseball, building his strength and improving his coordination and timing. His involvement with the Falcons ended only when he began playing American Legion baseball. It was there, he recalled, that he got an early baseball thrill when he got his very first baseball uniform.

Robert Jones of Donora said that, "In the days before television, you had to find other means of enjoyment," and sports was a big part of that. The town featured what were somewhat organized football and fast–pitch-softball games. Jones continued, "There were no uniforms, maybe just T-shirts with the sponsors' names on them, but the games were popular, and they used to get pretty good crowds at Palmer Park [where a field would later be named for Musial], Legion Field [where he played his high school ball], and Americo Park [where he played some summer ball]." Team names included the 10th Street Tanners, the Castner Dragons, and an all-black team known as the Monarchs that Jones recalled as being "hot stuff; they were pretty good."

Musial's mother said that his first baseball equipment was nothing fancier than "a dime-store bat and ball when Stan was four." She added that while he was good at all sports, "he was crazy about baseball." She also provided her son with homemade baseballs frequently.

Stan's first exposure to the game of baseball came when he was around seven, playing a plethora of pickup games with boys from the neighborhood on a makeshift field. Joe Barbao Jr. stated, "Tom Heslep had a coal mine and there was a small field we used to play on [near the mine]. It wasn't manicured and it wasn't grass, just dirt." In Musial's autobiography, he wrote of how he quite often played baseball with older kids. He wrote that they tolerated him during their pickup games because he didn't "foul up their fun."

Apparently, not all the older boys felt that Musial didn't hamper their games. O.J. Stewart, eight years older than Musial, lived just a few blocks from him on Heslep Avenue. He remembered Musial approaching the older boys, relentlessly looking for a baseball game he could join, seeking his daily fix of baseball. Stewart yelled, "Go home, kid. You're not good enough to play with us." His brother, Dale Stewart Sr., added, "The little kid would mess our game up," and Musial was summarily chased away. Undaunted, and with boundless energy, he would move on, eventually finding a game where he would, little by little, hone his skills.

The Donora newspaper later reported, "While still a kid in knee pants, Stan was very seldom at home and nearly always could be found wearing a dilapidated baseball glove while cavorting about a diamond."

Rudy Andabaker, who played in the NFL and once coached football at Donora High, said that townsfolk "always said Musial carried a glove and a baseball going back and forth up Fifth Street, catching the ball even in the winter time. He was always like that." And Joe Barbao said the "baseball-hungry" Musial "would rather play baseball than eat."

Finding good equipment, though, was another matter. Barbao's son, Joe Jr., said he had heard the stories of Musial's mother making baseballs for him. "She stuffed it up with rags, then wet it down and put tape on it." It was not unlike another trick of the day. Joe Jr. recalled taking the core of a baseball after its cover had ripped off and taping it up "with black [electrician's] tape and [continuing] playing. It got heavier, but in those days that's just what you had to do."

Ed Pado added, "We played baseball with wrapped-up cloth with a stone or whatever we could get in it. My father was an electrician in the steel mill, and he could get all the [black electrician's] tape he wanted." He joked that unlike the title of a famous book about black players in the pre–Jackie Robinson days titled *Only the Ball Was White*, for many boys such as Pado and Musial, the ball was *black*...and sticky. He said, "We made it look like a baseball, but it weighed a ton—you got hit with one of those baseballs, you knew you got hit. If you hit it, it didn't go very far."

Sometimes, though, kids had a cheap way of getting better baseballs. They would wait beyond the left-field fence of a popular local diamond, pounce on home-run balls, and steal them. "The only way you got a new ball," laughed Barbao Jr., "was when a ball went over that fence and you grabbed it and ran like the devil."

As Musial grew older, he took part in other childhood activities. It's likely that he explored Heslep's coal mine—especially since it was so near to the spot where Musial played pickup games of baseball—a dangerous yet tempting place to venture for an adventurous boy.

Neighborhood children were, of course, warned of the perils that lurked there. Nancy Rumora, daughter of Joe Barbao, stated, "We were never allowed to go south of Marelda in the hills because of those mines." An area around Eighth Street was also verboten due to mines. "We weren't allowed in that [location] either, but we did [go there]."

Barbao Jr. said, "The mine was closed down, but every once in a while smoke would come up through crevices in the ground, and they [firemen] would flood it with water, as much water as they could to settle it down for a while, but it was still smoldering under there, just fermenting in there."

Keeping Stan, by this time a teenager, away from the area behind Marelda would have taken both manacles and leg irons, for that locale was flat and conducive for informal baseball games in the era where sandlot games dotted small towns all afternoon long throughout the long, sweltering summers. No handheld video baseball games for the boys of *those* summers.

After school the children in the neighborhood would gather for simple games such as Kick the Can. Kovacik recalled, "We had a big fence in our backyard, and all the boys from the hill would come back there and play baseball—and I was the tomboy—and whatever the boys were doing, that's where I was."

Pado remembered other typical pastimes for Donora youths. "We did high school pranks—nothing bad. We always found something to do. Anything we would make up to do, we'd do, but nothing mischievous.

"Nowadays I really think there's too much parental interference. Little League is great, but in those days we picked up our own sides, we set our own rules, and we found out the rules and regulations from our bigger brothers."

Children would play outdoors all day, and when dusk began to set in they would cluster under streetlights until, as Musial neighbor Barbao Jr. stated, your "father would whistle, and if we were too far away to hear that whistle, then we were too far away from home."

Periodic steam whistles emanating from the steel mill pierced the Donora air as well, indicating lunchtime, the end of the lunch breaks, and various shift changes. Everyone from school children to workers knew what each blast meant and easily kept track of time with each whistle's blowing.

Some days young Stan, more concerned with the physical than the cerebral world, would wake up and rush to his window in expectation of the aftermath of a snowstorm, only to see a disappointing smattering of snow on the ground. Other times a wicked snowstorm, complete with blizzard-like conditions, would have battered the town, inundating it with as much a foot or so of the white stuff. Eventually, further accumulations would pile up, linger, and become an eyesore, a nasty blend of snow plus soot and grit from the residents' coal furnaces and from the smokestacks of the United States Steel works. It was a gradually diminishing blight that could take weeks to vanish. Such was the clime of Western Pennsylvania.

Stan's summer nights were penetrated by the lugubrious whistles of passing steam engines. He would play outdoors all day, fleeing his stuffy house in those pre–air conditioning days. Hucksters toured the streets, hawking fruit and vegetables, and, after it rained, a man made his way through town offering to repair umbrellas for a fee.

To place a phone call, one picked up the receiver and asked the operator to be connected to Frontier-9 (for the digits 379 as the town's prefix) and then the rest of the number, not unlike Barney Fife's, "Sarah, get me Juanita down at the diner."

Ray Bradley stated, "I loved Donora. It was just a great place for a kid to grow up. Everybody got along.... There wasn't that much trouble in Donora of any kind."

Growing up in Donora shaped Musial in many ways. Trudging up the myriad steep hills had a plus side. Barbao Jr. believed that "playing on the hills all the time was a good thing because our legs [got] stronger." That, and enduring the harsh Western Pennsylvania winters and smoldering, blast-furnace-like summers helped forge Musial into a rugged individual.

Already in love with baseball, Stan, now a young man, was ready to play the game at an organized level. He began his journey on the diamonds of Donora, with his ultimate destination being Cooperstown.

## CHAPTER TWO

# The Making of a Man

In his teens, Musial developed through his experiences on and off the sporting fields. In school and around town, he was well liked, a typical kid growing up in a small town, becoming a man along the way.

Musial's family certainly could not afford to travel to Pittsburgh to watch Major League Baseball. Stan was 17 when he first saw the Pirates play. Vance Bunardzya said, "My dad took Stan to his first major-league ballgame [at] Forbes Field. My dad suggested he play hooky from school to go see the Pirates. When he walked into the ballpark, he said, 'Gee, Johnny, what a beautiful ballpark.'" He also stated that he believed he could handle big-league pitching. It would only be a handful of years until Musial played in that park and, indeed, handled major-league pitching with ease.

The weekends in Donora were full of activity. "There was always some place to go," said Ray Bradley. "Everybody either went to the Elks Club, the [American] Legion, or the Vets [Veterans of Foreign Wars]. We had three movie [theaters] at one time."

Bradley said that while times were tight, many of the high school basketball players, including Musial, would sometimes drop by local drugstores such as Milton Duvall's. "We'd go out and get ice cream or stop for a sandwich at Lee's Restaurant."

Musial might glance through the local newspaper to check out the sports and the funnies, which carried comic strips with quaint titles, such as *Homer Hoopee*; *Oh, Diana!*; and *Oaky Doaks*, but serious news items were of little interest to him.

Ed Pado said, "The big thing of the day was to go downtown and walk McKean Avenue [the main street] as far as we could go, go on the other side

and walk back. A lot of times they had tea dances after a high school basketball game. They'd have records and they'd put them over the loudsystem
speaker and hold dances for high school kids up until 11:00."

Joe Barbao Jr. recalled bowlers in Donora taking their turns on the
lanes, crossing the street to grab a quick beer at the Sons of Italy, and then
returning to their duckpin game. Their skills diminished as the night wore
on, but, said Barbao, "You were happier."

Michael E. Kelley said local "coal miners and steel mill workers were
practically weaned on Stoney's beer. Those men worked hard, they played
hard, and they drank hard."

Still, said Pado, "It was a nice community; they had some tough cops in
those days—they didn't mess with you. You'd get a kick in the can before
they'd report you; a good bunch of guys. They all got our respect."

Bradley said Musial, as a high school student, "wasn't on the honor
roll, but he was right below it. He was more interested in sports. He loved
sports, and I don't think he really had to do [much, if any, work] around
the house." He did take on a summer job in 1937, pumping gasoline, but
mainly his family tried to make sure he would have time for his involvement
in sports.

Another classmate, Frances Delsandro stated, "He was an average
student, a good *C* student. Never any trouble, and we had some kids that
did cause problems. He was just a decent, all-around kid. He was someone
you'd like to be your brother or your son, because he [was] so nice."

"I never thought of Stan as an intellectual giant," said Steve Russell, "but
he had a lot of polish. I found it very interesting that a man who didn't have a
lot of education became so closely associated with author James Michener."

Dorothy Kovacik reminisced, "He was horrible in shorthand class and
would never do his nightwork [homework]. I helped him many times with
his shorthand assignments; I did a lot of nightwork for him. The only
trouble was, Stan never learned to read or write shorthand and couldn't
read any of the homework I did for him. And when he got into the class,
Miss Perry, our teacher, would ask him to read a letter which I had written
in shorthand, and he couldn't. Miss Perry gave him the dickens for not
doing the work himself. Nor could he transcribe anything when the class
had a typing assignment. He would get hollered at for that. At reunions
we'd always laugh about that."

Kovacik saw Musial as being a boy "who loved being on the ball field"
more than anything else, but he was also a skilled prankster. "He was good

for doing…we called them antics. He would trick somebody who didn't know what he was [up to], and he'd have a big laugh over the whole thing. He loved drawing tic-tac-toe on the blackboard before the teacher would walk into the classroom. Fellow students always had to rush up and erase the blackboard before the teacher caught them. And any time he would get into trouble, his sister Rosie would come to his rescue."

In adulthood Musial continued to be fond of what might, outside the realm of baseball, seem like puerile practical jokes. "At private parties," wrote Irv Goodman, "he will resort to shaking hands with a false thumb or perform…a belly dance." All false facades of suavity were often shoved aside with Musial.

Cardinal Carl Warwick remembered a time he was sitting in the lobby of a New York hotel. "We only got $10 a day meal money then, and he and Red [Schoendienst] were walking through the lobby. Stan asked, 'Carl, did you have dinner yet?' I said, 'No, I'm not going to eat tonight, I'm saving my meal money.' He said, 'No, you're going to eat with Red and I.'" Warwick protested, but Musial insisted, and they hopped into a waiting limousine.

"We went to Toots Shor's, and when they brought the check to the table, Stan looked over to me and said, 'Carl, your part [of the tab] is $62.' We were on a 10-day road trip, and all I had was $100 in my pocket, and I liked to choke. Then he said, 'You can breathe again now, I was just kidding. There's nothing on this check. Mr. Shor is picking it up.'" Considering the top meal money Musial ever received was $9 per day, a $62 bill for Warwick would have been astronomical.

Musial's after-school time was mainly dedicated to sports and to the girl he met while in high school, the girl who would eventually become his wife, Lillian Labash.

Lil was a pretty blonde of Czeckoslovakian and Russian descent. Lil was the daughter of Sam and Anna, and the Labashes were a family who, according to Stan's niece Susan Naylor, "all came through New York City, went to Braddock [a Pennsylvanian steel town], and then they all moved to Donora."

The close-knit family consisted of eight children who lived off profits from their grocery store on McKean Avenue in the area of town known as South Donora, prospering enough to purchase a car. It was a typical store of the day, complete with a large block for Sam's use when cutting meat before he carefully wrapped purchases in butcher's paper. Then there was the large penny-candy display case that caused children to salivate as they pressed their noses to the glass.

Lil enrolled in commercial courses at Donora High School and graduated the year before Stan, although she was only two months his elder. She
was bright, petite, had pretty brown eyes, and answered to the nickname
"Shrimp." She took part in the school's Sewing Club and Personality Club
and was on the yearbook staff.

Her brother Monte said Lil was an ordinary girl who just happened to
fall in love with and get married to a man destined for greatness.

Her father had taken her to Palmer Park to watch the gangly 14-year-old
Stan Musial play in a sandlot game. He was impressed, telling his daughter,
"Look at that Polish kid pitch." Lil, too, was quite impressed. After that,
she believed "it was inevitable that [they] were going to see each other, be
together." Later she said she became taken with him, falling for the sight of
his legs in his basketball outfit. She joked that Stan had, in turn, fallen in
love with the lunchmeat and milk at her father's store. Monte related, "The
first thing Stan would do when he came to the store was to take salami out
of the meat case and cut himself a hunk of it."

Lil was hardly unique in her admiration. Kovacik remembers watching Musial practice on a back field by the high school. "The girls were all
gaga over him because he was such a good player," She said. They were also
attracted to his physique, his prowess, and his curly brown hair.

One of Musial's closest friends was Dick Ercius, who dated Lil's sister
Ann and introduced Lil to Stan in the autumn of 1937. Just a few months
later, as winter blew in, the two went on their first date. Lil recalled going to
a skating rink with Ann and Ercius after a basketball game. They continued
seeing each other. Then, Lil said, "The following year Stan and I started
going steady."

Ed Pado reminisced, "We were pretty close. We went together to the
junior-senior prom; Stan was a good dancer. He went with Lillian Labash,
he was already going with her for quite a while, and I was going with a girl
from Donora. My brother had just got a brand new Chrysler Royal,and
Stan says, 'Hey, Ed, you mind if Lillian and I go with you?' In those days
not too many guys had cars. My brother told me I could use his if there
wasn't any drinking." Musial, of course, readily agreed.

Normally Stan, having no access to a car, hiked from his end of town to
Lil's South Donora home to pick her up. Then they walked somewhere else
for their date, he walked her back home, and then he traveled the length of
the town once again. The distance from Stan's house to Lil's and back was
about three miles, so each date with Lil involved a long journey.

Musial was accustomed to such walks. "We would walk together to school," said Kovacik, "and we had a long trek over the hills; it was nothing but hills, and hills, and hills to go to the school. It took 20 minutes to get there." The students made their round trip twice daily because they had to return to their homes for a long lunch break during the day. "We got out at 20 after 11 and didn't have to be back until, like, 10 minutes to one."

By her senior year, Lil and Stan were pretty serious, and in her yearbook's "Class Will" section she bequeathed her "basketball hero to Mr. Russell [the team's coach]."

Laurel Grimes declared her uncle Stan and her aunt Lil "were very, very handsome, like a movie-star couple." Unlike the majority of Hollywood couples, whose marriages do not last long, the Musials celebrated their 70th wedding anniversary in 2009, and Stan has, by all accounts, been totally faithful to Lil.

Lil's nephew, Ron Nagy, added, "Lil is really important to him," and vice versa. "God forbid, if one ever passes away before the other, the other [will] really be [devastated]. They are really close."

Musial's personality and his values were certainly cemented by his high school days. For example, Bradley noted that back then Musial "never smoked and he never drank." Though at his farewell bash before he departed town to play in the minors, beer flowed plentifully. "I guess it was safe in those days because very few of us had cars, and there wasn't much traffic on the highways, not like it is today. So nobody ever thought that much about having beer [at a party]."

There was always an aura of facileness around Musial. Tim McCarver, a Cardinals teammate of Musial's, commented, "He could relax because he was born under a lucky star. He'd play poker and draw inside straights…. He'd win all the time and have no clue how to play. Everybody in the game would be a better player, yet he'd win. That was Stan."

New York Giants infielder Bill Rigney marveled at how cool and collected Musial became as an adult. "I'd watch him play doubleheaders in St. Louis in 100-degree heat. I'd look like I'd been in a mud bath, and he'd have maybe three beads of sweat on his entire body, and his uniform would be nice and white."

Musial never felt the need to display a pretense of urbanity. Helen Jones of Donora recalled Musial "was always at the class reunions, and he'd bring his harmonica." He continued his love of the harmonica, whipping it out and playing for any audience at the drop of a batting helmet.

Only Musial could get away with playing an instrument considered so unsophisticated, but for years Musial has unabashedly played it in front of baseball royalty and has managed to carry it off. He even appeared on *Hee Haw*, wearing bib overalls and animatedly playing his instrument.

Long after he grew up, Musial remained loyal to old friends. Todd Ririe, whose parents were friends of Musial, also brought up Musial's regular attendance at class reunions. He speculated, "I think the reason he liked to come back to the reunions is he was more or less treated like just one of their other graduates of Donora High School. I think that's probably the reason he went to so many of these things, because it wasn't like [the reunions] were in a fancy location, and it wasn't like they had a big fancy celebration. But I think that was all part of probably why he liked it." In such a setting, Musial could relax.

Kovacik observed that when Musial came back to town, "he was just Stan from high school. He did not use any of his popularity to be anything but what he was, a good guy, but we looked up to him because he made it."

As a young man, Musial never had many opportunities to display his munificence simply because he had very little money. That changed when he became financially secure. Ted Musial was passing through St. Louis once, and he and two friends headed to Musial's restaurant. "The story around town was anybody from Donora that came, the meal was on Stan," said Ted. "So, we went to the steakhouse, and when we ordered our steaks, we told the waitress that we were from Donora, and she said, 'Well, the steaks are on the house'" after they showed her a "Donora: Home of Champions" license plate on their car for verification.

Musial would also develop into the kind of man who gave of his time, encouraged everyone, and was supportive of others. Ron Necciai was a wild fastballing pitcher. Born just across the river from Donora in Gallatin, he stunned the baseball world in 1952, when, as a 19-year-old, he struck out 27 batters in a nine-inning game for the Bristol Twins and followed that up with a 24-strikeout performance. He admitted with a chuckle, "I could throw it hard, and I could curve it, but where it went was another story."

Necciai's dazzling strikeout totals earned him a call-up to the Pirates in August 1952. Necciai recalled that after a game he had pitched against the Cards in St. Louis, "Stan sent their clubhouse man over to the Pirates clubhouse to get me and bring me over there to talk to him. He knew I was from Gallatin. I sat there for at least 20 minutes. He was very encouraging. He said, 'You're able to pitch in this league, you'll do fine. You've got the kind of stuff, you just have to work on your control and [have] a little confidence.' He was very complimentary. Here I was, Mister Absolutely Nobody in the National League and he's the greatest name in the National League, and he sends for me. He didn't have to do that."

Dodgers pitcher Carl Erskine said, "I knew him as an opponent and respected him a great deal, but I knew him off the field and learned that he was a real gentleman and a real class act. So what I'd heard about him was true, that he was a first-class person. We just had a respect for each other."

Big-league pitcher Bill Monbouquette recounted the time he took the loss in the first of two All-Star Games held in 1960. Later, sitting in his hotel's lobby, he ruminated over what had gone wrong. Musial strolled over to him and invited him out to eat with a group of players. "He was on the National League team, but he still was that kind to me. He even treated everyone to dinner."

Growing up poor taught Musial to be frugal when need be. In 1943, back when players bought their own spikes, Musial purchased a pair of new cleats, which he soon discovered were too tight. Being cautious with money, he refused to discard them, wearing them until the team trainer took him to a store and purchased a pair that fit properly.

One of Musial's nephew's, Ron Nagy, insists, "He wasn't tight, he wasn't a spendthrift." A Donora mayor, John Lignelli, contended, "He provided probably as much [money] as he could for the town's Little League. Maybe some people think he should have done more. He did a lot, absolutely.

"He never forgot where he came from and, to me, anyone who excels the way he did and still remembers Donora—his heart was always in Donora. He always bragged about Donora, always." Only decades later, when Musial's health slipped, did he, according to Lignelli, "fade from the [local] picture."

From childhood on, Musial had a reputation for having a sense of fair play, for being a true teammate, for avoiding subgroups on his team, for treating rookies the same as veterans, and for caring about winning more than his personal stats.

Dr. Ferretti said, "As a kid, everybody loved him and he got along with all [races]; and in Donora we had all kinds of cultures."

Another Musial classmate, Helen McCulloch, said, "He was a really nice, nice kid. Always. I remember him as always being a polite, quiet boy. He wasn't a showoff or anything."

Emil Badzik, a childhood acquaintance of Musial's, commented, "He was unassuming, happy-go-lucky. Some [young athletes] were pretty mouthy, and they'd argue about things. No, he was easygoing all the time."

As far as Musial's athletic feats went, by 1935 people had begun to take note of his sports prowess. Charles "Jerry" Wunderlich, his junior high gym teacher said, "He had the kind of grace in sports that always seems to put a boy at the right place at the right time.... Some boys have it. Some don't. You could take one look at Stan and know that he had it."

The 14-year-old prodigy played (and was listed as a manager) for the Heslep All-Stars in the informal Junior City League in town. His first item for his scrapbook came from a newspaper account of a game in which he hit fifth, banged out four hits, and whiffed 14 in a five-hour contest. Later the local paper noted, "Musial's relief twirling was a shining light of the fray. He fanned 15 in the six innings that he hurled" for the All-Stars against the Herald-American Newsies, but the league soon folded.

He also played both mushball—a game played with what amounts to a softball—and fast-pitch softball. Bradley stated, "We played softball on a field next to the mill in a fast-pitch league; a couple of those guys pitched it so fast you couldn't believe it. Stan didn't stay with softball very long because he went down to American Legion ball when he was about 17, but anything that he tried to do, he was good at."

Musial excelled at numerous sports throughout his high school career. For instance, Musial's notable basketball play began around 1936 when he played in a city league for St. Mary's. Then, as a sophomore, he played well enough to work his way up to the starting five by March. That team went 8–6.

Bradley remembered, "Stan was on the first string, and I used to guard him all the time in practice. I was a reserve guard and he was a first-string guard. He was a guy who could stop and go on a dime. He could shoot with either hand, he was a good ball handler and a very good passer. He was very, very smooth, just like he was in baseball. He had that knack. He was one of the best basketball players I ever saw. Of course he was only around six foot, [but that] was big in those days. He could have had a scholarship, I think, to any basketball school in the country, and Pitt and Duquesne offered him scholarships."

Doc Carlson played football under the legendary coach Pop Warner and went on to become Pitt's basketball coach, where he won two national titles. Steve Russell said that after Musial's showing as a junior,

"Carlson desperately tried to recruit Stan." But basketball was not Musial's calling.

Former Donora native Hugh Forsyth said that his uncle, Emil Badzik, taught Musial how to play tennis and, "within two weeks, Stan was beating my uncle." Emil stated, "He was a natural at everything. Every time you'd hit the ball, instead of hitting it back left-handed, he'd turn around the opposite way. He would always get in position to hit a backhand; he'd go to his right and use his backhand, but he was good. He was good at everything. At school he picked up a ping-pong paddle, and in a week's time there was no one who could beat him. A basketball player? He was one of the best. There must have been 50 schools after him."

Bradley said, "I never knew him to kid around that much. I thought maybe he was a little bit serious, especially after he was around 16, 17." The resolute Musial just followed his coach's instructions and "never really screwed up [or around] like some of the other guys we had."

Musial, a self-proclaimed perfectionist, observed, "I don't like to do anything I can't do well." Bradley continued, "He always wanted to win. Always looking for ways to win; he used to steal more balls in the back court than any guard I've seen. If guys were passing the ball back and forth, he'd just wait, and all of a sudden, wham, off he'd go and he had a layup. He had that knack, a fast start; he could move real quick."

Bradley said that while Stan was intense, he seldom became ruffled. An exception came during his adolescence. "I first met Stan in junior high in ninth grade. We were playing basketball and Stan got into an argument with a farm boy by the name of Dave Rabe. This kid lived out in the country and did all the plowing. He was real short but real stocky and strong. He didn't know how to play basketball—he was rough. He pushed Stan out of the way, and he was running into Stan a lot. So, pretty soon they got into a little fight, but Dick Ercius stopped it right away. And it was a good thing because this kid was so powerful, so strong, I don't know what would have happened if it had kept going.

"Stan didn't have a temper, you never saw him get real mad. That was the only time I ever saw him get into a fight—it was just pushing around—and I saw him a lot of times."

The Donora High School 1937–38 hoop team went 11–1 playing before, as the yearbook put it, "capacity crowds amid spills and thrills." Eugene "Fats" Norton led the team in scoring, followed by Ercius and Musial, and all three garnered All-Section honors. Musial, a junior who averaged 10 points per game, also was named to the All-Western Pennsylvania team. Musial helped the 1936–37 Donora High basketball team advance to a national scholastic basketball tournament in Chicago.

The *Varsity Dragon* reported that the 1938 powerhouse basketball team "brought honors to the hometown and to the schoolboy, becoming the champions of Section IV for the first time in the history of Donora." Musial wore jersey No. 16 on a team outfitted with dark high-top sneakers and shiny, satiny, and very short pants with buckled belts, incongruous by today's fashion standards. He was listed as a forward on a team that was talented but not very deep.

They rolled on, win after win, including a 36–31 opening-round playoff victory versus previously undefeated Washington, Pennsylvania, in Pitt Stadium.

The school yearbook reported the next contest, the Western Pennsylvania Championship Game, was a "hard but glorious defeat" to a much taller and more experienced Har-Brack team in overtime. The yearbook added that, "Trailing by a margin of 13 [a huge deficit in this low-scoring era] points in the first stanza, the Dragons made one of the most thrilling comebacks in basketball history," tying it up in the closing minutes of regulation and forcing overtime play. Then the Dragons "simply ran out of gas," resulting in their 39–33 loss.

Norton said Musial often scored on set shots and loved to cut "across to the basket. He was quick, a good ball handler, and had a good shot."

Robert Jones remembered, "He had a real good hook shot [sometimes using it from as far out as the foul line]. He'd dribble into the corner of the gym—I can still see it—and his being lefty came into play because [backed into that corner with the two converging baselines protecting his shooting arm] no one could cover him. He'd throw it up over his left shoulder and, boom. He was deadly with it."

Dr. Ferretti contends Musial "was a better basketball player than baseball. He stood out on the basketball court like a sore thumb. Man, when he was on that basketball floor, he was unbelievable, just fluid motion."

Badzik noted, "Stan never seemed to care [as much] for football. I don't think he was a rough and tumble fellow, he was just easygoing. He and Joe Montana played on the same high school field, though." Montana played on Legion Field as a high school quarterback decades later.

Jones stated, "Stan was a little bit frail for football—he was well built but not exactly muscular, he was kind of lean—so he never even went out for football." Jimmy Russell, who coached football and baseball at Donora High, tried to recruit him to play quarterback, but his parents thought the sport to be too rough. Russell stated Musial "would have been a marvelous T formation quarterback."

His biggest early baseball influence was former minor-leaguer Joe Barbao Sr., a neighbor 22 years Stan's senior who also pitched and coached the Donora Zincs team in a semipro industrial league. Musial would wait almost daily for Barbao to get off work, then join him in a game of catch while also learning the many basics and intricacies of the game. Barbao took to Musial and soon awarded Stan the job of batboy on his team. Ken Barbao recalled his father telling him that Musial "had the makings of being a good ballplayer, that's the reason he took so much interest in him." His sister Nancy added, "Stan and Honey were a fixture at our house at one time. He was at our kitchen table a lot, *a lot.*"

Perhaps the legend of Musial begins on August 4, 1936, when Barbao asked the slender boy, in a scene that could have been lifted from a modern sports movie, if he wanted to work mop-up duty after his team was trailing badly. Barbao reasoned that he would let the batboy have some fun. "Get in there. Let's see what you can do," he instructed Musial, who, ignoring the oppressive heat of his heavy wool uniform, began firing in pitches. He threw hard with a flapping left-handed motion. Literally a boy among men—some in their thirties—the boy is said to have worked six innings, retiring 13 batters on strikes (although one source shows he recorded 12 outs, five via the strikeout).

When Musial was younger and had to play with kids his own age, it had always been a mismatch. Ed P. Sukel, son of Ed M. Sukel, who once played in the same youth league as Musial, stated, "My dad told me Stan *really* stood out—'like he was a man among boys.' Everyone knew that he had special baseball talents, but they didn't know how far he would go with it."

Musial's first performance with the Zincs didn't exactly shock Barbao, who had, for some time, worked with the budding pitcher. Barbao taught Musial three basic pitches: the fastball, curve, and change-up. Most of his strikeouts came on fastballs and what Barbao called his "little old cutty-thumb curve."

John Benyo Jr., whose father played on Musial's team, said that "the general impression when he first started pitching for the Zincs was, 'What the hell can this kid do?' After he was signed by the Cardinals, a lot of scouts went and scouted those industrial leagues in the Mon Valley."

Some players were offered contracts in the low minors but chose instead to keep their better-paying mill jobs and still play competitive baseball on industrial leagues.

The Donora Zincs were one of 10 clubs in the Monongahela Valley League that was composed mainly of players from local industries. Another was the Donora Croatians, and there were others from nearby towns.

The Zincs players were required to sign a contract certifying they would agree to play out a full season with the team, barring their being released or traded, and "to obey all the rules set forth by the said league."

Over the years, large headlines concerning the Zincs' feats sprawled over the local newspaper. One particularly colorful one read, "Near Riot as Zincs and Croats Tie Again." Clearly the town took its baseball seriously.

Barbao Jr. stated, "The Depression was over, but times were still tough. The teams in the Mon Valley League didn't have much equipment. There were no hard hats, no helmets. When an inning was over, the first baseman would flip his glove into the coach's box, and sometimes players from the other team would borrow a glove from [an opponent]."

He also remembered, "One time my dad was coaching first base and Stan lined one down the first base line and knocked him right on his can, hit him on his leg around the ankle. So my dad just reached right over and picked up the first baseman's mitt that was laying there, leaned it up against his ankle [as if it was a shin guard], and naturally everybody in the stands [was] laughing. They kept the game going, but they found out the next day it was broken, and he was on crutches for six weeks."

In 1937 Musial began playing American Legion ball, impressing everyone. At around the age of 16 he reached his adult height of six feet but weighed only around 145 pounds. Musial ripped hit after hit. As a young pitcher he could—in the parlance of the game—throw BBs through a brick wall.

In September 1937 Musial's world was altered forever. Andrew French was the business manager of the Penn State League's Monessen team in Class D, and, having seen Musial play on sandlots, he extended an invitation for Stan to workout under the scrutiny of player-manager Ollie Vanek at Monessen's home field, Page Park. Vanek related Musial's appearance the first time he saw him throw. "He looked like a grammar-school kid rather than a high-schooler. He was built like a split matchstick and wore dungarees, a T-shirt, and blue canvas sneakers. I can still remember his pink cheeks and gangling arms." French evaluated Musial as being a future prospect but nevertheless wrote of him as a "green kid." Still, he and Vanek, suitably impressed after several workouts, wanted to secure the signature of Lukasz on the contract for the underage (then not yet 17 years old) Stan.

Lukasz believed his son's getting an education and working an honest, *real* job were of paramount importance. Stan was in a quandary. Dr. Ferretti spoke of the Donora High School librarian, Helen Kloz, who helped Musial with his dilemma. "His father wanted him to go to Pitt; he wanted a Joe College, you know. So Stash was perplexed. He went to Miss Kloz and said, 'My dad wants me to go to college, but I want to play baseball.' She said, 'Stanley, you do what you love.'"

Legend has it that, learning of her son's desire to sign a pro contract, his mother provided the impetus to allow her son to play ball. Stan had approached her first, sensing she was the ally he needed. He knew his father's obdurate ways and his beliefs. As his mother related, "My husband came from the Old Country. He never allowed any sassing. Our children had to obey. They were taught to work hard and not to grumble." Arguing with his father would be as unthinkable as it would be futile.

So Stan pled his case to his sympathetic mother, using Darrow-like logic with a touch of raw emotion sprinkled in. Soon both his oration and his tears flowed like water from the nearby Monongahela River. His mother capitulated yet realized her husband "couldn't comprehend such devotion [as Stan had] to a silly game."

Greg Oslowski related that local legend contends that Lukasz not only "didn't want him playing baseball. He told him, 'Go get a real job.' Stan would hide his shoes, glove, and ball because his old man would throw them in the coal furnace, burn them, and say, 'Go to work. Go in the mill.'"

Mary insisted otherwise. "My husband was so stubborn because he wanted Stan to go to college. He thought baseball was just a game and he wanted Stan to amount to something."

Musial later wrote that French and Vanek "visited my home…a couple of times to soften up my father." Legend further has it that it was after the penultimate visit Stan wept, believing his father would never relent. His mother said, "Stan was all upset…he was sure he'd never get another chance." Having seen enough of his anguish, Mary reportedly told French and Vanek to return the next day. "Lukasz will grant his permission," she vowed. She then approached her husband obliquely, aware that it would require guile to influence her strong-willed husband.

She asked him why he had come to America. He took the bait and replied, "Because it is a free country." She replied, "All right. And in America a boy is free *not* to go to college, if that's his choice." Finally, the necessary papers were signed, allowing Stan to leave Donora later and head to Williamson, West Virginia, for his first days as a professional ballplayer.

Without his mother's intervention, it seems safe to say Stan would have wound up being a carpenter—he displayed a knack for woodwork in shop class at Donora High School—or he would have found himself working shifts in the United States Steel Mill for a living.

Donora High had gone 15 years without a baseball program. That dry spell ended in 1938. Veronica Duda, wife of Michael "Ki" Duda, related, "When Stan was going to be [a junior] in high school, my husband initiated the baseball program there."

Coach Duda, knowing he wasn't a baseball expert, had Chuck Schmidt help him coach the Dragons. When Schmidt was once asked what made Musial such a good player, he replied succinctly, "God."

After playing for just one year on the team that Mrs. Duda said had been basically created just for Musial, he turned professional and, she noted, "was not allowed to play any more after that." When he lost his senior year eligibility, it wasn't as if he was missing much. Rudy Andabaker stated, "People don't understand that around here baseball players don't have the time to get in a lot of games because the weather's not conducive like Florida and some other states. And when they call the games, they don't make them up."

But the year he did play was magnificent. Musial pitched, played outfield, and batted cleanup, reviving the dormant program, and the Dragons of Section VIII excelled early on. A school publication reported that on April 13, 1938, "Stan Musial, star hurler for the Dragon Diamondeers, honored Donora with a high school record of 17 strikeouts [of 21 total outs in a three-hitter] while playing against Monessen in the inaugural game of the season." Donora won 3–2 with Musial driving home Buddy Griffey, Ken Griffey Sr.'s father, with the contest's final run on a scorching single.

Coach Duda observed, with a smattering of hyperbole, "The trouble with him as a schoolboy pitcher was that we couldn't find anyone who could catch him. He might strike out 18 men, but half of them would get to first on dropped first strikes."

In Musial's next game, a two-hitter, Donora crushed Rostraver 22–3 in their home opener in front of 500 spectators. He next pitched five relief frames, giving up one hit and one run while fanning 10.

Musial classmate Lou Ferretti spoke of a memorable Legion Field homer against Monongahela. "Stan hit the longest goddamn home run [ever hit there]. It went down the right-field line, down the length of the football field, [and beyond]. He just pulled that son of a bitch. He could *hit*." By the time the outfielder flagged down the ball, the speedy Musial had crossed home plate. Since home plate was tucked into a corner of the football field's end zone, the ball flew the distance of the field, including both end zones, and beyond. The ball traveled an estimated 388 feet in the air and rolled to the fence a reported 452 feet away from home.

Buddy Griffey also homered in that game, and Musial contributed a double as well. His heroics earned him the April 27 *Herald-American* headline, "Musial's 4-Run Homer Wins for Dragons." Donora won 6–3 on his fifth-inning slam after being down 3–2 entering the fifth. Two innings earlier they had walked Musial intentionally, but with the bases jammed, there was nowhere to put him in the fifth.

Badzik recalled Monongahela fearing Musial's power "so they 'surrounded' the outfield. They figured he was going to put a long ball out, so they put the shortstop, the second baseman [out there]; they had five outfielders. He hit the ball to right field and put it over the fielder's head; that was one of the longest balls out at Legion Field. They didn't think he was going to hit it *that* far."

Musial's high school field was quite unusual. Barbao Jr. stated that "the left field foul line was on the goal line, so left field was fairly short." To compensate for the short dimensions in left, a ground rule was put into effect: A batter who deposited a ball over the fence anywhere between the left-field foul pole to a marker situated by the power alley in left was awarded a double. One had to drive a ball over the fence to the right of the marker to earn a home run. The distance to the left-field fence was, said Pado, "about 310, 315 feet from home plate, and the fence was, I think, six or eight feet high."

Earlier Musial had developed the ability to hit the ball to the opposite field. He had played pickup ball on a diamond with a short right field just in front of a hill. The children played with just one baseball, so if he pulled it to right, there was a good chance the game would be delayed while the boys hunted for the ball. In left field, though, there was an inviting slope for a target. To hit it there was to guarantee a hit.

Badzik stated, "When he was in high school, he was mostly a pitcher, and he was a pretty good pitcher, but he was a good hitter, oh, he was good." He possessed many tools and was labeled in a *Saturday Evening Post* article as a "boy who can run like a deer and hit like a Cobb." One report had him making the trip from home to first in a brisk 4.2 seconds, while others swear that, in full stride, his feet resembled a blur.

Bradley commented, "Back then, every once in a while he'd fool around at first base, and he'd play the outfield—he moved real quick and gracefully—but mostly he'd pitch. He could throw a ball awful hard. He had a good fastball and a good curve, and when he stepped on the mound you knew that he knew what he was doing. He struck out a lot, and he had [several] shutouts."

While his high school coach saw him as a pitcher, Stan said, "I didn't like to pitch, because I could always hit, but in high school if you have the best arm, they always make you the pitcher."

Pado, who threw the first no-hitter in the school's history, said, "Stan was a good pitcher, as good if not better than anybody I ever knew in high school, but he had a little temper. I had to end up catching for him because the catcher that we had was Pete Piskor, and every now and then they didn't see eye to eye. Then he split his finger on one of the pitches that Stan threw—he told me that Stan might have got one of the signals mixed up—and I was asked to catch."

The 1938 team went 9–3 as Musial racked up a 4–2 ledger, with sloppy defense contributing to both defeats. In one loss, three defensive misplays cost him the game despite his 14 strikeouts. He was down 2–0 at the end of the first inning, then threw no-hit ball for four and a third innings. In the other defeat, 5–4 to nearby California High School, the Dragons were guilty of five errors. Musial went the distance, whiffing seven and surrendering just three hits.

On May 13, 1938, in his final high school contest, he had a perfect day at the plate with a homer, triple, and single. His home run in his last at-bat came on a drive that soared over the center fielder's head and landed in the weeds, guaranteeing Donora a second-place finish in their section. He struck out 12 in defeating the Monongahela Wildcats 4–1 with only an unearned run tallied against him, and he gave up a mere two hits. Overall, he topped all section hitters at .455, earning a spot on the All-Section team.

In his senior year, Musial helped coach the Dragons baseball team, which won the Mon Valley High School Championship. He also continued to play for the Zincs until his minor-league season began with Williamson.

As Musial's senior year began he weighed, said Bradley, "around 160 pounds. He was slender, but he was built, though. He didn't have any fat on him, I'll tell you that. He was like Ted Williams, slender and very athletic. I'd say he was wiry."

Around this time, the average weight of a football player on the Donora High School 26-man team was only 156 pounds. Musial would go on to become big-league baseball's equivalent of Sugar Ray Robinson, perhaps the greatest player ever on a pound-for-pound basis.

In the meantime, the 17-year-old kid walked the halls of Donora High knowing he was already a pro athlete, but it didn't show. Bradley stated, "He was never big-headed, never acted like that, he was just a regular guy."

Despite having been the target of baseball scouts "inundating the high school campus," Musial remained "modest and humble," said Musial classmate Dorothy Kovacik. One friend said that Stan, "for as famous as he was…was *very* laid back. Always just a nice, nice guy."

While the word "nice" is juvenile, as time went on it became the word universally used to sum up Musial—from friends, classmates, relatives, and even sportswriters who often grow jaded and cynical. Musial went from being a nice boy, considerate of others, to being the same kind of man. One Musial admirer labeled him "numbingly amiable."

Steve Russell said Musial kept his "wonderful attitude on life" even though he was a product of Dickensian poverty. Stan's nephew, Ed, stated, "Whatever you saw with Stan, that was the genuine thing. He didn't put on airs for anybody and [with him] whatever you see is what you got there. He was a generally nice person."

Ed added that his uncle didn't tend to talk about his exploits. "He would always just agree when people tried to get him to tell some. Like he would just say, 'Oh, yeah, I remember that [feat or event],' if somebody would try to drag something out of him like, 'Oh, you remember when you hit this home run,' or 'Remember when you hit those five home runs?' It just didn't seem like he wanted to brag, put it that way." He would rather talk to or about other people than about himself.

Sportswriter Edwin Pope said, "Stan Musial had an honest and deep interest in how you were doing, how you were feeling. This is something you never get from a professional athlete; they don't care how you feel." Donora star athlete Bimbo Cecconi agreed, "He makes you feel that you are as important as he is, and he has never changed that attitude."

Musial would, in fact, always remain accessible, not aloof nor distantly regal like DiMaggio or bellicose like Williams. Bob Costas observed, "When he [Musial] walks into a room, for a lot of people it's like they're seeing an old friend. DiMaggio walked into a room, a hush came over it."

Because of Musial's humility, his high school peers didn't particularly seem to look up to the "Donora Greyhound." As Robert Jones of Donora put it, "Not really. He didn't even know how good he was. He just developed. He was a natural-born athlete. He could hit one out [to left] any time. People take credit for helping him, but I think he did it all on his own."

The Donora High yearbook from Musial's senior year offered a terse summation of the future legend, listing his activities and distilling his personality, while displaying not an iota of prescience: "Stanley Musial: commercial [classes]; baseball; basketball; Monogram Club; intramural [Ping-Pong] and tennis." The caption by Musial's photo continued in sophomoric terms: "Stan's far more than just an athlete. He's friendly, full of fun, and neat."

Clearly the style and quality of high school yearbooks has remained unchanged over the years. Make no mistake, though, Musial was a stellar athlete who played tennis after having virtually no training—who didn't just *play* but excelled in the sport—and who took part in, of all things, intramural Ping-Pong. He was, according to all accounts, almost too good to be true.

Upon graduating, Musial left home full of talent and aspirations but with positively no inkling that his future held a rendezvous with baseball greatness. He left town as a boy, returned one baseball season later a man, and ultimately would turn himself into *the* Man.

## CHAPTER THREE

# The Minors and the Million-Dollar Accident

Having signed his baseball contract as an amateur free agent, Musial headed out into the world beyond Donora, joining Branch Rickey's Rickey Chain Gang in 1938.

Like so many Donora natives, Musial was staunchly proud of his town while, at the same time, realizing that it was no utopia. As he told former Milwaukee Brewers CEO and president Ulice Payne Jr., who also had grown up in Donora, he wanted to leave for wider opportunities. Payne said, "He talked about how when he was a young man, knowing how small Donora was, he was glad to get out of there. In his view, St. Louis [became] his home, and he spent almost all of his life there."

Due to the voluminous amount of players Rickey signed, many a talented youngster languished in the minors, trapped inside the system, some never reaching the majors or doing so near the end of their careers. The players were tied to the club and would leave the system only when the organization felt it was to their benefit to move a player. Also, when a player did begin to progress and start to pull down a decent salary, the team frequently would plug in younger players at much lower salaries. This was the meat grinder environment Musial was plunging into.

Musial's future was strongly linked to Branch Rickey, who headed up the Cardinals front office. Known as "the Mahatma," Rickey had already been around baseball for more years than Musial had been alive. Although Rickey made it to the big leagues in 1905, two years later he set a dubious record when he gave up a staggering 13 stolen bases to the Washington Senators in one game. He lasted for only small portions of four seasons.

Rickey remains one of baseball's most unforgettable and most influential characters. Bobby Bragan, who played under Rickey, believed he "made more contributions to sports than any other man."

Red Smith called Rickey "a God-fearing, checker-playing, horse-trading, cigar-smoking, double-talking" man, a teetotaler who had an "agile mind" and a "facile tongue." Smith recounted an incident in which Rickey was asked a question by John Drebinger of the *New York Times*. After a reply that meandered for over 15 minutes, Rickey asked, "Does that answer your question, John?" A befuddled Drebinger replied, "I have forgotten the question."

On another occasion, Rickey grandiloquently rambled on during a speech only to be interrupted by a man in the audience, who blurted, "Gawd, guys get drunk and don't say things like that."

Bob Friend said, "I always had a lot of respect for Rickey. He produced a lot of good ballclubs, but he was tough to deal with." Some, however, felt it required a micrometer to measure his heart.

New York Giants executive Garry Schumacher came up with a set of rules to follow when dealing with the cunning Rickey: "Don't drink the night before [and] keep your mouth shut and your hands in your pockets." Rickey once discussed salary with Marty Marion and tried to entice him by saying Marion should simply accept the "terms I have offered, and I'll take care of you." Marion wisely replied, "Give me what I want, and I'll take care of myself."

Elroy Face said once when Ralph Kiner, who led (or tied) his league in homers in each of his first seven seasons, tried to negotiate a raise from the Pirates, the crafty Rickey asked him, "Where did we finish last year?" Kiner replied, "Last." Rickey retorted, "We can finish last without you."

Bobby Bragan, who played for the Phillies during his first three years in the majors, had a similar tale of Rickey. "I was traded to Brooklyn, and I was looking forward to meeting Mr. Rickey. I was making $4,500 a year, and I said, 'I'm coming from the poorest clubs in baseball to one of the more affluent teams and that should warrant some kind of a token raise.' He said, 'You got it all wrong, Bobby. You played every day over there in Philadelphia; you're going to be on the bench over here so long they'll start calling you Judge. Sign that contract.' So I signed it. And then I played every day. So in June I stopped by his office on Montague Street again, and his secretary said, 'He can't see you today, come back tomorrow.' So I went back the next day. I went in, and he said, 'Bobby, my secretary said you came by to see me yesterday, and I've been racking my brain ever since, [thinking,] *What could that young man want to talk to me about?* And I prayed to God it wasn't more money. Either you're the kind of a person that can live up to your contract, or you're not—isn't that right?' I said, 'You're exactly right, Mr. Rickey. I just came by to say hello.'" Needless to say, Bragan played that season for the same money he had in Philly.

When George Shuba was asked if Rickey was *really* as tough to deal with as baseball lore has it, he laughed, "Oh, of course he was. Gene Hermanski, our outfielder, said he went to talk to Rickey for a raise after having a good year. After he left his office, one of the sportswriters asked him, 'How did you do with Mr. Rickey?' Gene said, 'Well, Mr. Rickey has a heart of gold—and he aims to keep it.'

"We had so many ballplayers, if you went in to get a raise, he would always say, 'You gotta remember now, [on top of] this salary you'll also get a share of the World Series money,' figuring that we'd be in the World Series all the time. And if you would say to him, 'What if we don't get in the World Series?' he'd say, 'There's a pretty good chance you'll be with the ballplayers that we have.'" He was praising the team's talent but at the same time refusing to pay them a decent salary.

Of course, while Rickey never went to the ballpark on the Sabbath, having made that promise to his mother, he would call to check on the attendance and never refused his club's share of the Sunday-game gate receipts. He never swore but laced his speech vociferously with "Judas Priest," his strongest epithet.

Rickey, unable to afford to buy players, grew his own talent, building a huge and productive farm system.

In his book, *The St. Louis Cardinals—The First Century* Mario Vricella stated that, contrary to a misconception, "The Cardinals under Rickey did not invent the minor leagues or even the farm system, but they did show the way to better build a ball club from the minors on up." The Cardinals also employed the largest big-league scouting staff and held more tryout camps than all of the other clubs.

Rickey's philosophy concerning his farm system was simple but effective. David Halberstam wrote that Rickey would attempt to "sign every talented kid they could for very little money, put them in a giant farm system, let them fight their way to the top..." Between 1938 and 1942 his Cardinals sold many of their better players for a then-astronomical

$625,000 yet still improved at the big-league level. Rickey's plan helped him lead the club to six pennants from 1926 to 1942.

Rickey had an uncanny ability to spot young talent, and, even though many of them fell by the wayside, enough would, in true Darwinian style, be strong enough and fit enough to survive. He likened his system to mass production, resulting in assembly line–like efficiency. At one point Rickey and the Cardinals owned all the players in the entire Nebraska State League and had 800 players under contract spread out over some 32 minor-league clubs. One player was Stan Musial.

After Musial had completed his junior year in high school in June 1938, he was shipped to the Class D Williamson, West Virginia, Colts in the Mountain States League. It was the start of a new life for a boy who had traveled 240 miles from his hometown; but to him it seemed like a long journey, and homesickness soon set in.

Musial earned $65 per month in Williamson, forcing him to subsist on a staple of hamburgers and hot dogs and stay in a $5-per-week boarding house.

In his first mound stint as a pro, he lasted just a few innings as he had trouble finding the plate, and Huntington batters had no problem solving him. A few days later he spun a three-hitter, trouncing Bluefield 10–3. He was raw and erratic.

He ended the year with a mediocre 6–6 slate and a steep 4.66 ERA (while hitting .258). He threw 110 innings and allowed an alarming 194 men to reach base via hits and walks. The team, under manager Nat Hickey, finished below .500 at 58–60, 14 games behind the Logan Indians.

The Cardinals dispatched Wid Matthews to work with the youngster. Matthews later wrote a report to St. Louis: "Arm good. Good fastball, good curve. Poise. Good hitter. A real prospect."

Off-season jobs were mandatory for players of Musial's era. Barbao Jr. stated, "In the wintertime he worked in the Zinc Works," on a job Barbao's father got for Musial. "His job didn't entail much real work, it was a menial job; he was basically told to take it easy and don't get hurt." There, laborers near the zinc smelters had to endure temperatures as high as 120 degrees. Working in the steel mill also entailed palpable danger. A man by the name of Andy Posey died when he fell into a ladle of molten steel. Posey, with the ladle serving as his crypt, was buried on United States Steel property, a modest marker indicating his final resting place.

In 1939 Musial experienced two rites of passage. He got his diploma in June, becoming the first member of his family to graduate. Because he had joined his minor-league club before his graduation ceremony, Lil accepted his diploma on his behalf. The other rite of passage was his marriage to Lil on his 19th birthday.

Carl Warwick said, "She was a very sweet lady, and his kids were too. It was just a fantastic family. She was supportive of Stan, and he always made sure that Lil was okay, that everything was fine."

Dick Groat said Lil "stayed in the background. She was always well liked by the [players'] wives." Despite her status as the wife of a superstar, she didn't act as if she were better than the other wives. Former Cardinal Charlie James stated, "She was very family oriented, she took good care of their kids. She was easygoing."

Stan and his wife would become good parents, and Lil once said that he was the same type of parent as he was a player—unflappable. Even when one of their children misbehaved, the most he would do was raise his voice a bit, and she said that mild display of anger would cause their children to "stand there with their mouths open, as if to say, 'Look at Daddy. What's the matter with Daddy?'"

Stan rarely became frazzled with the public attention he garnered either, and he was consequently very fan friendly. Steve Russell said Lil took care of the household and was "sharp enough that [Stan] didn't have to worry about any of those [daily routine matters]." Freed of chores, Musial spent much time with his fans. Sometimes to the point where Lil felt she had to become, said Russell, "very protective of Stan.

"I have the impression that Lil would keep people away from Stan if she could, but Stan was very big on his fans. His fans were very important to him, and a couple of times he told his wife, 'Be very careful with my fans.'"

Once Warwick's wife Nancy and Lil Musial stood outside a ballpark waiting for their husbands after a game. "Stan came out, and there [were] a whole bunch of kids just surrounding him," remembered Warwick. "He was signing autographs, and Lil walked up to him and said, 'Stan, we need to get going, we've got to get to dinner.' Nancy said he was very polite. He said, 'Lil, these are people that clap and support me. I will sign for everybody here, and then we'll go to dinner.'"

"Stan's a very natural person," said niece Laurel Grimes. "He just enjoys people; he's a people person." When Grimes visited St. Louis in 1992, Lil invited her out to dinner. They were seated in "a raised-up area, so every-body could see us, I think," said Grimes.

"A young boy came over to my uncle and asked him if he could sign some balls. My aunt said, 'Well, how did you happen to come to a restaurant and have baseballs?' He goes, 'Well, my dad's a coach.'" Thinking they might know the boy's father, Lil prodded and finally learned he was just a Little League coach. "My aunt and I looked at each other, and my uncle just put his hand up like, 'Stop. Don't interrogate my fans. Not another word.'" That, said Grimes, "sort of encapsulated their life—she was the one in their private life who ran things and kept things together, but their public life was always center stage; they lived their life in public. When it came to that, that [public attention] was most important, and he respected his fans no matter how old he got and who they were. They were *it*.

"We just both shut up; and he signed and made this kid feel like he was so important. He walked away, and we still never figured out why he came into a restaurant with baseballs."

Grimes said Lil is "a resourceful person, like a lot of women who've had to raise their kids while their husbands had a job that's on the road. For many years she was Mom and Dad because he was away a lot—not only just during the baseball season, but because he was such a major celebrity. He would always be invited to banquets all over the country. They've definitely been a team. He's said that she's his rock."

As far as baseball went, in July 1939 Williamson's new skipper, Harrison Wickel, unimpressed with Musial, called him undependable and "by far the wildest pitcher I have ever seen" and recommended he be released. Musial, however, remained on the team and hit .352, pinch-hitting and filling in as an outfielder when injuries hit the skimpy 14-man roster. He went 9–2 with a 4.30 ERA and struck out 86 in 92 innings. Unfortunately, he also walked 85.

Williamson rebounded from a mediocre 1938 campaign to win the regular-season championship at 76–51. Advancing to the two-round play-offs, they took the opening best-of-three set over Huntington, with Musial winning two consecutive decisions before dropping the best-of-five championship round to Bluefield. Though they lost the championship, Musial had a magnificent performance in the second game with five hits, two of them homers, and five RBIs.

In the off-season Stan and Lil again returned to Donora, where Stan would work until spring training. They moved into a house on Modisette

Avenue owned by Steve Nagy, who had married Lil's sister, Helen. They rented the upstairs while the Nagys lived downstairs. The house sat in a quaint section of town known as Cement City.

During several off-seasons Musial worked in Labash's store and/or the zinc mill. Between work and raising a family, Stan's time shot by, but his mind was always occupied with his next baseball season. That, and the turmoil in Europe. A September 1, 1939, headline proclaimed, "Hitler Warned by Britain to 'Cease Firing,'" with an accompanying prophetic article titled "It Is Your Suicide, Hitler."

By 1940, the Cardinals owned a slew of players. Musial related, "We'd have 300 players at spring training. Everyone was known by a number, not his name. You'd look on the board in the morning, and if your number was up there, it meant you were going to play."

The 19-year-old Musial went 18–5, again in Class D—this time for the Daytona Beach Islanders. He fanned 176 batters over 223 innings while posting a commendable 2.62 ERA, but he discovered he was not truly cut out for pitching. For one thing, his walk total was woeful at 145. He confessed, "The truth is that I was considering giving up pitching.... Don't let that 18–5 record fool you. I was wild...." He felt that he had peaked and would have been incapable of advancing to a higher level in the minors as a pitcher.

Musial's manager, Dickie Kerr, had gained fame as the winner of two games for the Chicago White Sox in the "fixed" 1919 World Series, the event that came to be known as baseball's worst blemish ever, the Black Sox Scandal. Bill Lee, a colorful pitcher of the 1970s, once called the southpaw the greatest pitcher ever. "Had to be," he claimed. "He won two World Series games when eight guys on his team were trying to lose." For his effort, he was anointed with the nickname "Honest Dickie Kerr." During that Series, Damon Runyon wrote of Kerr, "A new Napoleon has risen to the height of five feet seven to lead the bantam brigade."

Later, frustrated by the miserly ways of White Sox owner Charles Comiskey, Kerr bolted from the Sox and signed with a semipro team in Texas for $500 more than what Comiskey had offered for playing in the majors. He did not return to the big leagues until 1925.

Kerr's obscurity lasted until 1940, when he managed in the Florida State League and used Musial in center field and on the mound. Shortly, he became one of the most important and influential men in Musial's life. *Time* magazine later reported that Kerr "had a skinny Polish kid named Stan

Musial who thought he was a pitcher. Kerr watched the boy and decided that as a pitcher he made a superb hitter."

One Sunday, Kerr saw Musial enter his hotel at around 7:00 AM and asked him if he'd been out on the town. Musial answered, "No, sir, I'm coming from Mass." Kerr immediately realized the high quality of this young man.

Meanwhile, if there was any doubt of his assessment of Musial's future as a pitcher, it vanished when Musial injured his throwing arm while playing the sandy outfield in Daytona Beach on August 11, 1940, against Orlando, taking a rough tumble on his left shoulder while making a shoestring snag of a fly ball. When he dove, his spikes got caught in the outfield terrain, and his fall was an awkward one.

A knot developed on the shoulder, and Musial took to the mound only twice more in minor-league games, winning 5–4 over Sanford before Orlando "knocked him all over the lot," as writer J. Roy Stockton put it at the time.

After his injury, baseball lore has it that Musial considered giving up baseball, although Musial denied that. On $600 for six months' work he was, the story goes, unable to support himself and Lil, then carrying their first child, so he reportedly discussed the idea of going home and getting a job in the steel mills.

Kerr told him his pitching days were over but declared, "You've got more of a future in this game as a hitter." Kerr also came up with a money-saving suggestion, that the Musials would move in with his family during the base-ball season. Kerr's wife, Pep, proceeded to act maternally toward Lil, and the two families clicked.

Kerr added, "I convinced him that he wasn't much of a pitcher anyway. And as a hitter he was a natural. You might say Stan's was a million-dollar accident." One writer called Musial's injury "the seminal moment of his life."

Musial later said, "I was a thrower and got by in high school because I had a dinky curve which used to fool the boys."

Musial also had the support of his father-in-law, Sam Labash. For one, he had paid for Lil's trip to join Stan in Florida. Sam's granddaughter Laurel Grimes stated, "When Stan married Lil, my grandfather was very supportive of him pursing his dreams. I think that support helped them a lot, because when they're in the minor leagues they were making a lot less money than guys that were working in the mill. That mill was booming [especially during] the war time. So most guys had to give up their dreams to go support their families, and Stan's family certainly was poor. My grandfather was very enthusiastic. [He said,] 'Give it a shot. Go for it.'" Luckily, she continued, "Stan had talent and opportunity, and they came together, they meshed."

The Musials' first child was born in August. They named their son Richard in honor of Kerr and gave the baby the middle name Stanley, after his father.

Late in the season, after Musial's arm had healed a bit, he was in the outfield on a full-time basis for the Islanders, going on to hit .311 with 70 RBIs over 405 at-bats. Musial displayed very little clout, hitting only one homer, just as he had the previous two seasons

Barbao Jr. said of Musial's move from the mound to the outfield, "You could equate him to Babe Ruth. Stan was a pitcher, a very good pitcher until he hurt his arm. Then, fortunately, they [the Cards] kept him around, like Rick Ankiel with the Cardinals when he couldn't put the ball over the plate, he was all over the place, and he's come back as a heckuva hitter right now [in 2007]."

Pitchers who develop bum arms usually are weeded out of the game— it's another case of baseball's version of survival of the fittest. There was no way for Musial to know it at that stage of his career, but his injury would lead to his eventual superstardom.

Because of his weakened arm, Musial's best position was probably in left, but he enjoyed playing right field better. For his entire career, he played 907 games in left field, 699 games in right field, 299 games in center, and 1,016 games at first. He once said that his only regret about his career was "[I] played without my good arm…. Of course, as long as I was hitting well, I never did worry about my arm too much." He noted that when he was young and speedier he had been able to charge the ball faster to compensate for his arm. Still, he conceded ruefully that if his arm had been strong, he "would've been known as a better outfielder."

In 1958, Kerr's kindness to Musial never forgotten, an appreciative Musial bought the Kerrs a $10,000, eight-room home in Houston, a white-frame bungalow.

Dr. Ferretti said it was natural for Musial and Kerr to get along, noting the manager had taken to Musial, "a typical Donora product [who] respected age and authority." Musial, in return, was so taken with Kerr he would have followed him with a blind faith and devotion.

The mild-mannered Musial, Clark Kent sans glasses, respected Kerr so much that when a Daytona teammate once said something negative about Kerr, Musial literally had to be pulled off of him.

It was because of Kerr and his unique ability to see Stan's strengths that Musial's career was about to take off in a huge way.

## CHAPTER FOUR

# A Supernova Appears— "Nobody, but Nobody, Can Be That Good"

In 1941 Musial, still under contract as a pitcher, reported to the Cardinals' Double A camp in Hollywood, Florida, weak arm and all, with a total of 233 other prospects. Burt Shotton, a former big-league manager, now worked for the Cardinals and immediately recognized that Musial's arm was bothering him. Shortly after that, Musial annihilated a pitch during an intrasquad game. Shotton stepped off the distance at around 450 feet. Musial recounted being told, "From now on, you're not going to be a pitcher."

Branch Rickey reportedly had also seen Musial's swing and commented that it "was so level that if you put a coin on the top of his bat, it wouldn't fall off."

His mound days over, he was eventually sent to a camp in Columbus, Georgia, where he was placed in a large pool of players. One day minorleague manager Clay Hopper used him as a reliever to face the barnstorming big-league Cardinals, and Musial worked his way out of the inning. The next inning, though, Terry Moore and Johnny Mize (whose grandmother was the sister of Claire Ruth, Babe's second wife) belted massive homers. A couple of days later, Musial worked against the Phillies and was tagged for four hits, six walks, and seven runs in one inning.

Manager Ollie Vanek, the same man who had earlier recommended Musial as a prospect, ran Springfield, Missouri, a Class C team short on outfielders. When Musial asked Vanek if he could work out with his club, Vanek consented.

Later Class A and B managers were asked if they wanted Musial on their rosters. None did. One version of Musial's revival act states that Vanek then accepted Musial but only after Rickey exerted some pressure on him, and with the understanding that when he could find a better outfielder, Musial was gone. Musial insists Vanek unreservedly gobbled him up because he liked his offensive tools and his prospects. Vanek later affirmed that he "knew this fellow could hit—he had showed me that with every team he played with from junior high school to Daytona Beach...."

In any case, Musial joined Springfield of the Western Association, earning $150 a month. He began the season in right field batting cleanup, and after going 2-for-13 over his first three contests, he started turning heads. In one game with Rickey on hand, Musial banged out a single, triple, and homer, good for all his team's runs. Soon his arm grew a bit stronger, and runners no longer took as many liberties against Musial.

Musial's power numbers surged as he pounded out 27 two-baggers and 26 home runs (including four over as many games and a one-game explosion of three homers), good enough to lead the league in homers, even though he didn't play there the entire season. It would mark the only time in his pro career that he led a league in home runs. He also hit .379 with 94 RBIs over 87 contests.

"I led the league in hitting; I was hitting home runs; I was doing everything," said Musial. Actually, the recognized batting champ (Musial did not have enough plate appearances to qualify) was Ed Yarmul, who hit .356. Still, Musial had indeed done everything. When he left the league, he had topped everyone in hits, runs, RBIs, total bases, and homers.

Musial was quickly proving to be a natural. Soon his definition of a slump would become, for example, an 0-for-12 spell, a mere 24-hour virus in an otherwise robust, unending stream of hits.

Musial, coveted by Rochester manager Tony Kaufmann, then made the gigantic leap to the Triple A Red Wings. The team was bogged down in fourth place when Musial jumped on board and played his first game in Syracuse on July 23. He homered the next night and connected again on July 29 in his home debut, one of four hits that day. In August he met Babe Ruth, who put on a pregame hitting display in Rochester. Musial was disillusioned when he saw the Falstaffian Ruth down a pint of whiskey during the game.

Now earning $400 a month, he hit .326 over a 54-game spell, once again a figure good enough to lead his league had his stay there been long enough—the official league-leader, Gene Corbett, hit .306. Plus, Musial was now hitting against pitchers who were extremely close to the majors, further evidence that this boy was a keeper.

Kaufmann praised the young star, saying, "This kid is an iceberg. If you tapped him, you'd find ice water in his veins. Yankee Stadium or a cow pasture—just another place to play ball to him."

One of the earliest national pieces on Musial stated his standout play in the International League playoffs was threefold: he hit well, ran the bases with aplomb, and made fantastic catches.

When Musial's Red Wings reeled off 16 wins during their final 20 games, they squeaked into the playoffs. Over his last three contests he collected nine hits. Newark then knocked off Rochester in five games. Musial returned to Donora, exhausted. After attending church the next day, he received a telegram instructing him to report to St. Louis.

Musial noted, "In those days, to be able to go from Class C to Triple A to the majors in one season was remarkable. Harry Walker, my good friend, thought that was one of my greatest accomplishments." Rickey commented that he was in awe of the 20-year-old's "kaleidoscopic advances."

In this time period, wrote former big leaguer Kirby Higbe, rookies were lucky to get many cuts at all in the batting cage. Veterans monopolized batting practice time while a rookie "would get run out after five swings." Veterans felt rookies were a threat to either their jobs or their friends' jobs, hence the icy cold treatment. Musial, however, gained teammates' respect early on.

Solly Hemus said the Cardinals were a close-knit club, good about accepting new players. When he was a rookie, he remembered, the team "took you in like a part of the family—Musial, Schoendienst, Brecheen, Marion, all those guys. The Cardinals have always been very, very, very warm to their young ballplayers when they bring them into camp. They're made to feel like they belong there—that's the way I felt, and I tried to prolong the same [tradition] when I [later] managed. It's a great organization, great people, and some great ballplayers."

The Cardinals and Dodgers battled in a pennant race, which was white-hot when Musial joined the parent club. The Cards, two games in arrears of Brooklyn, were ready to pounce on the Dodgers if they faltered.

The Cardinals were trying to survive a spate of injuries, including those to starting outfielders Enos Slaughter—known to teammates as "Bosco"—and Terry Moore, who was astonished when he first discovered this Musial kid was the pitcher who had given up mammoth homers to him and Mize in the spring.

In Musial's September 17, 1941, big-league debut, the nightcap of a doubleheader, he faced Jim Tobin of the Boston Bees and picked up his first big-league hit. "The first time I popped up his knuckler [to third base], but the second trip, I doubled [off another knuckler] for two runs, and we won the game 3–2," said Musial, who collected another hit later in the game.

After the top of the first inning, Musial, as was the custom of the day, tossed his glove onto the outfield grass as he trotted to the dugout, doing so as nonchalantly as a litterbug might flip a gum wrapper aside—perhaps flipping it aside as if to validate his presence in the majors.

Precisely 20 years after his debut, he remembered, "There were three out-fielders who reported the same day in St. Louis. Erv Dusak, Walt Sessi,... and me." Because Dusak and Sessi had been sluggers in the minors, Musial said, "[I was] somewhat surprised when [Billy] Southworth started me...." Over his first 22 at-bats, he cranked out 12 hits, vociferously announcing his arrival in the majors and confirming Southworth's good call.

On September 21, 1941, Musial turned in a six-hit performance in a twin bill versus Chicago. The opener was tied when the Cubs sent the 3-for-3 Musial a message pitch (i.e., "Don't get too comfortable and dig in on me, kid"), which left him sprawled in the dirt of the batter's box. Undaunted, he jacked a line shot to right-center field and then advanced to second on an infield out. An intentional walk ensued before Coaker Triplett dribbled the ball in front of the plate. Catcher Clyde McCullough grabbed it and threw to first. When the umpire called the runner safe, the Cubs catcher and first baseman began to argue. Meanwhile, Musial rounded third and crossed the plate before the Cubs could react, scoring the winning tally on a ball that had traveled 10 to 15 feet.

In the journalistic lingo of the day, Musial managed to score "without slackening his streamlined stride." McCullough had failed to cover the plate, distracted when the first-base umpire called Triplett safe on his tardy throw. Southworth stated, "That kid was born to play baseball." Jimmy Wilson, the Cubs' manager, chimed in, "Nobody, but *nobody* can be that good."

On September 23, 1941, the Cardinals visited Pittsburgh for a dou-bleheader, marking Musial's first trip to the big-league park nearest his hometown. His father was in attendance and especially enjoyed the night-cap. "In the second game," stated Musial, "we beat Rip Sewell 9–0, and I hit my first major-league home run [off him]. The odd part of it is that Steven Posey, a friend of mine from Donora, was sitting in the right-field stands and caught the ball."

Two days later, Donora officials organized a day for Musial, called off school, and showered him with luggage and money. Unfortunately, that was the day the Cards were eliminated from the race when Brooklyn blanked Boston. The blazing Dodgers had never relinquished their slim lead late in the season, and St. Louis, with 97 victories, wound up two and a half games out.

Having made the jump from the low minors to the big leagues, Musial would never again move to a new club. Unlike players who were often traded, baseball nomads who carried a hobo's bindle rather than a bat on their shoulders, Musial stayed put in St. Louis.

Facing only the Cubs, Pirates, and Braves, Musial had responded beautifully to his big-league call-up, hitting a gaudy .426 over his auspicious 12-game, 47 at-bat stint with the parent club. "Not bad for an ex-pitcher," he joked.

Respected baseball historian Bill James ranks Musial's late-season showing as one of 10 all-time bests. Twenty hits, five for extra bases, seven RBIs, and eight runs certainly made for a solid foundation on which to build.

During the off-season, Musial signed with Bob Feller's All-Star Team that went on tour, playing against the Kansas City Monarchs of the Negro Leagues, a team led by Satchel Paige. The barnstorming competition was the first for Paige since he squared off against Feller in a scorching pitchers' duel in Iowa in 1936.

Sportsman's Park was booked for an October 5, 1941, barnstorming contest. This brought up important social and political issues, as the park suffered from, as the *Kansas City Call* stated, "an unsavory reputation [as] the only major league park in the country where Negroes are relegated to the bleachers and pavilion and denied grandstand seats." That publication later reported, "several Negroes have managed to obtain grandstand seats," and soon the ballpark opened its grandstand to anyone who wished to buy a ticket. The result was "over 20,000 black and white fans commingled and watched a minor classic with major historical implications." The contest went to Feller's squad 4–3, with the key blow coming from Musial, who smacked a Paige fastball over the pavilion roof in right field.

Playing his home games in Sportsman's Park benefited Musial, as the facility clearly was one better suited for left-handed batters than righties. A poke down the right-field line had only to travel 310 feet to reach the foul pole, 41 feet shorter than the pole in left. The right-field power alley was 354 feet from home plate, versus 379 to the alley in left.

It was an interesting old park—the Browns began playing there not long after the turn of the century, and the Cardinals called it home from July 1, 1920, to May 8, 1966, resulting in more big-league games taking place on that diamond than at any other park.

It was unusual, too, with its flagpole standing in fair territory in the outfield until the 1950s, and a goat that had grazed that same outfield earlier. An advertisement read, "The Cardinals National League Champs Use Lifebuoy Health Soap." Unlike the Lifebuoy ad in Philadelphia's ballpark, no graffiti artist had added the words, "And They Still Stink."

In the meantime, the Donora Zinc Works Employees Athletic Association decided to fete Musial with a testimonial dinner held at the town's Methodist church on October 14. The menu that day featured tomato juice, celery, olives, Swiss steak, mashed potatoes, buttered peas, mints, coffee, and apple pie a la mode. The high school orchestra provided music. In short, it was a wholesome, all-American evening. The only things missing were hot dogs and Chevrolet. The local newspaper announced plans to run a regular feature titled "What Stan Musial Did Yesterday" during the next season.

As the year closed and Musial's early fame spread, he remained so quiet and polite he wouldn't even correct those in the media who pronounced his surname incorrectly, saying "mews-zee-al," rather than the proper "mew-shil." Some were even calling him "Muzal," voicing the same pronunciation as the name (Bob) Meusel of the Yankees, until Musial finally clarified matters.

Just two months and a day after the 1941 Series was completed, a surprise attack by Japanese forces turned Pearl Harbor into an abattoir and drew America into World War II.

Nothing, though, could totally diminish Musial's optimism. The year ended with his future looking bright, even if his bank balance was only $128.

By 1942 Donora's steel mills were absolutely popping with activity, mass-producing materials crucial to the war effort, and, for the first time ever, Pittsburgh's steel mills operated on Christmas Day.

Newsreels captured patriotic moments, such as Paramount News showing a reenlistment ceremony and releasing it as a piece titled *Hank Greenberg Now Battling for Uncle Sam!* The first major leaguer to be drafted also made news. He was Hugh Mulcahy, whose many defeats—he twice suffered 20-loss seasons over his 45–89 career—spawned the insensitive nickname "Losing Pitcher."

On January 15, 1942, President Franklin Roosevelt responded to baseball commissioner Judge Landis, who had wondered if baseball should continue during the war. Roosevelt wrote, "I honestly feel that it would be best for the country to keep baseball going. There will be fewer people unemployed and everybody will work longer hours and harder than ever before. And that means they ought to have a chance for recreation and for taking their minds off their work even more than before."

While Roosevelt supported baseball, he also decreed that no ballplayers would be granted any special exemptions (Musial was excluded from the war until nearly its conclusion due to his family's dependency upon him). Roosevelt would allow "no provision for soft defense jobs" for big leaguers as had been the case in World War I. He also asked that more night games be scheduled so that citizens who worked during the days could still have the opportunity to see a big-league game. Landis quickly complied with the president's wish.

Coming off Musial's September "cup of coffee" in 1941, his first real taste of big-league spring training came in St. Petersburg, Florida. He remained unassuming, a proper rookie, even though he had already impressed the Cardinals brass. In that era, though, there were no guarantees, and veteran players were as difficult to unseat as political incumbents. Jobs on big-league diamonds, with a mere 16 major-league clubs in existence, were scarce.

Roger Kahn found Musial to be the type of man "who seem[ed] to know instinctively just how to conduct himself on the day he first [saw] a major-league camp."

A March 9, 1942, newspaper article proclaimed the six-foot, 175-pound Musial—whom they called "a pink-cheeked Polish boy"—to be the best of the 125 National League rookies. "He has the physique, the speed, the natural ability and the competitor's heart." His collective RBI output of 1941 was 122, prompting Cards manager Billy Southworth to glow, "In all my experience I don't think I've ever seen a better looking ballplayer come up."

One writer penned, "If there's anything the matter with Musial nobody has discovered it." He was, the reporter concluded, destined to be the league's Rookie of the Year.

Despite the kudos, the Grapefruit League season did not begin well for Musial, who later stated, "After getting a couple of hits in the first exhibition game against the Yankees, I didn't do much of anything. I was really the lemon of the Grapefruit League."

Never a great spring-training hitter, Musial believed the St. Petersburg facility was not conducive to his hitting. He said, "I couldn't see very well down in Florida…. They had those palm trees waving back and forth." He told his wife to stay up north, afraid that he might not make the big-league team out of camp.

Southworth said, "I can't quit on him. He won't give up, and I certainly won't." With that, he benched Musial for about a week, then reinserted him into the lineup against a right-handed pitcher. Late in the game, Southworth was tempted to pinch-hit for Musial when a southpaw entered the contest but stuck with Musial, who crushed a two-run, game-winning triple.

Meanwhile, in April, the federal government declared a "dim out" of coastal regions, fearing that the bright lights of cities silhouetted vessels, "making them easy targets for U-boats" lurking in the ocean. In New York, for the first time in 25 years, Times Square's neon lights were turned off.

Musial broke in during a time period when uniforms were boxy and baggy with tops that either buttoned or zipped up and featured half-length sleeves and a T-shirt worn underneath. The big-league garb was far from being sleek or streamlined and was equally far from being sartorially stylish, but for Musial, donning a major-league uniform was the culmination of a lifetime dream.

Early on in the regular season, Southworth still protected Musial some-times by sitting him against starting lefties. He didn't want to put Musial into situations where he might be outclassed. Such treatment did not last long, however.

The war had not depleted the Cardinals of stars, and their dream outfield featured Musial in left, the hard-nosed Enos Slaughter in right, and Terry Moore, who was stupendous in center. Moore, who never went beyond grade school, had, like Musial, begun his career as a pitcher before hurting his arm.

The infield featured the smooth glove work of George "Whitey" Kurowski at the hot corner and a new first baseman in Johnny Hopp. Kurowski's hands were fast and strong, and he was one of the best at hitting under pressure. On the debit side, said shortstop Marty Marion, "he didn't have much range to his left, so I would cheat toward third. And if I went far to my right for a ball, George would hold his glove over his mouth and say, 'Thank you, Marty, thank you.'"

Kurowski had been declared 4-F during the war years due to a crippled arm. When he was seven years old, he had taken a tumble, landing on glass, resulting in a nasty cut to his throwing arm. Soon blood poisoning and osteomyelitis set in, and doctors had to remove four inches of bone. Marion said Kurowski's crooked arm resembled "a dog's hind leg."

The double-play combo was composed of Marion and second sacker Frank "Creepy" Crespi.

The pitching staff contained Mort Cooper, who possessed a good fastball, curve, and change; Howie Pollet, who threw baffling change-ups; and Murry Dickson, a finesse pitcher. Howie Krist had gone 10–0 in 1941 but couldn't crack the starting rotation in 1942. Virtually every pitcher on the staff was a homegrown Rickey product; Harry Gumbert and Lon "the Arkansas Hummingbird" Warneke were exceptions.

Finally, behind the plate was Walker Cooper, who, at a husky 6'3" was ursine in appearance. The payroll for the entire star-studded squad was $180,000.

In the spring, the team tore up Musial's $400-a-month contract that he had signed the previous autumn, boosting his pay to $700 a month. Feeling secure, Musial called Lil, instructed her to join him, and then went out to locate an apartment for his family.

Prior to World War II, the U.S. national anthem was played before baseball games only for occasions such as a team's home opener or for the World Series. That changed with WWII, though, and players solemnly stood before each game, caps off and often held over their hearts, listening to "The Star-Spangled Banner."

Brooklyn, the reigning league champions, a team that would boast of six pitchers to win in double-digits in 1942, bolted from the starting gate with St. Louis once again their main rival. In early May, the Cards, who had begun the year at 5–6, took two of three against Brooklyn. Southworth let it be known that he felt his squad would go nose-to-nose with the Dodgers all year long. "They haven't had their slump yet," he pointed out.

Opposing teams knew the Redbirds lacked right-handed punch, and they began switching up their rotations to use more left-handers against the Cardinals.

Musial began hitting in the second slot in the order. About six weeks later, he moved to the three-hole. For the next month he hit anywhere from third to sixth before earning the cleanup spot from late June on.

In late June the Dodgers, still slumpless, hosted the Cardinals for five contests in Brooklyn, winning four times, submerging St. Louis seven and a half games out of first. The atmosphere was charged during the series, and a fight between Joe Medwick and Marty Marion broke out.

Medwick, an egocentric player accused of worrying only about getting his hits, was also famous for his temper. He was known to fight opponents *and* his own teammates. Dizzy Dean, who spent time with Medwick on the Cardinals, asserted, "The trouble with Medwick is, he don't talk none, he just hits you."

While Musial would grow to become the most popular visiting player in Brooklyn, the rest of the Cardinals and other visiting teams were not made to feel welcome. The visitors' clubhouse was a shambles. Joe Garagiola said it "was in need of a good fire." Without air-conditioning, the window that opened onto the street was kept open in hope of catching a wisp of an errant breeze.

Ebbets Field was a most interesting baseball venue. Built by Charles Hercules Ebbets, the quirky and charming bandbox hunkered down on what had been a garbage dump known as Pigtown in Brooklyn.

Hall of Fame announcer Ernie Harwell remembered his days with the Dodgers. "In Brooklyn we had a lot of traditions. We had the Brooklyn Symphony. They [the group of musicians] had a guy named Shorty Laurice—he and four or five of his pals would come out to the park, and when a guy struck out they would go, 'Bump buh buh, bump buh buh,'" said Harwell, imitating a derisive musical accompaniment that would play as the strikeout victim marched back to the bench. "And when he'd sit down, 'BOOMP!'"

Bob Friend said the short right field at Ebbets helped Musial. "It had a great big high screen—Musial just peppered that thing—it was only about 297 down the right field line. He wore them out up there. Center field was 390, left field was 335; it was a great hitters' ballpark."

Carl Erskine noted that Musial "hit exceptionally well at Ebbets Field," yet he didn't pitch Musial any differently there than he did in St. Louis.

"We got irritated at our fans in Brooklyn. Some of the guys really got upset because our fans cheered Musial like he was playing for us, and he was killing us," he chuckled, recalling those normally loyal fans who had dubbed Musial with the moniker Stan the Man. "It was because he hit so well in those close confines of Ebbets Field, and the fans loved him."

Musial turned Ebbets Field "into a Little League park" and ended up a .356 lifetime hitter there, his best average for any foreign venue.

Earlier Brooklyn fans called him "Musical" until, as the story goes, he went ballistic with the bat and hit .625 in a one particularly torrid series at Ebbets. Flowery journalists gave him other nicknames such as "the Pennsylvania Pole," which, gratefully, never caught on.

In one of the first games Musial ever played in Brooklyn, he made a great running catch. A fan shouted, "Hey music box, how in de woild kin ennybody run so fast and see so good, yuh bum, yuh?" A "bum" appellation, wrote J. Roy Stockton, was, as a rule, reserved for Dodger stars; calling Musial by that label was "a rare caress for a Flatbush fan."

Despite Musial's success against the Dodgers, they didn't knock him down much, and they certainly didn't hit him with pitches often. Even headhunter Don Drysdale, who faced Musial for 68 official at-bats, never hit him. Likewise, Sal "the Barber" Maglie (so called because of his propensity for giving batters a close shave and worse with his pitches), who pitched in the National League with the Giants and Dodgers, went up against Musial for 18 at-bats and gave up three Musial homers yet hit him only once. Such was the respect held for the Man. Over his long career, he was hit by a pitch just 53 times. Still, that didn't stop him from saying, "If your side is black and blue all season long, you know you're having a good year. They used to hit me when I was younger, but you can't be worried about getting hit."

Kirby Higbe joked that Musial's "only weakness was low behind. But he was one hitter we learned not to knock down, because it just made him mad and a better hitter, if that was possible."

Erskine stated, "Now he beat me in Ebbets Field one day by a squib bloop.... I was protecting a lead, and I came in relief, and he squibs a ball, should've been the third out. I fooled him on an off-speed pitch, and he hit it off the end of his bat, but as I told you, he got some [cheaper] hits occasionally, to go with his line drives, because he always made contact. And he just blooped a single that cost me a game because it brought up, I think, [Ken] Boyer, the next hitter, and he hit a home run. Instead of getting Musial out and ending the game, he kept the game alive. There again, that was his style, he always made you handle the ball; he hit it someplace."

One Donora resident spoke of the time in Brooklyn when Musial had a stretch of five hits "and every one went to a different part of the stadium—left field, left-center, center field, right-center, and right field." Larry King stated Musial tattooed each of those hits off the outfield wall.

At the All-Star break, Musial, now entrenched as the team's left fielder, had driven in just 17 runs over the season's first 55 games. His average, though, was at .315, and his Cardinals were on pace to win 94 games. However, the Bums were winning at a clip that projected 102 wins.

"I was sorta disappointed that I didn't make the All-Star Team in 1942," Musial later said. The other two Cardinals outfielders did make the squad, but 1942 represented the only time Musial didn't make the team other than 1945, when he was in the Navy.

When the rival Cards and Dodgers met in July, another fight took place. This one boasted a main event with the marquee billing of Musial vs. Webber. Under orders from the abrasive Leo Durocher, a man who many felt was as subtle as a sucker punch and as welcome as a chronic case of eczema, Les Webber knocked Musial down with four consecutive fastballs. In a rare flash of anger, Musial, who would never again charge the mound, set out after Webber before being restrained by coaches.

Musial said he was familiar with Durocher's habit of shouting out "to his pitchers from the dugout, 'Stick it in his ear!' all the time. But it [usually] didn't bother me." As for his uncharacteristic charging of the mound, Musial later admitted, "I didn't know what I was going to do once I got out there."

Normally Musial, a pacifist, was on the outskirts of scrums, not at epicenters. Former Cardinal Joe Cunningham said, "He didn't want to take a chance on getting hurt. He and Red [Schoendienst] more or less said that these fights are just trouble, you can get hurt and then you'd be out of the lineup. I don't ever remember Stan or Red getting in the middle of a fight."

Solly Hemus remembers differently. "Oh, he'd get in the middle of it. He had the respect of the other ballplayers. Opposing players admired him, and they didn't want to get involved with him either." In other words, Musial might help break things up without worrying about someone taking a cheap shot at him from behind.

Musial once opined that Durocher's attempts at intimidation were "just stirring up a nest of hornets," that his tactics "backfired on him more often than not" and caused Musial to get "charged up before" games against

Leo the Lip. Durocher's style, wrote Musial, "turned us from tabbies into tigers."

Dodgers catcher Mickey Owen related a story about Musial and Webber. It began when Musial hit a line shot to the box, which struck Hugh Casey on the hand. The next Dodgers pitcher, Webber, seeking revenge for Musial's hitting his buddy, tried to plunk Musial. He missed Musial twice. Stan turned to Owen, laughed, and said, "That S.O.B. can't hit me if he throws all day." Sure enough, Musial nimbly eluded the next two would-be knock-down pitches, foiling Webber.

Musial's rare bursts of anger were triggered by his attitude toward Durocher, a man who, Musial felt, was frequently guilty of bush-league antics. Many players saw Durocher as penny-ante in the high-stakes world of big-league baseball. Once Durocher so rankled a pitcher, he swiveled toward Durocher's dugout and launched the ball in his direction.

A line from the movie *Inherit the Wind* described a pompous, self-assured character as being "the only man I know who can strut sitting down." Durocher had that same talent. Further, he used his acerbic ways to help his team win, and he certainly must have felt he could get under Musial's skin.

Hal Smith said Durocher "was not a favorite of all the players, you know. Even a bunch of his own players [didn't care for him]. He liked the superstars. He ran with them, he didn't have much to do with the guys that didn't hit over .300 and knock in 100 runs and hit 30 home runs. If you weren't a superstar, you weren't his idol."

In any case, after Musial calmed down after being buzzed four successive times, and Webber continued pitching, the Cardinals went on to sweep the doubleheader, making up precious ground. The nightcap featured outfielder Pete Reiser slamming full-tilt into the concrete wall and suffering a concussion in a vain attempt to snare what became an inside-the-park home run off Slaughter's bat. Higbe felt the injury cost the Dodgers a pennant.

He may have been correct. Brooklyn had won 71 of their first 100 contests, good for the second-best pace in league annals. Then, beginning on August 14, the Cards won an unbelievable 37 of their last 43 games.

Right around the time they began to click, the team selected a Spike Jones novelty song, "Pass the Biscuts, Mirandy," as their victory tune. After each Cardinals win, they played the song with team trainer Harrison J. Weaver, known as "Doc" to the players, on the mandolin and Musial playing a mean slide whistle or beating out a rhythm using makeshift drumsticks.

Former Cardinal Wally Westlake remembered how Musial sat on a metal stool in the clubhouse, "and he'd turn that radio on to that Oakie [much like today's country] music and hit on that stool with a pair of wire coat hangers—and I mean he would strum up a storm. We used to kid that he was getting himself cranked up for the game."

When Brooklyn's lead had been seven and a half games, Larry MacPhail, who had built this Dodgers club, paid a rare visit to the clubhouse, where he warned manager Leo Durocher and his players to fight complacency, but the team acted as if the pennant was already theirs. Instead of heeding MacPhail's advice, the players, in an almost flippant and clearly a buoyant mood, hopped a train for a late-season trip to St. Louis. As the train rolled on, they held a wild party, as if to celebrate their sure-thing success. Red Barber reported it was to be "the last party the 1942 Dodgers had." They dropped three out of four to the Cards.

Just prior to a September 11–12 two-game set in Brooklyn, and after a stretch in which the Dodgers went 10–9, Brooklyn still led the blistering Cards by two games, a lead as tenuous as a puff of cigar smoke, with 18 games to go.

Mort Cooper, going for his 20th win, opened the short series. Cooper, interestingly, had begun switching his uniform number around mid-August. He had never before won 13 games, and when he remained stuck on his 12th victory for some time, he decided to try wearing No. 13 to change his fortunes. When that superstitious move worked, he began switching jerseys after each of his victories, borrowing uniforms when necessary, no matter the fit, in order to wear the number of the next win he was aiming for. Thus, on that September day, he was wearing the No. 20 jersey of teammate Coaker Triplett. Cooper would don No. 21 the next time out, after dissecting the Dodgers, tossing a three-hitter while allowing no runner to reach second base.

Max Lanier, a pitcher who threw lefty since childhood after twice breaking his right arm, followed that up with a 2–1 victory. Immediately after the final out had secured their 29th win over the last 34 contests, Musial and his teammates joyfully jogged off the field, tied for first.

On September 13, St. Louis lost a 2–1 heartbreaker in the ninth inning to the cellar-dwelling Phillies but took over first place when they salvaged a win in the nightcap and Brooklyn dropped a doubleheader to the Reds. The Dodgers, frustrated and defanged, dashed off a telegram to the Reds, in which they accused the team of using their best pitchers to squelch the Dodgers' pennant chances.

Due to their frequent late-inning rallies, the Cards became known as the "come-from-behind kids." They went 43–9 over the last third of the season.

When the Cardinals' lead reached one and a half games, Durocher called a team meeting, exhorting his Dodgers to go hard for their final eight games. The team responded, winning all eight contests. The Cardinals, unfazed and refusing to lose, swept their final six games and wrapped up the pennant.

Everything clicked for them, including Musial's first grand slam, a September 22 smash off Rip Sewell, who had also been the victim of Musial's first big-league homer. Despite being in the middle of a pennant race often as tight as the seal of an O-ring, the Cards had drawn well under 10,000 spectators to see Musial's slam, which secured the team's 102nd win.

In the pennant-clinching game of September 27, Musial triumphantly snagged a fly ball in left field off Clyde McCullough's bat for the final out. Brooklyn, which had held a 10-game lead on August 5, was through, despite winning 104 times, the best win total ever by a second-place club.

The Cardinals won a staggering 106 games, the most in the National League since 1909. The Cards, a team almost devoid of pure power—Enos Slaughter led the team in homers with a mere 13 with Musial close behind at 10—had won 21 of their 25 contests in September. They became hot at just the right time and discovered they needed nearly each of those wins to seize the pennant.

Slaughter later said, "That '42 Cardinal team was the best team I ever played on, better than all the Yankee teams and everything else. We had a young team...we had desire." Others called the unit "a team of poor, unspoiled country boys who worked extra hard." Ironically, their manager, Billy Southworth, griped that his team was "pampered."

Musial ended his first full year in the majors hitting .315, second-best on the club. His reputation growing, the boy known as the "Donora Greyhound" could just as well have been called the "Donora Magician," a precursor to Lance Burton. He was in the batter's box one moment, then, poof, he would reappear on second or third base (he reached double figures in both two-base hits and triples), employing sleight of foot on the base paths and his quicker-than-the-eye hands at the plate.

The 1942 Yankees entered the World Series on a quest for their sixth world championship in seven seasons. The last time they had lost a Series was in 1926, to the Cardinals. Since then, the juggernaut of a club had won eight championships and had lost just four of their 36 postseason games.

Sportswriter Maury Allen believed that, "the Yankees were going to really give them a lesson and show them what baseball was all about, and this is another Yankee sweep." Marion agreed but disagreed with Allen. "Even though the Yankees probably had better talent than we did in that particular year, we knew they could not beat us because we were very confident."

The Cardinals had good reason for such confidence; they were armed with 20-game winners Mort Cooper (22–7 with a lustrous ERA of 1.78) and rookie Johnny Beazley (21–6 with a 2.13 ERA). These two men were destined to start four of the five games in the Series.

The opener was held at Sportsman's Park on the final day of September. Spectators shelled out $5.75 for a reserved seat in the lower stands. By way of contrast, a ticket for a seat in outfield Section 103 at Philadelphia—hardly the best seat in the house, and one that went for around $27 in the regular season—had a face value of $225 for the 2008 Series.

Many Cardinals fans arrived via the Grand Avenue streetcar, dismounting at Grand and Dodier. The park—bedecked in red, white, and blue bunting—stood proudly in the middle of a rather shabby neighborhood. Inside, the atmosphere was electric—all that was missing was ring announcer Michael Buffer.

The Yankees spanked the Cardinals, who, having given up the fewest runs all year long in the National League, surrendered seven runs, some of them gifts, as St. Louis committed four errors. Cooper's mound opponent, Red Ruffing, had a no-hitter brewing until Terry Moore broke it up with a two-out single in the bottom of the eighth. In the ninth, the Cards staged a furious rally, cutting the lead to 7–4. However, with the bases jammed, Musial grounded out to first to end the game.

The next day, St. Louis could muster only six hits versus Ernie Bonham, but they won 4–3. Charlie "King Kong" Keller's homer in the eighth helped erase a 3–0 Cardinals lead. But Musial answered in the Cards' half of the eighth with a timely two-out single to score Slaughter, giving the Cardinals the lead for good.

The Series moved to Yankee Stadium, a venue as venerable, some might argue, as the Roman Coliseum. Arrogant Yankees gloated that there would be no need for any additional games in St. Louis. Their prophecy would prove correct but, for them, in an ironic, demoralizing way. In Game 3 Ernie White and Spud Chandler locked up in a pitchers' duel. White prevailed 2–0, making him the first pitcher to blank the Yankees in a World Series contest since 1926.

A record throng, just 98 fans shy of 70,000, packed Yankee Stadium for the fourth encounter. Keller came up big again, contributing a three-run homer, but the Cardinals, who blew a 6–1 lead, bounced back to win 9–6. Two-thirds of their runs came in the fourth inning when Musial began a rally by bunting down the third-base line for a single. Then he topped off the scoring by pulling a run-producing double to right. His two hits in one inning tied a World Series record, one that would prove as difficult to tumble as six "milk cans" at a county fair.

Game 5 was held on October 5, and the Cardinals felt momentum was on their side. For the third straight game, the two teams drew over 69,000 fans to a bulging Yankee Stadium. The Yankees would leave the game, played in a crisp hour and 58 minutes, disappointed, the losers of four Series games in a row for the first time since 1922.

Amazingly, the Cards once more were guilty of four errors. Despite such sloppiness they went on to win 4–2, giving them their first title since 1934 and their fourth championship versus two World Series defeats.

Bedlam reigned in the Cardinals clubhouse, and champagne flowed freely. Several players snatched the hat off National League president Ford Frick's head and ripped it apart. It felt good being the champs.

A newspaper account summarized, "The Yankees were simply outhit in the clutch, outrun on the base paths and outgamed by a desperate, gambling gang of kids who played them for what they were—swell opponents— rather than what they were rated to be, a super-human baseball machine." The Cardinals had simply refused to be awed by the Yankees.

St. Louis had dethroned the supposedly invincible Yankees. What made the win so shocking was the way the Cardinals, after their opening loss, swept the next four contests. Over that span the Yanks dropped as many Series games as they had in their last eight World Series from 1927 to 1941.

Years later, Musial picked the 1942 squad as the best Cardinals team he ever saw. They "fought together," he said. "We thought we could beat anybody, and we did. They'd knock us down; we'd knock them down."

Musial hit just .222 with just one extra-base hit, a double, in the World Series, but he did draw four walks to give him an on-base percentage of

.364. After earning $4,200 for his regular-season output (just $27.27 per game), he beamed upon receiving the winners' share of the Series booty, $6,192.50. By way of contrast, in 2009 major leaguers received $89.50 in per diem money, or $7,249.50 a year just for incidentals.

At the train station, when the rest of the team headed back to St. Louis to take part in a parade, Musial bid his teammates farewell; he was headed back home to meet his wife and son. He shook hands all around and wept as the train pulled away from the station.

Still only 21 years old, Musial commented that he could now "walk down the streets of Donora as a member of baseball's world champions."

October 14 was declared Stan Musial Day in his hometown, and a testimonial dinner, limited to 400 friends and relations, paid tribute to Donora's hero. He kept occupied until spring by attending football games at Donora High, touring the South, and visiting a few army camps.

Just 24 days after winning the championship, Branch Rickey, his contract with St. Louis having expired after the Series, quit his post as the Cardinals vice president. He and team owner Sam Breadon were no longer compatible, so, after their more than 20 years together with the club, Rickey was through.

Three days later Rickey signed a $40,000 per year (plus bonuses) contract with the Dodgers to become their president and general manager.

With the New Year came a command from Landis—all major-league clubs would be required to hold their spring-training camps "north of the Mason-Dixon Line." Landis even had teams' 1943 schedules altered so that they would only make three, not the customary four, trips into opponents' cities during the season.

Major-league teams were thrown into a tizzy, forced to find new locales for spring training. "The Florida 'Grapefruit League,'" wrote William B. Mead, "was replaced by the Indiana 'Limestone League.'" The Chicago Cubs and White Sox trained in French Lick, Indiana, the future home of National Basketball Association superstar Larry Bird. The Reds worked out in Bloomington, Indiana, at the university there, and the Tigers, Pirates, and Indians also found spring homes in Indiana.

Even though Landis had forbade camps being located south of the Ohio or the Potomac rivers, the two St. Louis teams were given some leeway. The Cardinals' spring coop was in Cairo, Illinois, a city typically 15 degrees warmer than St. Louis, and the Browns trained in Cape Girardeau, Missouri, about 120 miles south of St. Louis.

Problems due to training up north ensued from the start. The White Sox's field was drenched in four feet of muddy water. Some teams had to spend some of their training time indoors, often inside college field houses. Cardinals manager Billy Southworth found occasional indoor work to be "a good break" and not a hindrance to his normal plans. "You see," he began, perhaps rationalizing, "the early outdoor work makes the muscles sore and the indoor work warms them up and takes out the soreness."

By way of contrast, Yankees skipper Joe McCarthy grumbled from his Asbury Park, New Jersey, location that he was training a baseball team, not "a basketball team or a track squad." His troops, he insisted, would work outdoors only. They did but suffered from the area's coldest and windiest spring in years.

By the last day of February, the number of minor-league players who were in the military or who had retired since October 10, 1940, reached 2,431, and the drain on player personnel was having an impact. Due to the war, the Texas League suspended all operations, reducing organized baseball to nine minor leagues doing business.

Furthermore, big-leaguers who had customarily traveled in private train cars and were given lower berths now had to mingle and eat with citizens and soldiers and sleep in upper berths as well. Everyone in the States had to endure shortages and rationing. First came restrictions on tires, cars, sugar, and gasoline. Later came the rationing of coffee, shoes, meats, and fats. Players often had to eat fish instead of their preferred sizzling steaks. Boxes of Cracker Jack candy, which had come with their slogan-promised "Prize in Every Box" toy since 1912 (four years after their product gained immortality by being mentioned in the lyrics of "Take Me Out to the Ball Game") no longer packaged trinkets produced in Japan.

In pro football, the Philadelphia Eagles and the Pittsburgh Steelers, their rosters badly depleted, merged for this season only, becoming the Steagles, an odd NFL hybrid squad.

The Cardinals felt the impact of the war, as did other clubs. By late October, 170 American League players and 155 National Leaguers were serving their country, and many of the teams' minor-league prospects were at an age that made them ripe for the draft. In addition, the 1943 Cards lost Terry Moore and Enos Slaughter, leaving Musial as the only returning outfielder. Harry Brecheen, who had been groomed in the minors since 1935, replaced Beazley's spot in the pitching rotation. Nicknamed "the Cat" for his agility and fielding prowess, the 160-pounder gave the defense further strength up the middle. "He threw that soft stuff up there, curveballs, sliders, change-ups, but with pinpoint control—in and out, up and down. He'd put it [more speed] on, take it off; drive you crazy," said Westlake. Over his career as a Cardinal, Brecheen won 63 percent of all his decisions.

With the team undergoing a face lift, a young Musial had a ton of pressure thrust upon him. He was expected to carry the offensive load and become the team leader.

Stu Miller said his Cardinals teammate Musial was not a rah-rah leader but rather led by example in the clubhouse and on the field. As Musial grew older, he became more up front with teammates. Bobby Del Greco said Musial "was a pretty good joker in the clubhouse. He played pranks on people now and then. He was really talkative and he was a great guy." He did magic and other tricks as well, especially for rookies, as a way to loosen them up.

"When he went out onto the field, he was all business. In those days we used to root for guys on the bench, screaming and hollering, but I don't think they do that anymore. But he was good like that. We used to chatter a lot when we played in the '50s and '60s: 'Let's get a hit,' 'He's [the opposing pitcher] not that good,'" Del Greco recalled.

As Musial later became more assertive, he assumed the role of the unquestioned team leader. Musial, said Del Greco, would "come in to the dugout and try to hop us up a little bit. He never got angry, well, maybe a little bit when we lost a few games, but other than that he was always cool."

Bill Virdon, who would also later become a Musial teammate, noted that, as a leader, "He was very complimentary. 'Congratulations, nice running, good job.' You couldn't have had a better person to encourage you as you went into games."

Carl Warwick felt "Musial was always friendly, kidding people. There was no doubt Stan Musial was the leader of that ball club. Any time his presence was around the players, everybody was in awe, ready to listen to him. He wanted to win. I guess Stan could have walked in the locker room every day and never said a word and everybody would follow him. He probably could [have done] that too, but he was an outgoing person with all the players. There was no distinction between him being a superstar and anybody on the ball club."

Tim McCarver added there was a special presence about him. "Any time Stan Musial was around, you got the feeling that everything was going to be all right."

While teammates lionized Musial, club owner Sam Breadon didn't agree early in 1943. He offered Musial, then employed in the Zinc Works, a $1,000 raise. On March 5 Musial wrote back requesting a hike of $10,000, later lowering his demand to $7,500. Breadon, so tight-fisted he once advised the team's traveling secretary to unplug his electric clock at night in order to save money, was infuriated and disappointed in Musial. He eventually dispatched Eddie Dyer to offer Musial a compromise, a contract for $6,250, which he accepted after his first-ever holdout, reporting to camp a week late. Breadon, still furious, considered Musial to be an upstart and an ingrate.

In 1943 and 1944, War years, the Musials had no car and lived near the ballpark so they could walk to home games.

*Into the Temple of Baseball* tells how Sportsman's Park, circa 1943, was "a grimy stadium...a tired ballpark echoing the murmur of a slack-jawed crowd aroused from time to time by the crack of a base hit or the cry of 'Cold beer here!'" Wagers were made right there inside the park, as Jewish, Irish, and black bookmakers were stationed at various spots throughout the park; but placing a bet "required a certain amount of stealth." The facility reeked of the customary unholy trinity of odors: cigars, urine, and stale beer. The playing surface, however, "was pristine"—from a fan's perspective, that is.

From a player's point of view, the field was far from being beautiful. Marty Marion called the infield "a rock pile" and groused, "There was hardly any grass because the sun burned it off." Brooklyn's George Shuba recalled the field in Sportsman's Park, used by the two St. Louis clubs, as being "very hard and the grass in the infield dried up because of all the use it got." Players also complained that the ballpark's lighting system was poor, thus not conducive to good hitting.

As far as the dimensions of the ballpark went, Shuba said a batter's best target was "in right field where you would hit it on top of the stands or over the stands, but the left-field and center-field fences were very far. It was a much better hitters' park for a left-handed hitter," a fact that pleased Musial.

The park's dimensions included these depths: 350 feet to left, 379 feet to left-center, 420 feet to dead center (but the deepest part of the park during Musials' era was 426 feet), 354 feet to right-center, and 309 ½ feet down the right-field line.

Glamorous or not, the park hosted 222,949 fans for 14 night contests, which was the league's limit for games played under the lights that season. The next year they were permitted to host 21 night games, alleviating the stifling, humid conditions of the midsummer.

Around this time, the typical outfit that Musial wore to the park was a beige suit, a white-on-white shirt, and a silver-and-brown-striped tie to go with well-shined tan loafers. Plus, adorning the fourth finger of his right hand was his 1942 World Series ring.

Steve Russell said that while Musial couldn't afford to wear fancy attire as a youth, he became a sharp dresser, "but that goes along with the territory of being a baseball player. Once you take on that role, one of the things that's expected of you is that you dress very elegantly, almost like G.Q. When you're not in that baseball uniform, you're expected to present an image, especially clothing-wise. Stan picked that up."

When the season began, the Cards were shut out in their first two games, both extra-inning affairs. Their first run of 1943 scored in their third game, when Musial slid across the plate on a steal of home.

One game began on a sun-drenched field before dark clouds rapidly rolled in, thunder rumbled, and cool winds caused the temperature to fall drastically. Suddenly a lightning bolt crackled and ripped into the center-field flagpole, singeing the American flag and, below it, the banner of the 1942 World Champion Cardinals. In retrospect, it seems somehow evocative of Roy Hobbs' pyrotechnics and was not, as some fans feared, a bad omen.

On June 12, 1943, the Cardinals settled into first place. They never again dropped lower than one and a half out and from July 2 on never relinquished first place. They were destined to finish a colossal 56 games above .500.

When July rolled around, the Dodgers' pitcher Les Webber once more tried to hit Musial with a few pitches. Walker Cooper quickly retaliated. Keeping with the mores of baseball during this era, he stepped on Augie Galan's foot at first after grounding out. Mickey Owen jumped Cooper from behind, and yet another scuffle ensued. What also followed were four straight victories over Brooklyn, and the Cardinals cruised to a comfortable lead in the National League.

The regular season took its annual hiatus on July 13, 1943, for its All-Star Game at Philadelphia's Shibe Park. A record eight Cardinals, including five starters, thickly dotted the NL roster. It was Musial's first Midsummer Classic and the first one to be held at night. It was also the only All-Star Game of the 20th century without a single Yankee appearing in the box score. Responding to charges that he showed favoritism toward his Yankees players in selecting his starting All-Star lineup, New York manager Joe McCarthy sat his five Yanks on the bench for the entire contest. Musial played in both left then right field, batted third, drove in the game's first run in his first All-Star at-bat, and went 1-for-4, a double. The AL won the game 5–3, and it was broadcast to GIs through shortwave radio.

The early part of August found the Cardinals in first place by 14 games, thanks largely to a stretch in which they took 18 of 20 games dating back to July 18. Their play in doubleheaders also helped, as they swept 14 twin bills and went 42–18 in doubleheaders (excluding those that resulted in a tie contest).

At the end of August they needed to stay afire in order to match their 106 wins from 1942. They rambled on, winning 26 of 32 games, but came up a tad short at 105–49. Their cumulative record for 1942 and 1943 was 211–97, the finest over a two-year span since the Cubs won 223 from 1906 to 1907. St. Louis wrapped up the pennant on September 18 with two weeks remaining on the schedule; only three National League clubs had ever clinched earlier.

In September baseball players—including Musial, double no-hit artist Johnny Vander Meer, Bill Dickey, and Rudy York, who was half American Indian—agreed to play in exhibition games in the South Pacific for American troops. The trip was canceled later by the War Department supposedly due to the decision of Secretary of War Henry L. Stimson, who "felt that the troops would resent the sight of apparently healthy ballplayers not in service uniform."

That year Musial put together a 22-game hitting streak, led the league in hits with 220, and won his first batting crown (.357). With just 152 games' experience entering the season, Musial had gone on to cop his first MVP Award. One writer suggested that he possibly could have topped the .400 plateau had it not been for the use of the balata ball.

That ball was made of a substitute for rubber near the core of the ball, because rubber was direly needed for the war effort. The dud of a baseball was heavy, and the game's offense seemed to suffer as a consequence—11 of the first 29 games staged resulted in shutouts.

Musial managed to do fairly well, but his best drives were being caught short of the fences. He commented that he sympathized with players from the past who lived through the dead-ball era. A test of the balata ball revealed it was 25.9 percent less resilient than the 1942 baseball.

Eventually the ball was juiced up a bit to combat the dearth of runs scored, but initially the balata ball had led to teams playing small ball, relying more heavily than usual on tactics such as the bunt and the hit-and-run play.

At season's end, St. Louis ended up leaving Cincinnati in the dust, 18 games out. The Yankees had also waltzed to their pennant, finishing 13½ games ahead of the Senators.

Murry Dickson had entered the army during the last week of the 1943 season but obtained a 10-day pass that permitted him to join the Cardinals and work in the World Series.

The Yankees, having lost Joe DiMaggio and Phil Rizzuto to the war, were hurt more than the Cards had been. The only non-pitchers who were Yankees returnees from the 1942 Series were Bill Dickey, Joe Gordon, and Charlie Keller. The Cardinals had a handful of players, such as Walker Cooper, Mort Cooper, Max Lanier, Marion, and Kurowski, who would not miss as much as one full season due to the war. Still, the Yankees came into the fray as the favorites.

Due to travel restrictions, the 40th World Series, a rematch of 1942, began on October 5, 1943, in New York for three contests before it would move to St. Louis on October 10 for the rest of the games.

The Yankees won the opener 4–2 behind Spud Chandler and his stellar 20–4 record. St. Louis used lefty Lanier as pitcher, who took the loss, hurt by his own error and wild pitch. Musial, in his No. 3 spot in the order, had a quiet 1-for-4 day.

The next day, Mort and Walker Cooper learned their father had died early that morning. They decided to play, then travel to the funeral. Mort went the route, issuing six hits. Musial's single to center off Tiny Bonham to open up the top half of the fourth helped. After a sacrifice, he scored on a Kurowski single, and the Cardinals went on to win 4–3.

A new World Series record 69,990 spectators crammed into Yankee Stadium for Game 3, a contest riddled by four Cardinals errors, including costly ones by Harry Walker and Kurowski in the Yankees' five-run eighth, which handed New York a 6–2 victory.

In Games 4 and 5, the Cardinals' bats went mute as they scored only once, losing by scores of 2–1 and 2–0. The now-forgotten Marius Russo handcuffed the Cards in the fourth contest, and Chandler frustrated the Redbirds in Game 5, working out of jams and stranding 11 runners. Suddenly it was all over for St. Louis.

Musial again had a sub-par World Series. He mustered just five hits (.278), all singles, and did not drive home a run. Still, he took home a check for $4,321.99, the losers' cut of the Series pot.

Musial returned to Donora's zinc works, then joined a six-week USO tour of Alaska and the Aleutian Islands to entertain United States troops. Howard T. Kosbau, the sports editor of a service newspaper, wrote, "The soldiers here would rather talk with big-league ballplayers than with Betty Grable." The trip was a success, but not *everyone* concurred that they preferred baseball to Grable.

As the seemingly endless days of winter wound down, Bimbo Cecconi of Donora remembered practicing basketball for his high school team in 1944. "Musial would come in the gym and get prepared physically with Jim Russell, who was from [nearby] Fayette City and played for the Pittsburgh Pirates. They'd come in and warm up and get their bodies in shape before they went to camp, but Musial was a skinny sucker. He was not a muscular person. In those days weight lifting and bodybuilding [weren't big]—this was all natural. He worked in the mill; I don't remember him lifting a weight. He was not made by stuff you drink, pills, stuff that makes big muscles. He was a natural athlete."

Finished with his workouts, Musial would deliver groceries for his father-in-law in South Donora, and he would do so until it was time to head south.

By the start of the 1944 season, more than 340 Major League Baseball players and over 3,000 minor-league players were in the military.

The boot-camp drudgery and the ennui of spring training complete, the Cardinals and Browns traveled back to St. Louis for their six-game City Series. Due to inclement weather, one game required no turnstiles, drawing a you-can-count-their-heads "crowd" of just 354, and one game was washed out. The Cardinals took four of five from a pitching staff composed entirely of overage and 4-F moundsmen. The Browns' offense, not unlike a placebo, sorely lacked any true punch—only the White Sox hit for a lower AL team average that season.

The Cardinals' fortunes remained bright with five of their starting regulars and two of their top pitchers from the 1942 champion team still on hand. They also knew they would not lose the 4-F Mort Cooper or Kurowski. Additionally, Walker Cooper and Marion the Octopus had physical problems that caused them to move down the draft list. In all, five of their pitchers were classified 4-F, so the team was not as decimated as most big-league clubs.

Musial had a deferment that, in some communities, would not have been granted. Each draft board considered factors such as occupation, number of children born prior to the Pearl Harbor attack, and age. Some boards took almost every able-bodied man between the ages of 18 and 38 available to them, while others had a pool of men so deep that some went to war and others stayed at home. "There was no hint that Musial sought or received special consideration; he was just lucky," wrote William B. Mead.

Musial was only 23 years old and was in top shape, but his son had been born before the attack on Pearl Harbor. Further, he was supporting his mother and father, who suffered from black-lung disease contracted when he worked in the coal mines. The fact that Musial worked in the steel mills during the off-season also helped him get a deferral.

Actually, by May 16 Musial had been accepted by the navy, having had his physical moved from Donora to Jefferson Barracks in St. Louis, but he had yet to receive a call-up date. Initially, though, the team believed they'd lose Musial within six weeks.

The Cardinals team was so rich in talent that *The Sporting News* opined, "If the Cardinals are able to maintain their current lineup for even half the season, it will be downright murder."

Joe Nuxhall's name played prominently, albeit briefly, in the sports pages, first when the Reds signed the ninth-grader to a big-league contract and later when he joined the team. True, there was a paucity of skilled ballplayers due to the war, but a *15-year-old player?*

Nuxhall stood around six feet tall when he was 12 years old and was discovered by the Reds two years later. Although Cincinnati wanted to sign him right away, Nuxhall turned down the offer because he hoped to help his Wilson Junior High School basketball team win their third consecutive conference title.

Armed with only a fastball, he soon became the youngest player ever to sign a pro-baseball contract. Due to his school obligations, he ordinarily showed up at the Reds' home park only on weekends and for an occasional night game during the week.

On June 10 he took to the hill in a major-league game at Crosley Field, the youngest player ever to appear in the bigs, now just two weeks removed from being a junior high school student/athlete. Reds manager Bill McKechnie needed an arm to mop up a 13–0 annihilation at the hands of the Cardinals. Nuxhall trotted from the dugout to the bullpen, reportedly tripping and plopping on his face, then proceeded to warm up before entering the game in the ninth inning.

In front of a short-sleeved Saturday-afternoon crowd of just 3,510, Nuxhall issued two walks and retired two hitters, including George Fallon, the first major-leaguer he faced. Then the first superstar he would oppose, Musial, settled in at the plate.

Nuxhall later said he was wild, but Musial "just dug in...he stood up there like I was a needle threader." It was no contest. Musial stroked a run-scoring single. Nuxhall then lost his cool. In all, he faced nine hitters and gave up five walks and two hits, uncorking a wild pitch and surrendering five earned runs over just two-thirds of an inning, for an ERA of 67.50.

The proverbial floodgates had gaped open so wide that McKechnie sauntered out to the mound and said, "Well, son, I think you've had enough." The young hurler, visibly relieved, headed to the showers. Nuxhall later said, "I kind of tended to agree with him."

The Cardinals went on to win 18–0 on 21 hits. Despite the offensive barrage, the game lasted just two hours and 28 minutes. They improved their record to 30–16, the best in baseball.

In a sort of parallel to the Moonlight Graham tale from *Field of Dreams*, another young pitcher, Jake Eisenhart, made his big-league debut that day. The 21-year-old worked just one-third of an inning in what would also prove to be his final day in the majors.

Two days after Nuxhall's debut he was shipped out for more seasoning in the Sally League. It took an additional eight seasons before he made it back to the majors.

A few days after Independence Day, a young army lieutenant named Jackie Roosevelt Robinson was court-martialed for refusing a driver's instructions to get to the rear of a military bus in Fort Hood, Texas. He was acquitted but realized, he wrote, that he not only had to fight a war against foreign enemies but also had to wage combat "against prejudice at home."

Around this time Cubs pitcher Hank Wyse toyed with a new approach in pitching to Musial. A friend of his advised him to wait Musial out, to go into his normal arm-pump prior to his big windup but to hesitate until he saw Musial's right knee relax, before releasing the ball. "If it don't do it on the second pump," Wyse was advised, "pump again. If you don't see it then, pump again."

The ploy seemed to work. When Musial began to notice his luck against Wyse had turned, he scrutinized pictures from his at-bats against him. Soon after, as Wyse recounted, Musial hit a rope "right between my legs about a hundred miles an hour. He got on first base and laughed. He said, 'You're not going to do it anymore. I know what you're doing.'"

On August 16 the Cardinals won their 80th game, marking the quickest any team ever reached that level. When the Pirates reeled off 10 straight wins that month they gained a mere one game in the standings.

In early September Musial collided with Debs Garms. Anxious to help the team when they began to sag (at one point they went 5–15), Musial returned too quickly and was not the man he normally was. He was further out of sync because he had to return to Donora to minister to his ailing father for a period of 10 days.

Still, the team had glistened right out of the opening gate, winning 73 of the first 120 contests. By the first week of September, their lead was so great that the Cardinals started taking ticket requests for the World Series. They faltered a bit in September before winning nine of their final 13 games and clinching the flag on September 21.

The Cardinals ended with an outstanding 105–49 record and led the NL in virtually every important team statistic while becoming the first NL team to win 100-plus games three years running.

Mort Cooper, 22–7, notched his third straight 20-win season. His win-loss percentage of .759 was just the third-best *on his own team*. The Cardinals owned the top three win-loss percentages in the league with Ted Wilks (17–4, .810), Brecheen (16–5, .762), and Cooper. Marty Marion won the MVP Award, giving the Cards the league's top player in each of the last three seasons. Marion won his trophy despite hitting just six homers (his career high) with 63 RBIs and a .267 batting average, the lowest ever for an MVP winner. He said, "I didn't know whether I'd get it or not, but I sure appreciated it." Today it hangs on a wall in his living room, and he sees it every time he speaks on the telephone.

An argument for Musial's being the MVP is valid, as his stats outshined Marion's. Musial hit .347, drove in 94, and scored 112 runs (to Marion's 50) but came in fourth in MVP voting.

Perhaps the biggest surprise of the year was the success of the St. Louis Browns, winners of 89 games. It was not a franchise with a glorious background.

In their finest hour, 1944, as author Mario Vricella noted, "The Browns had not caught up with the league; the league had finally caught up with the Browns by sinking to their level." They hit an anemic .252 as a club, and, essentially, aside from Vern Stephens (.293, 20 HR, 109 RBI) the Browns' bats were as useless as a soggy loaf of French bread.

It took the Browns until the final day of the season to clinch the AL flag, and they won by a scant one-game margin over the Tigers, while the Cardinals had been out of first place only four days all season long and won their race by 14½ lengths over Pittsburgh. The Cards won their 91st game by September 1, while the Browns won two fewer than that all year long.

Willard Mullin, the man voted the top sports cartoonist of the 20th century, was most famous for the creation of his character the Brooklyn Bum, a potbellied hobo who represented the Brooklyn Dodgers. Mullin personified other baseball teams, including the Cardinals, whom he signified with a character named Swifty because of the team's base-running prowess. Swifty wore a beaver hat, a mustache, a flowered cravat or string tie, a double-breasted long coat, and a constant sneer. On the other hand, Mullin's St. Louis Browns character was a sleepy Missouri hillbilly who wore a scraggly beard, a tall cone hat, a polka-dot shirt over long flannels, and long boots. These two embodiments faced each other in the World Series.

Delirium raged in St. Louis. Subway Series are rare and usually associated with the city of New York, not St. Louis. The Browns had won the AL flag, true, but as Pulitzer Prize–winning writer George F. Will put it, "It took a global conflict to bring that about." Most seasons the Browns could be defined as the Washington Senators had been: first in war, first in peace, and last in the American League. In fact, one writer altered that classic line about the Senators to more fittingly describe the Browns' normal fate: "First in shoes, first in booze, last in the American League."

St. Louis residents pulled for the Browns, the team that entered the Series as one of only three clubs never to have won a world championship (the Dodgers and Phillies are the other teams). Musial stated, "It was amazing.... I guess they were rooting for the underdogs."

Actually, it was the Cardinals, with an ailing Marion and with Musial's recent knee injury, who reeled into the Series after pulling a September somnambulism act, dropping 15 of 20 games. The Browns had no players with any World Series experience. Bookies in the city installed the Cardinals as favorites with a 1-to-2 line versus the Browns at 8-to-5.

As the Series neared, the city's mayor, Aloys P. Kaufmann, declared the week of October 2–8 to be St. Louis Baseball Week, and a federal grand jury in town ruled that such an occasion called for a recess.

Sportsman's Park was ready for the all–St. Louis World Series, labeled the "Trolley Series." The last time an entire World Series had been played in one ballpark was in 1922, when the Giants and Yankees, who shared the Polo Grounds, met. Now, tickets sold briskly in St. Louis—six reserved seats went for $37.50 with scalpers asking for $150. The bleachers in center field, where fans could not sit during the regular season in order to keep a good (e.g., no distracting white shirts) hitters' backdrop, were sold out for the World Series.

The Cardinals dropped the first game on October 4, 2–1. Denny Galehouse, somewhat of a surprise starter, worked a seven-hitter. On the offensive side, a George McQuinn two-run homer versus just a ninth-inning sacrifice fly for the Cardinals did the trick. In the third inning Musial had sacrificed two runners up a notch, but they were stranded.

Surprisingly, Southworth had his number three hitter bunting. It was not a matter of could Musial do it, but should he be doing it? In Musial's first two full seasons in the majors, he laid down 15 sacrifice bunts. In 1944 Southworth had Musial sacrificing just four times. After 1944 he would record only 16 more sacrifice bunts and in 11 of those remaining years he had zero.

The Cards charged back the next day behind Max Lanier's starting pitching and Blix Donnelly's four innings of shutout ball in relief to secure the win. Tied at two runs apiece entering the eleventh, the Cards squeaked out the win on a Ray Sanders single, a Kurowski sacrifice bunt, an intentional walk to Marion, and a pinch single by Ken O'Dea.

The third game was played as a home game for the Browns, and they took a convincing 6–2 decision. Ted Wilks, who served up five consecutive singles in the third, took the defeat.

Game 4, played on October 7, featured Brecheen on the hill and Musial homering in the opening frame, a two-run poke over the right-field pavilion. He added a walk, a single, and a double later in the game and scored twice. His two ribbies matched his total from his previous 13 World Series games over 48 at-bats, while his home run would be his only Series blast ever. It was, however, a big blow, as the Cardinals never trailed and sailed to a 5–1 win. Brecheen surrendered nine hits, but all but one were singles.

The next contest, a rematch of starting pitchers from Game 1, found Cooper and Galehouse locked in a tight one. Cooper, backed by two wind-blown solo shots by Sanders and Danny Litwhiler, prevailed 2–0, scattering seven hits while fanning 12 (one shy of the Series record), including all three of the pinch-hitters the Browns sent to the plate in the ninth. Galehouse, also turning in a complete game, whiffed 10. The pitchers' combined 22 strikeouts established a record that lasted 19 years.

Finally, on October 9—the entire Series was played without an off day because no travel days were necessary—the Cards, despite hitting just .240 as a team, wrapped it up with a 3–1 win, thanks once more to the fine mound work of Lanier. The Cardinals, having committed only one error, had a fielding percentage of .996, a new high for a six-game World Series. The team's pitching staff (1.96 ERA) gave up just 12 runs to the impotent Browns.

The Browns staff, victimized by no offensive support and by 10 errors, wasted a fine effort—their ERA was microscopic at 1.49. Predictably, the clueless Browns, with their popgun offense, hit for a pathetic .183 average but had somehow managed to win two contests.

Cardinals owner Sam Breadon said his team was a good but not great squad. Had they lost to the Browns, he declared, "It would have been a disgrace." After all, by the season's end, a glance at the all-time American League composite standings illustrated his point—the Yankees had the best record, the Browns the worst, a staggering 802 ½ games in arrears.

The Series finale had drawn 31,630. That same day, in Baltimore, a Little World Series game pulled in almost 53,000 fans. Players' shares, $4,626.01 for the winners and only $2,744 for the losers, represented the lowest payouts since 1920. The players were also given 10 percent of their earnings in war bonds, not cash. Still, with the Musials' second baby (Geraldine) due in December, the money was welcome.

The 1944 World Series was the third straight one for Musial, and this time he enjoyed his best postseason. He hit .304 and collected seven hits, including two doubles and his home run.

For the second time in three years, the Cardinals wore the crown of world champs under Southworth, the man Marty Marion felt was the best skipper he ever played for, averaging just over 105 wins per season. Moreover, it was the Cardinals' fifth title overall, good for a new NL record.

On November 25 baseball commissioner Kenesaw Mountain Landis passed away. His death allowed the door to the majors to squeak open an inch or two for black ballplayers. After the Black Sox scandal, baseball hired Landis, thick white mane of hair and all, as the game's first commissioner. He had no intention of breaking baseball's "gentlemen's" agreement concerning segregation, an agreement as unyielding as any mountain. When pressed about the possibility of black players in the majors, Landis, according to Red Barber, would always "change the subject or walk away, or both." Landis' replacement, Happy Chandler, an affable figure vastly different from the scowling Landis, was amenable to integration.

There was no doubt that black players were as good, many better, than major-leaguers. Before the demise of the Negro League, in postseason meetings between white major-leaguers and the black stars of the Negro League, the big-leaguers won only 129 of the documented 438 matchups. Simply put, the all-white major-league squad could not even win one-third of the time.

This was an era when white and black barnstorming players traveled separately, were housed separately, and ate separately. Soon, though, things would never again be the same in the world of professional baseball.

On January 23, 1945, Musial, no longer exempt from serving in the military, enlisted in the United States Navy. Musial reported to the Bainbridge Naval Training Center in Maryland for basic training. He played baseball there, moving closer to the plate and hitting for more power.

His Bainbridge manager was Jerry O'Brien, who said Musial's "play was as spirited for us at the below $30 boot's pay as it had been the season before and the season after when he was a considerably higher paid professional."

Musial's next service stop was at Pearl Harbor, where he was assigned his official duty as a ship repairman. There Musial played in a league made up of eight teams, each with about five big-leaguers. He played roughly four times each week and thereby avoided having his skills corrode.

Joe Barbao Jr. said, "Your star athletes did get [placed in] Special Services because they could play ball, they could entertain, which is what the troops needed, too." Many of them, aside from playing the games "didn't have to do anything hard" or dangerous, he said.

Some stars did see some serious action, though. Serving on the battleship USS Alabama, Bob Feller, who would win five campaign ribbons and eight battles stars, said he "kept in shape by jogging around the deck between Japanese air attacks." Warren Spahn lost three years serving abroad and took part in the Battle of the Bulge. Hank Bauer earned two Purple Heart medals, and Yogi Berra was a navy gunner's mate in the D-Day invasion.

Back home, teams continued to fill their rosters with some misfits, some castoffs, and many 4-Fs. In what other age would a 41-year-old, bespectacled Paul Waner linger on, trying his best to track down elusive fly balls in right field? A year earlier, Al Simmons had come out of retirement and tried to recapture a modicum of his former greatness, but at 42, he could hit only .203. There was even a pitcher, Bert Shepard, who lost a leg in the war, came home, and appeared in one big-league game. He gave up just one run over five and a third innings, walking one while whiffing two batters in a 1945 contest.

Pete Gray was a one-armed outfielder who had lost his right arm due to a childhood accident that took place when he was six years old. While he would play in only 77 games for the Browns and hit a mere .218, remarkably he struck out just 11 times over 234 at-bats. In 1943 and 1944, he had been a full-time player for Memphis of the Southern Association. In 1944 he swiped 63 bases, hit a crisp .333, topped all outfielders in fielding percentage, and walked away with the league's MVP Award.

Most of the men who were starting position players in 1945 would see little or no action the next year. In short, the quality of baseball was strained.

A bold team owner could have tapped into the Negro Leagues for a wealth of talent, but there were no takers. Teams gave, at best, token treatment to the concept of integration. In staid Boston, for example, the Red Sox were pressured into staging a tryout at Fenway Park on April 16, 1945, for three black players: Jackie Robinson, Sam Jethroe, and Marvin Williams. Red Sox manager Joe Cronin and his coaches looked them over, then nonchalantly dismissed them. None of the three men were ever contacted by the Red Sox. "They'd had their 'chance,'" wrote Red Barber.

Meanwhile, Rickey reflected on his past and how it related to his (and ultimately baseball's) future. He had once coached baseball at Ohio Wesleyan, and his best player was a black catcher named Charles Thomas. In 1904 Rickey took his squad to South Bend, Indiana, to play several games against Notre Dame. When Thomas was about to sign in at the Oliver Hotel, the clerk yanked the register away from him, refusing him lodging.

Rickey arranged for Thomas to sleep in the second bed in his room yet not officially register. After getting the team settled in, Rickey joined Thomas in their room. There sat his catcher, weeping openly and "pulling at his hands as though he would tear the very skin off," recalled Rickey.

"It's my skin, Mr. Rickey...it's my skin! If I could just pull it off I'd be like everybody else...It's my skin, Mr. Rickey," Thomas said. In March 1945 Rickey recounted that story to Dodgers announcer Red Barber, saying that all through the years he continued to hear Thomas' lament. "Now I'm going to do something about it," Rickey said.

In April 1945, the month Hitler, Benito Mussolini, and Roosevelt died, Landis' successor as baseball's commissioner, A.B. "Happy" Chandler, was asked what his position was on African Americans in baseball. The man who had given up his position as a U.S. Senator from Kentucky to take baseball's highest post (and earn a raise from $10,000 to $50,000) replied tersely, "If a black boy can make it on Okinawa and Guadalcanal, hell, he can make it in baseball."

*He* may have felt that way, but according to Ken Burns' documentary on baseball, a secret poll of the owners of the 16 big-league clubs of the day showed that 15 were steadfastly opposed to integration. Only Rickey was open to the concept. The Burns documentary states that "Rickey believed in fair play and big profits." His signing Jackie Robinson to a contract was evidence of this credo. He was convinced, as he state candidly, "The Negroes will make us winners for years to come." Such an attitude made him a not-so-great emancipator, in that he was motivated in part by money and not entirely by altruism, but he was an emancipator nevertheless.

In the spring of 1945 the Cardinals held their spring training in Cairo, Illinois, until floods chased them back to St. Louis. Manager Billy Southworth, coming off three straight pennants, had a passel of question marks to cope with. Musial was gone and Danny Litwhiler would soon be drafted. Freckle-faced rookie Red Schoendienst, a natural shortstop, was plugged into Litwhiler's spot in the outfield.

Then came the difficulties with Mort and Walker Cooper. The brothers had inked a contract for the season that called for each to earn $12,000 with the understanding that no teammate would get paid more. When the brothers discovered what owner Sam Breadon was paying Marty Marion, they fled from the team on April 14, 1945. They asserted they'd rather sit at home than play for a penny less than $15,000, a demand that ruffled the penurious Breadon.

The issue became moot for Walker when, just five days after he stomped back home, the draft board informed him that he would soon be a private in the U.S. Army. He quickly enlisted in the navy and reported for duty on May 1, 1945. It was yet another blow to the Cardinals. Furthermore, Breadon, pushed by Mort's demands for a three-year contract, traded his ace to the Boston Braves.

In Hawaii that August, Musial briefly resurrected his pitching career and blanked an Army all-star team with a four-hitter in Maui.

World War II ended when the Japanese surrendered on September 2, 1945. Lukasz's homeland, Poland, was devastated by the war and lost a higher percentage of its population than any other country, about 20 percent. A few months later he came down with a case of pneumonia that left relatives fearing he would die. Stan later said he believed his father never did fully recover.

Stan eventually got an emergency leave, visited home, ministered to his father, and then was assigned to the navy yard in Philadelphia.

In the meantime, by September 25, 1945, the Cubs' magic number was dwindling—they led the Cardinals by one and a half games with just six games to play. The Cards visited Wrigley Field, lost the opener, then came back with a win the next day before time soon ran out. The Cubs swept consecutive doubleheaders.

So the wartime Cubs met the wartime Tigers in the Series, and when sportswriter Warren Brown was asked who he believed would take the World Series, he replied, "Neither team is good enough to win it."

Meanwhile, Rickey announced he had assigned his finest scouts to seek out the best black players around. He claimed his plans were to field a team in the Negro Leagues called the Brooklyn Brown Dodgers, but his real purpose was to find a black player suitable for his design to integrate baseball. At one point he dramatically declared, "I don't know who he is or where he is…but he is coming."

On October 23, 1945, Rickey met with Robinson, who was under the impression he would be asked to play for the Brown Dodgers. Instead, sitting under a picture of Abraham Lincoln on a wall in Rickey's office, Robinson signed a contract to play ball for the Triple A Montreal Royals. What was to become known as baseball's "Great Experiment" was officially under way.

Rumblings of future discontent were evident, especially with Brooklyn's Dixie Walker's reaction to the signing of an African American ballplayer: "As long as he isn't with the Dodgers, I'm not worried."

## CHAPTER FIVE

# A Cornucopia of Batting Crowns

The year 1946 found 12 Nazis, the most notable one being Hermann Goering, condemned to death at the Nuremberg trials. The United States ushered in the Atomic Age, conducting a test of the atom bomb on the Bikini Atoll. In an odd juxtaposition, Hollywood premiered *It's a Wonderful Life* with its upbeat, life-affirming theme.

With the war's end, the face (or, more accurately, *faces*) of baseball changed quickly. During the previous season, one source listed 384 big-leaguers who had been in the military, but only 22 of them were still there by the summer of 1946, and the vast majority of the reported 4,076 minor-leaguers who had served their country were also back. Obviously, the spring-training sites were packed with contenders and pretenders for big-league spots. The terms of the GI Bill called for employers to give returning military veterans the opportunity to reclaim their old jobs, but baseball ignored that provision when it was convenient to do so.

Right after World War II, baseball monopolized and "mesmerized the American people as it never had before and never would again," wrote David Halberstam. When the stars such as Musial returned to baseball, "their very names seemed to indicate that America could come pick up right where it had left off."

Ballplayers were glorified, but their salaries were not on such a grand scale. Erskine said players of his era were virtually forced to sign their contracts as if at gunpoint. If a player became a holdout, the team very well could say, "Well, we can't use you," and the player was stuck. "We couldn't sign with another team, so you went home," Erskine said. He added, "Your contract had to be renewed annually. And so you didn't have any security." Because the contract guaranteed a player who was released at any time be given just two things: 30 days' pay and transportation back home. Players had almost no leverage at all. Things would soon change.

In St. Louis in 1946, Breadon, no doubt still upset with Walker Cooper, sold him to the Giants in January. The next year Cooper, slow afoot but tsunami powerful, went on to set the single-season record for the most RBIs (122) by a catcher.

In February the Montreal Royals made news again when they signed their second black player, a man who became as obscure as the trailblazing Jackie Robinson became famous. He was John Wright, a 27-year-old pitcher, a returned serviceman, and a veteran of the Negro Leagues. The club would soon sign 24-year-old catcher Roy Campanella and Don Newcombe, moves that would pay off big in the near future. Jim Crow was far from being dead, but he had been given a swift slap to the face by a cadre of pioneers on baseball's racial frontier.

The Cardinals, not known for being aggressive or progressive in signing black players, inked Vincent "Manny" McIntyre, a 26-year-old shortstop from Canada who had played hockey in the Quebec Interprovincial League from 1944 to 1945. However, when he committed 30 errors in 30 games for Sherbrooke, he was quickly released.

In the meantime, the 1946 season also featured another case of integration. Eddie Klepp, a white pitcher, signed with the Cleveland Buckeyes, an otherwise all-black team. Like Wright and Jackie Robinson, Klepp had to cope with hardships, including eating alone and staying apart from teammates in white hotels. He also endured hazing by fans and harassment by Birmingham, Alabama, city officials during spring training.

The new year also brought an early whiff of the woes that were percolating in Mexico. Wealthy Jorge Pasquel and his brothers Alfonso, Bernardo, Gerardo, and Mario, ran the Mexican League and decided to expand the league by two clubs. Needing to fill roster spots, Jorge approached major-leaguers. First he signed several Cubans from the majors, causing a bit of a squawk by big-league officials.

However, by March, when he signed Americans such as Mickey Owen, it kicked off a baseball war. The biggest fuss came when Pasquel later announced he was going after the thunderous Ted Williams. The Splendid

Splinter, wooed from spring training and on into the summer, reportedly walked away from a multiyear pact calling for $500,000.

The exodus of other players to Mexico was described as a kind of gold rush fueled by large contracts. In all, 27 United States players took the bait.

Spring training opened with the Cardinals' base returning to St. Petersburg. Under the blistering Florida sun, new skipper Eddie Dyer, a star halfback at Rice who had never managed in the majors, had to select his nucleus and weed out his prospects from the suspects. Dyer had worked his way up from the team's minor league and was now being rewarded for his loyalty dating back to 1922.

After Musial was honorably discharged in March, he hitchhiked from Philadelphia to Donora, spent time with his family, then joined the club for spring training. Early on, he slipped in the sandy soil of Waterfront Park and strained some ligaments in his knee. It was an injury that bothered him from then on, hampering him badly in his older years.

Dyer wanted to get a look at hurlers such as control artist Ted Wilks, who had a splendid 14–4 season in 1944 when he led the National League in win-loss percentage before being limited to 18 appearances in 1945 due to an arm injury. Dyer wondered, too, what to expect from Murry Dickson, a somewhat proven talent who had gone 8–2 in 1943 before departing for the service.

Early on, rookie Dick Sisler, son of Hall of Famer George, was pegged as the starting first baseman. Musial recalled he enjoyed playing the outfield and believed he would remain there, until Sisler started slowly. "So, one day our manager, Eddie Dyer, came to me and said, 'Why don't you take over at first base for a few days, until we get Sisler squared away?'" Those "few days" lasted 114 games and would soar to 149 the following year. From 1946 on, Musial would bounce around from the outfield to first base and back again, depending upon his managers' perspectives.

In retrospect, it was fortuitous that Musial moved to first, because it gave the Cardinals what writer Bill James called "the best infield of the 1940s."

Lil and Stan were kept busy in the spring, preparing to move to Southwest St. Louis City. It would mark the first time that they had not lived in a cramped apartment or hotel. In the meantime, they lived in a rented bungalow.

Commissioner Happy Chandler attended the traditional season opener in Cincinnati on April 16, 1946. There, he addressed the issue of players jumping to the Mexican League, announcing that all former big-leaguers who had signed on with the outlaw league were now officially suspended, possibly for up to five years. Earlier he had offered those players a "grace period," which extended up to the opener. Now he declared, "Those who did not return...are now out."

The threat that Mexican millionaire Jorge Pasquel posed to the majors was as real as it was imminent. The Pasquels continued using big money to attract U.S. stars. Horace Stoneham, owner of the Giants, was so enraged by what he perceived to be the disloyalty of some of his players, he fired pitcher Sal Maglie, first baseman/outfielder Roy Zimmerman, and second baseman George Hausmann merely for speaking with Mexican League representatives.

While Musial was starting his fourth full season, Jackie Robinson made his pro debut on April 18, 1946, at Roosevelt Stadium in Jersey City, New Jersey. He went 4-for-5 with a three-run homer and two stolen bases in a 14–1 win.

Robinson, a four-letter man at UCLA, was a tremendous athlete. For the Bruins, he averaged 11 yards per carry as a halfback in his junior season and was touted often as the best running back in America. In basketball, he led the Pacific Coast Conference in scoring for both his junior and senior seasons. Despite those scoring sprees, when the results for the voting on the conference's top players were tabulated, he was not selected to the first, second, or even the third team. Robinson won the 1940 NCAA long-jump championship and was said to be a sure thing for the 1940 Olympics had World War II not canceled the games. Finally, he even competed in tennis and won a national African American tennis tournament as well as several championships in swimming. It was baseball, though, that would ultimately pay his bills. His path would soon cross Musial's and the Cardinals'.

By 1946 the Cardinals roster was abounding with stars. The Musial, Moore, Slaughter outfield was back, as were key pitchers Dickson, Howie Pollet, and Al Brazle, who could drive batters crazy with an assortment of nonpower pitches. Brazle, whose real first name was Alpha, was, said a teammate "kind of a beanbag, kind of squirrelly," but it was good to have him and the rest of the group back.

When Dyer was hired, he had boldly stated to the assembled media, "It'll be my fault if we don't win the flag." He began his managerial machinations almost immediately, shifting Red Schoendienst, who as a rookie in 1945 had led the league in steals, to second base and replacing Emil Verban.

Del Greco commented, "Schoendienst was feisty on the bags, on double plays," and in the dugout he would scream to extol his teammates, displaying leadership qualities that eventually helped him earn a job as a manager.

"He was a lot like [Dick] Groat," noted former pitcher Vernon Law. "Exactly. A tough out and a real competitor. He didn't have the greatest arm in the world, but I tell you, the ball always got there in time, just like Groat."

In addition, rookie Joe Garagiola, who had first been scouted when he was a 13-year-old playing on the sandlots of St. Louis, was gradually being eased into the catcher's role. He was a better hitter than he comedically gave himself credit for. Law said, "He challenged you, he was not an easy out. I think [ultimately] everybody expected more out of him than what he gave simply because he was kind of cut out of the same mold as Yogi Berra and people thought that he was going to be as good as Berra, but there were not too many that were." On defense, Garagiola, said Law, liked to get in the mix of things. "He'd get right down in the dirt and he'd take that dirt and rub it on his arms. He looked like the comic [character] Pig-Pen, but he was a good receiver. He knew the hitters and wasn't bad behind the plate at all."

The extroverted Garagiola later gained fame as a baseball broadcaster. Shuba said, "He would always talk to you when you were up at the plate, friendly stuff," almost as if he were auditioning for a future job in the media.

The first week of May saw Musial being named Player of the Week thanks to his 12-for-20 hitting outburst. Back from a year's hiatus, he was hitting .415 up to that point.

Also in May, Ebbets Field was again the venue of a brawl when Les Webber brushed back Enos Slaughter, who gained retribution by, in a time-tested move, bunting the ball toward the first-base line, where Webber had to field it, then plowing into the pitcher. Slaughter was, said Dick Schofield, "the type who sharpened his spikes before a game," a throwback to the days of Cobb.

Mike Schmidt wrote that Musial's era featured players "fighting for their livelihood on the field. There were no guaranteed contracts, and pitchers knocked you on your ass if you overswung on an outside pitch.... The game policed itself and only the strong survived."

May was also the month when pitchers Max Lanier and Fred Martin (who would later gain fame as a baseball innovator, introducing the split-finger fastball to the game) and second baseman Lou Klein defected to

Mexico, lured there by promises of big money awaiting them south of the border.

Lanier, who had burst from the gate with a 6–0 record, was bitter the Cardinals had offered him a measly $500 raise in spring training, lifting his salary to just $10,000, telling him, "Take it or go home." Economically forced to stay, he did his job. So well, in fact, it prompted a visit by a Mexican League recruiter. He was offered $20,000 plus a $35,000 bonus, "So I went," he said.

Lanier later reported that Mexico City's accommodations were top-notch, but anywhere else they were primitive. He spoke of fans in Tampico lobbing firecrackers onto the field and of how a set of railroad tracks ran through center field. Workers would "open the gates on both sides of the outfield to let the trains go through," he said. Of course, that was better than Puebla, where goats grazed in the outfield prior to games.

Lanier said that, in a startling contrast, Jorge Pasquel had a private box directly behind home plate. He would watch the games from that vantage point, "where his meals were served on silver platters."

Those rogue players who went to Mexico were derided in the media, labeled "Mexican jumping beans." Their playing days there were short-lived. The league was not robust and by 1948 was a financial flop that presented no threat to the major leagues.

Musial, too, was tempted to break his contract, which called for a salary of $13,500. He stated in his autobiography that Jorge Pasquel and Mickey Owen, an ex-major-leaguer, first approached him. He contends he never seriously considered the monetary offers made but added that Pasquel's "offer kept going up." Pasquel was dangling what he believed was nearly tantamount to a Don Vito Corleone can't-refuse offer. In an effort to win him over, Pasquel visited Musial three times.

The exact amount of money offered Musial varies depending upon which source is referenced. One account has Musial considering a $130,000 five-year contract, while Musial stated the deal was for $25,000 per season for five years plus a $50,000 bonus, which Pasquel had with him in cashier's checks during one of his visits. That offer, claims yet another source, left Musial saying he "would have to think it over."

Time magazine reported that after Pasquel offered Musial $75,000 cash to sign plus double his salary, "Stan promptly made a date with Cardinal Owner Sam Breadon to say goodbye." Dyer intervened, reaching Musial before he got in to see Breadon.

Musial was willing to listen to Dyer, who offered some advice. Dyer first listened to what Musial had on his mind, then appealed to him, "Stan, you've got two children. Do you want them to hear someone say, 'There are the kids of a guy who broke his contract'?" Musial certainly did not want that legacy. He refused the money and firmly decided to do the honorable thing and remain in St. Louis.

On May 25, 1946, Cardinals manager Eddie Dyer told *St. Louis Star-Times* writer Sid Keener that Musial—along with Moore, Slaughter, and Kurowski—had refused "fabulous offers" from the Mexican League.

However, Musial wrote that in early June his family was preparing to leave their Fairgrounds Hotel quarters and move into a bungalow he rented. He further stated that it was on June 6 when reporters hounded him "when they saw him packing" and asked if he was moving. He replied he was moving but to his new home on Mardel Avenue, not to Mexico.

Yet another source stated that it was not until mid-June before Musial officially notified the media that the issue was dead. Sounding much like a Jimmy Stewart character, he conceded that Pasquel's offer had been a difficult one for him to refuse: "All that money makes a fellow do a lot of thinking before he says no."

The particulars and chronology may be a bit hazy, but in the end Musial remained a Cardinal. People speculated as to why he had apparently given serious consideration about leaving the club. Was he using the offer from Mexico as leverage for a raise? Was he, as a product of poverty, simply trying to get his fair share, or was he bitter about being underpaid by the Cardinals?

At any rate, in August Breadon gave Musial a $5,000 boost in salary to show his appreciation and to appease him. When he soon nailed down his second batting title, hitting .365, he was getting paid around $118 per game.

Despite their star-studded lineup, by July 2, 1946, the Cardinals sank seven and a half games behind the Dodgers, and gloom set in. Red Barrett, exiled to the bullpen by Dyer after he had won 23 for Southworth one year earlier, took to signing autographs "Red Barrett, Cardinals of 1945." But the Cards heated up and shaved the Dodgers' lead to four and a half games by their middle-of-the-month, four-game set versus their rival. Then they chased the Dodgers out of town, leaving Brooklyn barely clinging to their half-game advantage.

On July 9, 1946, the Cardinals sent a veritable busload of players to the 13th All-Star Game. Due to wartime travel restrictions, there had been no All-Star

Game the previous year. Now, three-fourths of the NL starting infield was made up of Cards: Schoendienst at second, Marion at short, and Kurowski at third. Additionally, pitcher Pollet, along with Slaughter and Musial, carried as outfielders, represented the Cardinals. The highlight of the 12–0 victory was Ted Williams' home run into the bullpen, his second shot of the day. It came off a novelty pitch, a blooper, lobbed by Rip Sewell.

An event took place on July 14, 1946, that would have huge significance for the Cardinals several months later. A drastic defensive shift to thwart Ted Williams, a strategic positioning of players originally known as the Boudreau Shift, was first unveiled by the Cleveland Indians during the second game of a doubleheader at Fenway Park. Williams had homered three times, one a grand slam, in the opener that day and cashed in with eight RBIs.

In the nightcap, in Williams' first at-bat after he had doubled, Cleveland manager Lou Boudreau ordered his players to assume a radical defensive alignment featuring six players on the right side of the field and the left fielder positioning himself in the spot normally manned by the shortstop, with the second baseman playing in shallow right field. Williams eyed the setup, stepped out of the box, laughed, then, seconds later, dropped anchor at second base after pulling a double down the right-field line. Boudreau later explained his reason for making the move quite simply: "We had to do something."

About six weeks later when the Indians and Red Sox met again and Williams faced the shift, a vaudevillian midget by the name of Marco Songini darted onto the field at Fenway, grabbed a glove left in the grass by a Red Sox fielder, and manned the empty third-base spot before police ordered him back into the stands.

Back in the National League, a spurt by St. Louis found them sweeping a four-game series versus Brooklyn in mid-July, leaving them just a half-game behind them on July 16. Dickson went through one stretch on a home stand in which he threw 26 innings while giving up only two runs.

The Cards again faced the Dodgers, this time in Brooklyn on July 30 through August 1, in a series Musial says gave birth to his nickname (although other sources vary on the exact date of the origin of his moniker). Bob Broeg heard the fans strike up a chant every time Musial batted. He later asked Leo Ward, the team's traveling secretary, if he had made out what they were shouting. Ward replied that it was, "Here comes the man!" Broeg, seeking accuracy, asked if Ward didn't, in fact, mean, "*that* man."

Nope, said Ward, it was definitely *the* man. When Broeg used the tale in his column, Musial's nickname stuck.

When August rolled in, Musial carried the bulk of the load down the stretch. His batting average stood at .356 by August 8, 1946, and a week later, after an explosion of hits (18 over seven games, including an outrageous 12-for-13 hitting spree), he topped the league in hitting at .374. Then, on August 26, Dickson's 2–1 win over Brooklyn propelled the Cardinals back into first place.

On September 12 and 13, the Cardinals once more were in Brooklyn, this time for their final scheduled series, a three-game set. At that point, the Dodgers, coming off a 19-inning scoreless tie contest the day before—called, naturally, due to darkness—were on a tear, having won nine of their last 10, but were still one and a half games out. Pollet breezed to a 10–2 win, but the Dodgers took the next two to slice the Cardinals' lead to a scant half-game.

The dog days of the season wore on, and by September 27 Brooklyn and St. Louis were tied for the National League lead with two games left on each team's schedule. The following day, Brooklyn hosted the Braves and mistreated them to a 7–4 tune but later, in a night game in St. Louis, the Cardinals defeated the Cubs to knot things up once more. The Cards, inexplicably, were seemingly invincible under the lights, winning at an utterly preposterous .658 clip in 1946 and, unthinkably enough, they would improve on that to .720 the following season.

On September 29 the Cubs retaliated, spanking St. Louis 8–3, despite a Musial homer. When the Dodgers fell—ex-Cardinal Mort Cooper shut them out 4–0 to cost them the title—the first tie for the pennant in big-league history took place. Fans in the two cities gnawed at their fingernails, but the Cardinals were confident, having beaten Brooklyn 14 of 22 times.

National League rules required a best-of-three playoff that would push the start of the World Series back four days from its scheduled October 2, 1946, beginning. NL president Ford Frick presided over a coin toss to determine which team gained a home-field advantage. The Dodgers won and elected to have the playoffs begin in St. Louis with a subsequent game or games to be held in Brooklyn. Baseball commissioner Happy Chandler declared all stats and records from the playoff games would count as if the games were part of the regular season, even in the win-loss column.

Meanwhile, the Red Sox officials decided that, to prevent the team from becoming rusty, practice games would be played. Boston manager

Joe Cronin requested American League president Will Harridge arrange for a team of stars from other AL teams to scrimmage them. The team Harridge assembled included greats such as first baseman Hank Greenberg, Luke Appling at shortstop, and outfielder Joe DiMaggio. Five left-handed pitchers—including standout Hal Newhouser, junkball artist Ed Lopat, and flamethrower Joe Page—were selected to help prep the Bosox for Cardinals southpaws. Three contests were to be staged at Fenway with normal prices charged for tickets and with the visiting players splitting the receipts.

During the fifth inning of the first of the practice games, Washington Senators knuckleball artist Mickey Haefner fooled Ted Williams, who was braced for a knuckler. His pitch cut in on Williams and struck him on the right elbow. X-rays revealed no breaks, but his elbow was badly swollen and he sat out the next two practice contests.

The games proved to be of little value; the bitter New England weather resulted in batters taking cuts on virtually every pitch in an effort to get their at-bats over with. The games averaged around an hour and 30 minutes and drew about 6,000 total fans.

Just before the Cardinals' playoff contest, each player was given an extra $100 beyond his salary for expenses. The stage was set for starting pitcher Pollet, who was 4–2 against Brooklyn that season—he was the only man to top them more than three times all year long. On October 1, he squared off against 20-year-old Ralph Branca. Manager Leo Durocher was pressed into using his swingman (Branca had worked just 67⅓ innings in 1946) because his normal starters were exhausted. Dyer's starter was also a bit of a surprise pick, in that he was sore and had been roughed up twice in the final week of the season.

At any rate, St. Louis scrapped for a run in the first inning on three hits, Brooklyn came back in the third to tie it, but the Cards put enough runs on the board—two in their half of that inning—to ensure the win. Later Musial would tack on another insurance run, scoring on a Garagiola single after he had tripled off the wall in right-center. Branca lasted just two and two-thirds innings, and Durocher had to dip into his bullpen four times. On the other hand, Pollet cruised to an eight-hitter. Final score: St. Louis 4, Brooklyn 2. Musial and company had a leg up.

The two teams then traveled to New York, where the Dodgers hoped to harvest the benefits of their home-field advantage. The Dodgers were still optimistic. "Leo told us we were going back to Brooklyn and beat them two straight," wrote Kirby Higbe in his autobiography. When the train chugged into New York, he wrote, "there were ten thousand fans to meet us at the station, and a big crowd spent the night in line outside the ball park. We all felt sure we could beat them."

The mound matchup for the second contest on October 3 was Dickson, 3–1 on the year against Brooklyn, versus Joe Hatten, Brooklyn's top lefty. This time Brooklyn drew first blood with a run in the opening frame, but the Cards embarked on a 13-hit onslaught against six Dodgers pitchers, including a Musial double. The final score of 8–4 wasn't indicative of the Cardinals' dominance for most of the game, but Brecheen did have to work the ninth in relief to shut the door, securing the Dickson win.

The Dodgers had rallied for three in the last of the ninth and had loaded the bases, bringing the potential tying run to the plate. At that point, a somewhat shaky Brecheen got Eddie Stanky looking, then pinch-hitter Howie Schultz swung on a payoff pitch with the runners in motion to end the contest. Moments after the final out, a Brooklyn fan attacked Slaughter near home plate as he made his way off the field. A host of other fans circled the two men before police broke things up.

At one point in the season, the Dodgers had perceived the Cardinals to be a team that was of little threat, a team that was just a distant blur in their rearview mirror, seven and a half games out on July 2. The Cardinals persevered, inching up on their rival, making up ground in the standings, game by grueling game, and their comeback was so much sweeter for the struggle they had endured.

With a final record of 98–58, the Cardinals moved on to the World Series, doing so with a scalding .628 win-loss percentage both at home and away. They had clinched their ninth pennant over the past 21 seasons. The playoff win also put $6,000 more in the Cardinals' pockets than what the Dodgers took home for their second-place finish.

The Cardinals, who led the National League in virtually every important team statistic from runs scored to lowest ERA, would have to take on Ted Williams—who had amassed 343 total bases that year—and his Red Sox. Thus the 1946 World Series pitted two storied franchises, although Boston's last postseason appearance was way back in 1918.

The focus of the Series was, of course, on the two leagues' MVPs— Williams, 27 years old, and Musial, just a handful of weeks shy of his 26th birthday. After all, hadn't Musial just come off a season in which he led the NL in myriad major categories including hits (228), triples (20), doubles

(50), and singles (142)? He also was tabbed as *The Sporting News* Major League Player of the Year.

While Williams and Musial were alike in that they were the game's premier hitters, their personalities were miles apart. Author Jayson Stark pointed out, "Williams always had a thunder cloud following him. Musial just played baseball."

Both Williams and Musial led their leagues in runs, slugging, total bases, and on-base plus slugging. In addition to hitting .342, Williams had, just a few months earlier, drilled a Freddie Hutchinson pitch approximately 500 feet, some 33 rows up into the seats behind the Boston bullpen at Fenway Park. It was a blast that broke a sleeping fan's straw hat and prompted club officials to have the seat painted red, amidst a sea of green seats. Despite such glistening stats, fans of luminaries Williams and Musial were in for a disappointment in the fall of 1946.

Boston was no slouch, having bolted out of the starting gate at 41–9 and having captured 104 wins in all. They were a very balanced club, leading the AL in fielding, batting, slugging, and runs scored. Further, they had two 20-game winners—Dave "Boo" Ferriss, who had begun the year at 10–0 and ended at a gaudy 25–6, and Tex Hughson, a pitcher with more pitches at his disposal than perhaps any other big-leaguer. His wide array of throws forced his catchers to come up with special signals, including ones for his staples, a curve he employed, usually off the plate a bit to tantalize hitters, and a fastball that tailed into righties, keeping them honest.

Kurowski called the World Series matchup "a case of their power against our pitching and speed."

On October 6, 1946, 36,218 fans, the highest attendance total for this World Series, shoehorned their way into Sportsman Park for the Series opener. This was the first peacetime Series since 1941 and, for the Red Sox, their first Fall Classic since they had sold a young pitcher by the name of Babe Ruth. While a plethora of the Cardinals had postseason experience, among the Sox only Rudy York and Pinky Higgins, who once hit safely over a record 12 straight official at-bats, could say the same.

Pollet, an avid reader of Shakespeare and the classics, and a 20-game winner, lost a tough one 3–2 when he faded late in the game. The New Orleans Creole surrendered a run in the ninth after he had come within one pitch of ending the contest and another in the tenth when he served up a home run to York. Musial, batting third and playing first, doubled sharply off the wall in right to drive in a key run in the sixth but anguished through a 1-for-5 day overall, failing to drive home the tying run from second base in the tenth.

The next afternoon Brecheen fired a four-hit shutout and drove in the game-winning run to knot the Series. Ironman Musial—he and Slaughter were the only National Leaguers to play in each of their team's 1946 games—contributed an RBI good for an insurance run they never needed as St. Louis won 3–0.

Fenway Park was the site of Game 3. York's first-inning three-run homer hurt the Cardinals early and a Ted Williams bunt down the line to a vacated third-base spot to beat the Cards' defensive shift took them off balance in the third inning.

Dyer had drawn up two versions of his Williams Shift, neither one quite as severe as Boudreau's. Dyer's more passive formation had Musial nestled tightly to the first-base line and Kurowski in a bit at third but shaded slightly toward the usual shortstop slot. Therefore, Williams was given all of the third-base line as if the Cardinals were inviting him, "Go ahead. Lay a bunt down for a single. We'll give you *that*." The other shift kept Marion at his normal spot with Kurowski situated in second-base territory with both Schoendienst and Musial to his left. Marion said the concept of both shifts was simple. "It was just the idea that we figured he'd pull the ball all the time," he said, so they borrowed and adapted the Boudreau innovation.

Musial ordinarily adjusted to pitches' locations and the defensive alignment, but, as Willie Mays noted, Williams was too obstinate. "When they shifted on him, everybody to the right side, he still kept trying to pull the ball for hits. If anybody shifted like that on Musial, he would have wrecked them by slapping base hits into left." Williams scrutinized each pitch as if he were a jeweler examining a diamond with his loupe.

Hall of Fame manager Earl Weaver commented, "Musial was the best at adjusting once the ball left the pitcher's hand. He'd hit the pitcher's pitch. [Ted] Williams was the best at making them throw his pitch." However, in this World Series, Williams was not destined to get *his* pitch very often.

Even after his bunt hit, Williams suffered as he continued, for the most part, to pull the ball. Williams later told documentarian Ken Burns that it was terribly difficult to "get a ball through all of that [defensive shifting]." He called the Series loss his biggest career disappointment, especially since he was convinced the Red Sox would prevail. "That was a total bust. I hit .200, we lost the Series." This coming from a man who detested failure.

Shift or no shift, essentially Game 3 was over after the first inning. Boston played out the string and won 4–0. Musial starched a stand-up triple in the ninth but died there. Despite York's homer, headlines blared, "Williams Bunts."

The Cardinals stormed back to tie the Series in the fourth game, shellacking Boston 12–3 on 20 hits, which tied a Series record set 25 years earlier. Incredibly, the Cardinals' fourth, fifth, and sixth hitters—Slaughter, Kurowski, and rookie catcher Garagiola—each collected four hits. Going into the 1946 Series, only 22 men (and just one rookie, Fred Lindstrom) had ever managed to turn in a four-hit day. So, when Slaughter took his position in the batter's box in the ninth inning, Charlie Berry, the home-plate ump, said, in an almost theatrical aside, that a fifth hit would give Slaughter the all-time Series record. Slaughter later stated that the pitch that followed Berry's comment was "the fattest" one he had seen that day, "and if that Berry had kept his big mouth shut I'd probably have hit it out of the park."

In the third inning, Musial, with his back foot nearly out of the batter's box, took an outside pitch to right-center to double home two runs, and St. Louis coasted to a ridiculously easy win. Starting pitcher Red Munger, who had been a lieutenant in the army until August, allowed the Sox hitters to sprinkle nine hits around the park but gave up just one earned run.

Over the years Fenway Park has been anathema to most left-handed pitchers. On October 11, 1946, in Game 5 of the Series, Pollet, a lefty who had never worked in that park, became yet another victim—although Al Brazle wound up taking the loss. Pollet's mound stint was brief, one-third of an inning, and he surrendered three hits, including a run-producing single by Williams, good for his only lifetime World Series RBI.

Boston's starting pitcher Joe Dobson had one of the best curves of his time and was Ted Williams' personal batting-practice pitcher. Dobson went the distance and gave up three runs, all unearned. The Red Sox scored a run or more in four of the eight innings in which they batted and staved off a slight ninth-inning rally to win 6–3, sending the Series back to St. Louis, where the Cards had to win two in a row or be eliminated. The Cardinals, having gone from a hit feast to an agonizing famine, wondered what the next few days would bring.

One thing was certain: they were delighted to depart Fenway Park, even if leaving there entailed an unbearable 36-hour train trip to St. Louis, clickety-clacking along at about 50 miles per hour for much of the trek. The Red Sox had posted a 61–16 record in Boston during the regular season, good for the fourth-best at-home win-loss percentage, .792, in baseball history.

On October 13 Sportsman's Park was groomed and ready to host Boston for Game 6, its mound taking on the stylistic appearance of three concentric circles with a ring of grass and an extra ring of dirt decorating the mound. In the third inning, after a Terry Moore sacrifice fly to score starting pitcher Brecheen, Musial slapped the ball to Johnny Pesky at short, legging out a single. Kurowski and Slaughter followed with RBI singles, and the Cardinals jumped ahead 3–0. Brecheen, relying heavily on his screwball while keeping Boston off balance with slow curves and change-ups, went the route, winning his second complete game of the Series, this one by a 4–1 margin. The game was played in a crisp one hour and 56 minutes.

The Cardinals entered the deciding game as a franchise that had never dropped the seventh game of a Fall Classic, and Boston had won each of their previous five World Series appearances dating back to the first World Series ever, in 1903.

Prior to the start of the game, Dyer gazed down at a stack of 50 telegrams he had received that day, each pleading with him to start Brecheen despite the fact that he had, just two days earlier, gone the distance. Could Brecheen be effective on one day of rest? Dyer decided that would be asking too much of him and gave the starting nod to Dickson, coming off five days' rest.

After seven innings the score stood 3–1, and St. Louis and Dickson had given up just three hits. However, as the game came down to crunch time, Dickson surrendered a leadoff single then a double in the eighth. Dyer felt he had to make the bullpen call for Brecheen. This time the results were mixed. Working out of the stretch, Brecheen blew the save when he gave up a two-run double to the bespectacled, 5'9" Dom "the Little Professor" DiMaggio. The ball flew over Slaughter's head and off the right-center-field wall, knotting the game at three runs apiece. The crowd of 36,143 grew nervous as momentum began shifting away from the Cards.

Brecheen then benefited from a single run in the bottom of the eighth on Harry Walker's line-drive double to score Slaughter. The details of that play are deeply etched into baseball history.

Slaughter had led off the inning with a sharp single to center off Bob Klinger, who was making his first appearance in the Series. Kurowski tried to move him over via a sacrifice bunt but failed, and Del Rice lifted an easy fly ball to Williams in left. At that point Slaughter was about to embark upon one of the most famous base-running ventures in the annals of the game.

Walker hit his double to left-center, where Leon Culberson, filling in for DiMaggio, who had sprained his ankle earlier in the game when he had tied the contest, was tardy in making a play. Culberson's hesitation permitted Walker to get a double out of what appeared to be a routine single and gave Slaughter, who never broke his long stride, impetus for his "mad dash" around the base paths. Likewise, when shortstop Johnny Pesky took the throw from Culberson, he too hesitated for a millisecond, and that hesitation proved to be his downfall.

Pesky, who would later call himself the goat for not anticipating Slaughter's attempt to score, took the throw with his back to the plate so he couldn't see Slaughter. Nor, with the cacophony of the excited crowd, could he hear any of his teammates' yelled instructions. Catcher Roy Partee went up the third-base line a bit to take Pesky's eventual relay, but it was too late.

Slaughter later stated that he had the steal sign on this play, giving him a good jump on his romp around the bases, "...and when I saw Harry Walker's drive into left-center, I decided to give it all I had."

The key two-base hit is often mistakenly remembered as a single that scored a runner all the way from first, but the official scorer ruled it a double. In any event, the Cardinals took the 4–3 lead on the memorable play.

After the excitement died down, Cardinals fans had little time to catch their collective breath when Brecheen became a bit unglued. When he gave up two hits by York and Bobby Doerr to open the ninth, Dyer considered lifting him. "I probably should have taken him out right then and there, but all season long he'd come through for me in the clutches. I had to go along with him. I owed it to him," the Cardinals manager said. As a rule, having Brecheen on the hill was as soothing and reassuring to a manager as the melodious sounds of a wind chime. The fact that the Red Sox had, thus far, hit a miserable 1-for-9 with runners in scoring position might have also helped Dyer's decision.

Brecheen recovered nicely, though, stranding York and Bobby Doerr, and the Boston rally proved fruitless. So it came to be that Harry "the Cat," a mere .500 pitcher on the regular season at 15–15, came up big in the clutch.

Officially, Brecheen had worked two scoreless innings and had nailed down the win. Now, with a career 4–1 World Series ledger, he became the first pitcher since Stan Coveleski in 1920 to win three games in a World Series and the first lefty ever to go 3–0 in a Series. His ERA for his first Series in 1943 was 2.45; in 1944 it tumbled to 1.00; for *this* Series it was an incredible 0.45. His overall ERA of 0.83 over 32⅔ innings in the World Series stood as No. 1 of all time. It ranked better than the previous record established by Babe Ruth (0.87), compiled as a member of the Red Sox staff, and better than Christy Mathewson (0.97 lifetime in the Series), who, in 1905, won three complete-game shutouts for the New York Giants, allowing an average of just five runners per game.

And so it was that Brecheen, Slaughter, and Walker—and not Musial or Williams, who had but five harmless singles and one run driven in—were the stars of the show.

Musial's uneventful 1-for-3 at the plate in the Series finale lifted his Series average to .222, paltry but 22 points higher than what Williams could muster. Williams had been a pilot and a hero in the war, but in this, his only World Series, he (by most reckoning) crashed and burned. Catcher Joe Garagiola disagreed, saying, "People say Williams didn't hit anything. That's where averages are really misleading because Williams hit some *shots* in that Series."

"We were pretty fortunate that we did hold Ted down in his hitting," said Red Schoendienst, "but he hit some balls awful hard. I was playing second base, and I was playing practically in the first-base position when he hit. I can remember him hitting balls at me that almost turned me over."

In Musial's defense, five of his six hits went for extra bases. Still, his 143-point decline from his regular-season average to his Series mark was the second-worst drop-off in NL history.

After the final out, Musial tentatively jogged toward the mound to congratulate Brecheen. On the periphery of the circle of Cardinals surrounding Brecheen, Musial timidly, almost stoically, tapped a few teammates on their backs before trotting off the field.

The Cardinals' coronation might have begun in a relatively calm manner, but the *New York Times* reported that to enter the victors' clubhouse after the game was akin to "risking life and limb" and that "caps, gloves, shirts, towels, belts flew all over the place" as the locker room "vibrated and shook." Dyer cried out, "We never lost a game we had to win."

In Musial's case, it almost seemed as if winning it all had become routine—he had appeared in the World Series in each of his four full seasons, winning three, yet he would never again play in the Fall Classic; 17 years without postseason play would follow for Musial (and 14 more such seasons for Williams).

The World Series, like a capricious lover, would rebuke the Cardinals' advances for almost exactly 20 years; the Cards' next trip to the Series, sans Musial, would not be until 1964. The win gave the Cardinals their sixth world championship over nine appearances since their first one in 1926 and their fourth title in a Series that went to a seventh game.

When the gate receipts were totaled, a full share for each Cardinal worked out to $3,742.33. Boston players got a check for just over $2,000, the most minuscule sum in nearly 30 years. So the Cardinals made less money than the Cubs had taken home the previous year for *losing* the Series ($3,930) and much less than the winning Tigers ($6,443) had earned.

Still, the Cardinals, playing in a small market (and in a city with two major-league clubs) drew over 1,000,000 spectators for the first time in franchise history. All in all, it had been a fine year for baseball with 12 of the 16 major-league teams establishing all-time attendance marks.

The Cardinals had no complaints, as the entire early-to-mid 1940s era had been terrific for the club. From 1942 to 1944 they won 106, 105, and 105 games, and they *averaged* 102 wins from 1942 to 1946, a stunning success story.

The completion of the 1946 World Series, on a simple 4-to-6 force out, marked the last time baseball would be labeled a sport in which only the ball was white. Jackie Roosevelt Robinson was ready to take center stage, emerging from the wings of Montreal, where he had helped them win the Little World Series.

Baseball was finally beginning to move out of its Stone Age.

However, Mark Ribowsky wrote that "the white game simply went on cashing in on the spectacle of black *versus* white." Bob Feller convinced Satchel Paige that they should "reprise their celebrated rivalry" at season's end. He obtained the permission of commissioner Happy Chandler to start a barnstorming tour while the World Series was going on.

The games were staged on the scale of Barnum & Bailey, and players traveled for a month, canvassing the country in two DC-3 airplanes, a method of transportation unused by big-leaguers back then. Feller once more signed Musial, who joined the club after playing in the Series. Feller fielded a team that also featured stars such as Johnny Sain, Phil Rizzuto, and Bob Lemon.

Those men received contracts calling for salaries in the $1,700 to $6,000 spectrum. Musial, despite playing only part of the team's schedule, earned more money on tour than his cut of the World Series pot. Paige's players, such as Buck O'Neil, Sam Jethroe, and Hank Thompson "were to get what the promoters deemed to give them." The 27 games were hugely successful, drawing about 400,000 spectators.

On February 1, 1947, baseball officially agreed to give players a pension. Players had to kick in $250 per year to be eligible, but for those who lasted five years in the majors, it was worth it. Those men would get a monthly check of $50 for life upon hitting age 50. Every extra year of service for a player added another $10 per month to his check up to a maximum of $100 a month for 10-year vets. Coming off a World Series in which the Cardinals and Red Sox had split a World Series pot of just $212,000, meaning the losing Sox were paid less than the umpires, the owners also conceded that they would establish a minimum pool for World Series participants of $250,000.

Musial wanted $35,000 for his next contract but was offered $21,000. Breadon insisted that was quite a hike from the previous year's $13,500. Musial argued that his salary, *after* the boost he received when he had refused the Mexican League offer, had been $18,500, so he wasn't asking for all that much more money. Breadon contended the extra $5,000 had simply been a bonus, thus Musial was, he contended, asking for nearly triple his 1946 salary.

In any event, after again becoming a holdout, he settled on a hike to $31,000 and instantly became the highest-paid Cardinal ever. He called the raise the "most significant" one he ever got.

The biggest news of the season, which concerned the Dodgers, was about to break. Leo Durocher was still the Brooklyn manager when spring training opened, but that would soon change. His Dodgers camp was in Havana, Cuba, because Branch Rickey wanted to avoid Southern states that had laws prohibiting blacks and whites from being on the same team. With less acrimony and chaos, Rickey hoped his players, many of them unhappy campers, would have the opportunity to see Robinson's skills and that they would request he jump from the Royals to the Dodgers.

That hope fell far from fruition. Approximately half of the squad was from the South and, during spring training, three of those players drew up a petition indicating they wanted no part of a black teammate. They sought out other teammates to support their declaration.

Durocher vehemently intervened. When he got sniff of his players' protestation, he called a late-night team meeting. In Durocher's autobiography, he wrote about his reaming the team: "Well, boys, you know what you can do with that petition. You can wipe your ass with it." All Durocher cared about, he stressed, was winning. "He's going to win pennants for us. He's going to put money in your pockets and money in mine…. He's only the first. *Only the first, boys!*" With that, the insurrection quickly died out.

Dodgers catcher Bobby Bragan was in the meeting (although he remembers it as taking place after a game) and recalled, "I know Leo Durocher called us in the clubhouse and said, 'I don't want to hear anything said about Jackie Robinson. I'm the manager of the team; I'll play who I want to. Everybody understand that?' And we did."

Higbe also related that after the incident Rickey was hell-bent on trading the dissenters but would bide his time to do so rather than make trades from a position of weakness, with other clubs well aware that he wanted to dump the players.

In any case, according to Higbe, many of Robinson's teammates soon saw how good a player he was and came to side with him. Another Dodgers teammate, Duke Snider, said he realized that those who spewed profanities and epithets at Robinson were the type of men who were "still fighting the Civil War." Snider stated that none of the Dodgers, other than the ones circulating the petition, signed it.

Stanky, one of the ringleaders in the rebellion against Robinson, did not endear himself to many players. A former teammate called him "a miserable little shit. Just the way he played, [but] the only thing I have to give him credit [for is] he made himself one helluva leadoff hitter. He came out there to kick your butt, but he was always pulling some kind of crap, mouthing off, and making remarks—he was just kind of an ornery little fart."

Rickey did not publicly reveal his plan to have Robinson break the big league's color line until the sixth inning of an exhibition game between Montreal and Brooklyn on April 10, 1947, at Ebbets Field, shortly before the regular season was to open.

According to legendary broadcaster Red Barber, Durocher's Dodgers were a "wide-open ball club for all kinds of gambling." When pitcher Larry French had been traded to Brooklyn in 1941, he observed, "Give any one of several players the right odds and he will bet you that your right ear falls off next Thursday." Durocher even gambled with his own players. Due to his shady connections and doings, he was suspended from baseball for the season and was not on hand to see Robinson's major-league debut.

Officially Robinson was the first African American in the majors during the modern era, post-1900. Robinson made his first big-league start on April 15, 1946, where he went hitless in front of an Opening Day Ebbets Field crowd of 26,623. Reportedly more than half of the fans were black.

Author Steve Jacobson wrote, "Black players would talk to friendly whites—Stan Musial was one of the best—who could see how good the black players were and ask them to talk up an end to big-league barriers."

Opinions vary on Musial's role in helping Robinson as he broke the barrier. Musial detractors charged him with being less than dynamic. For some his somewhat tepid support for Robinson, while true to Musial's personality, was not enough—they expected the Cardinals star to assert himself as a leader in this matter. Like many stars not known for their loquaciousness and aggressiveness, Musial tended to, as the baseball cliché goes, lead by example. In *Greats of the Game*, Ray Robinson and Christopher Jennison asserted that Musial was not "a professional crusader for civil rights."

Musial mainly skirted racial matters but got along well with players of all colors and backgrounds. Alex Grammas recalled Musial getting along with all of his teammates. "Well, I'm Greek," he laughed. "He was good to me. People were people to him—he never thought of them as black, white, or Italians, or Greeks. He's Polish himself so he understood we all come from the same place."

While Musial came across as easygoing, there was much more depth to him. Polish jokes were anathema to him, and not simply because of a sense of chauvinism; he was intelligent and would not put up with intolerance or injustices. Further, he refused to be mute when confronted with such situations. He once said he didn't find ethnic jokes amusing: "My dad came out of Poland and worked like hell all his life, and what was funny about that?"

Once, Stan was riding in a taxi with several of his teammates. One of them began mocking their cab driver, who happened to be Jewish, by talking loudly in an affected Jewish accent. Embarrassed and outraged, Musial ordered, "Knock it off," tipped the driver well, and, turning again to his teammate, said, "Do me a favor, please. Don't bother to ride with me again."

Joe Black was pitching against Musial in St. Louis once and Cardinals players began to ride him. "Hey, Stan," they shouted, "with that big black background, you shouldn't have trouble hitting the white ball." Musial approached Black the next day and apologized for his teammates' slurs.

Roger Kahn wrote that the Cardinals were "for decades the Ku Klux Klan's favorite team, an image that changed only slowly and grudgingly over many years with the ascent of Stan Musial…a liberal Democrat." That tribute perhaps best encapsulates Musial's esteem and influence.

Bill White, a black teammate of Musial, said he treated everyone well: "It didn't make any difference to him who you were." Former teammate Charlie James confirmed Musial never had trouble "getting along with *anybody*." Likewise, said Hank Sauer, "If you couldn't get along with Musial, you couldn't get along with anybody."

Steve Russell noted Musial was staunchly supportive of President Kennedy "on the civil rights issue, which was kind of a touchy issue back then. He had a philosophy that was ahead of its time, but being that he came from Donora, with an African American population, maybe he already had become somebody who was concerned about the rights of minorities."

According to an ESPN presentation, Musial was to the Cardinals as Pee Wee Reese—whose public acceptance of Robinson helped ease the tension that came with breaking the color barrier—was to the Dodgers.

In any event, in early May the story of a thwarted Cardinals strike against Robinson hit the papers. Sports editor Stanley Woodward of New York's *Herald Tribune* revealed that several Southern Cardinals had been organizing the strike, which was to take place on the Dodgers' trip into St. Louis on May 20. Their plan was to entice more players from other National League teams to join the cause, ultimately elbowing Robinson out of the game.

Musial would have no part of an uprising and insisted he had no problem with blacks. "I played against blacks in high school, played with Buddy Griffey," he once stated. Moreover, Musial openly let Robinson know he had his stamp of approval. Consequently, stated writer Peter Golenbock, "Robinson always credited Stan for standing up for him." One writer actually has Musial squelching the uprising, saying he would not even allow a team vote to occur—the Cards *would* play Brooklyn.

Golenbock, it should be noted, also wrote that the story of the Cardinals going on strike against Robinson was fabricated, that the team was "falsely accused." He said Musial, Marion, and respected journalist Bob Broeg "all deny categorically that the Cardinals ever threatened to go on strike against Robinson." He further wrote that the story of the strike didn't make much sense in that it reached print after the Dodgers and Cardinals has already played three incident-free games.

"We never considered it, talked about it, or had any ideas about it," Musial firmly stated. "There might have been grumbling, but we never had a meeting or anything of that nature." No vote, he insisted, ever took place.

In a 1989 book, Musial once again denied any knowledge of a boycott. "You could hear some mumbles in there," he said, but insisted "there was no kind of boycott of any kind."

The issue lived on into the 1990s, when Roger Kahn noted in his book, *The Era*, that at the time of the proposed boycott, "Musial was sick and feverish with raging appendicitis," so he was making no intentional attempt at distorting the truth; he was simply "too ill to know what was taking place." In any case, it seems the Cardinals' boycott issue is destined to be at least partially muddled forever, but Musial clearly had no truck with a racist movement.

In the meantime, Jonathan Eig wrote that Musial felt Robinson was simply seeking what *his* parents had wanted when they traveled to America: the chance to better himself. However, Musial either "lacked the courage to tell his teammates or he didn't know how. [Musial stated,] 'For me at the time—I was 26—saying all that would have been a speech and I didn't know how to make speeches. Saying it to older players, that was beyond me.'"

The truth concerning Musial's views on the integration of baseball seems, by and large, simple. Throughout life Musial tended to avoid controversial matters; he was not about to champion a cause. Buddy Blattner, a former teammate who went on to become a big-league broadcaster, once commented that Musial didn't burden "himself with the heavy baggage of the games [sic] policies or politics."

Roger Kahn wrote that Robinson compared Musial to Gil Hodges in that both were nice people, but, said Robinson, "When it came to what I had to do, neither one hurt me and neither one helped." Veteran sportswriter Stan Isaacs said, "I would tend to think what Jackie said is probably closest to it [the truth]—Stan wouldn't have been involved. I don't think he would have been a guy involved with boycotting. On the other hand, he's not the kind of guy who would be a leader and say, 'This is unfair and I won't be a part of it.'"

Isaacs added, "I don't think he would be a guy involved with issues other than playing baseball. He's a mild, likable guy. I don't think he's the kind of guy who would look for confrontation…. That's the essence of him."

Erskine said that if he were confronted by a critic of Musial claiming Stan's voice wasn't strong enough when it came to the crashing of the color barrier, "I'd say to him, the way a guy said to me when he wanted me to be a character witness for a fellow in my hometown, 'I don't know him real well. I [just] know who he is.' He said, 'Well, have you heard anything bad about him?' No. 'Have you ever heard that he was in any trouble or that he ever got arrested?' No. 'Do you think that, from what you know about him, that he's out to be untruthful?' No. He said, 'You're the greatest character witness that we could have. You live here, you're around everything in this community, and you never heard anything bad about him? That's the best recommendation you could get.'

"I'd say that about Musial. I never heard a bad word about him. I never heard a black player say, 'Musial snubbed me.' Musial was a kind person, a thoughtful person, a gentleman."

Erskine said that some writers did point out that Musial wasn't quite active enough regarding the integration of the game "as a general statement, but you have to go ahead and finish the thought and say, 'Okay, he didn't march with Martin Luther King or whatever, but what he did do—how many young people did he influence in having a good lifestyle and having a kind of a makeup that was an encourager instead of a discourager? And that's what Musial did. He used his station in life to encourage young people, to help young hitters, to help fans appreciate the game. I mean, his strengths were his personality, and it was being, maybe, on a more passive side, but his impact was great."

Apparently team owner Sam Breadon learned of his team's incipient boycott and flew to New York to discuss the matter with Ford Frick "even as he tried to downplay the gravity of the situation," but Frick believing the situation was as serious as a hospital's Intensive Care Unit, threatened to suspend any player involved in a strike against Robinson. Frick said he would stick to his conviction even if "half the league strikes. Those who do it will encounter swift retribution. All will be suspended, and I don't care if it wrecks the National League for five years."

While St. Louis isn't exactly a city embedded deep in the aorta of Dixie, it was a city not yet ready to accept Robinson. George F. Will recalled, "On Jackie Robinson's first tour in '47, St. Louis and Cincinnati were problems. The history of Missouri in the matter of race is very complex and bloody."

In fact, it was not until May 1944 that Sportsman's Park became the final big-league ballpark to integrate. Then, finally, black spectators were no longer required to sit in the remote right-field pavilion, watching games through a screen.

Generally Philadelphia—under acerbic manager Ben Chapman—and St. Louis are named as being the most hostile teams to Robinson. Chapman, from the safety of his dugout, would yell out to Robinson, "Jackie, here's my shoes. Shine them after the game."

Bragan stated Chapman, "a Birmingham boy, would holler [from his dugout], 'Get up. Let that black boy have your seat,' to our team. And he'd holler at Jackie when he went to bat."

Once Chapman approached Robinson in the runway that led to the clubhouse and gave what he must have thought was a compliment to Robinson. "Jackie, you're one hell of a player, but you're still a nigger."

In 1947, according to the Ken Burns documentary *Baseball*, "The most serious incident came in St. Louis against Rickey's old team, the Cardinals. Enos 'Country' Slaughter, out at first by at least 10 feet, nonetheless jumped into the air and deliberately laid open Robinson's thigh with his spikes." Bob Broeg took issue with the word "deliberately" and said the wound was not significant. Bragan recalled the play a bit differently. "Enos Slaughter kind of outran a ball to first base, and they thought he stepped on Jackie's foot. They had a little ruckus out there, but it didn't amount to anything." Still another source has Slaughter barely missing Robinson's Achilles tendon. One thing remains clear: Between Robinson and Slaughter, believed to be one of the main organizers of the proposed Cardinals strike against Robinson's participation, there was nothing but enmity.

It took great restraint for the livid Robinson to maintain a pacifistic approach to his vitriolic and bellicose antagonists, but he lived up to his vow to Branch Rickey—he would seek no retaliation against opposing players during his first three big-league seasons.

Musial only rarely flashed anger, usually remaining stoic. Once, though, he became enraged at manager Leo Durocher, who repeatedly ordered his pitchers to knock him down and who, during a game in which his Dodgers led the Cards 9–1, gloated and shouted obscenities at the Cardinals dugout. That time, Musial could stand it no longer. He reportedly glowered across the diamond at Durocher, pointed at him, and bellowed, among other things, "You're up and strutting now, but just you wait. We'll get you, you prick." Tim McCarver said it was the only time he remembered Musial lacing his speech with obscenities.

The contrast between the belligerent Durocher and Musial was vast. Talent-wise, Musial was a perennial offensive threat; Durocher's bat had been as threatening as a psychosomatic illness.

Durocher often clashed with Musial. Once, in 1947, the Cardinals knocked Robinson down, and Durocher retaliated by having his pitcher twice deposit Musial on his back. On the second pitch, the ball struck Musial's bat, and he was thrown out at first while still in a prone position. Later he addressed Durocher, "Hey, Leo...I didn't throw at your man." Durocher said that Musial should instruct his team to leave Robinson alone: "For every time my man gets one, it looks to me like you're gonna get two." Durocher stated that ultimatum ended all issues between Robinson and the Cardinals.

Durocher, again unlike Musial, was egocentric, concerned only with himself and with winning at any cost. He once said that if his mother was rounding third heading home with the winning run, he would trip her. Later on, conceded Durocher, he would apologize sincerely to her, but as he told Roger Kahn, "even my own mother don't get to score the run that beats me."

As the season progressed, the Cardinals' personality emerged. They were a team Johnny Sain called "rough-and-tumble," one that hustled and contained players who were "throwbacks to the Gashouse Gang." Musial was one of those men.

Early on in the season, Musial, then a .347 lifetime hitter, inched closer to the plate and was soon hitting with the fearsome force of a riptide. Harry Walker, however, suffered a horrible cold spell, hitting .200 by May 3, the day the Cardinals swapped him to the Phillies. Incredibly, he went on to hit .371 for the Phillies and won the batting title.

Preseason favorites, the Cards experienced early woes, dropping nine in a row at one point, while the Dodgers got off to a great start. In a swoon, the Redbirds were mired in the cellar from April 29 until June 3, an ignominious fall from their 1946 grandeur.

On May 8 Musial, in a hitting funk and complaining of sharp stomach pain, was flown from Brooklyn to St. Louis, where he was examined at St. John's Hospital. Dr. Robert Hyland diagnosed a case of appendicitis and decided to handle Musial's condition through "treatment and diet." An operation, he determined, could wait until the off-season.

When Musial returned to the lineup too quickly, he continued to suffer at the plate. He had lost 10 pounds, felt weak, and lost significant bat speed.

On May 19 his average hit a nadir of a mere .140, and he had reached a point where it took a bunt hit to end an 0-for-22 drought.

As the St. Louis summer heated up, so, finally, did the Cardinals, even though they struggled against lefties (losing 11 of their first 15 decisions to southpaws). Snapping out of their lethargy in June, they rattled off nine successive wins, good for their longest winning spree of the year.

It began when they swept a four-game set against the rival Dodgers beginning on Friday, June 13. With Musial having recovered from his health problems, he feasted on Brooklyn pitching, compiling seven hits. Not even a city transit strike could hold down the crowd, anxious to see Jackie Robinson that weekend. A season high of 29,686 content spectators attended the series finale, delighted that the Cardinals had stormed back into contention. By June 20 they were just three and a half games out.

In one contest against the Pirates, Musial blistered a line drive off Kirby Higbe. Hank Greenberg, playing first base in his final season, couldn't react to the liner; it went between his legs and into right field. "Hig, I should have caught that one," apologized Greenberg. Higbe replied, "Hank, if you had caught that one, it would have turned you inside out."

Having hoisted his average to the .280s around the last week in July, Musial reached .302 on August 10, and the Cardinals were in second place. He went on to up the ante by hitting .480 in August.

When September finally dragged its way in, the Cardinals and Dodgers met for the final time with Brooklyn up by five games. The three-game series began on September 11, a Thursday night, and 29,452 sweaty but enthusiastic fans jammed tiny Sportsman's Park. In the second inning Joe Garagiola lumbered down the first-base line trying to beat out a potential double-play grounder. In the process, he stepped on Robinson's foot. According to Dodgers announcer Red Barber, when Robinson came to bat the following inning, he and Garagiola argued and "menaced each other." Beans Reardon, the home-plate umpire, broke things up, but two innings later a still-fired-up Robinson crashed a two-run homer. With 15 games left to play, Brooklyn increased their lead to six games, a decent shield against a brief letdown, but not exactly an insurmountable lead.

The following night, in front of a throng of 31,957, the Dodgers tallied four times in their half of the ninth, but the Cardinals rallied for two, enough to win 8–7. The finale came on a Saturday afternoon, under the unforgiving Missouri sun. Despite the heat, this time 33,510 spectators were on hand (Robinson and his Dodgers drew more than 1.7 million fans on the road in his rookie campaign). Cardinals fans left the ballpark drained, having suffered a nerve-rattling 8–7 loss. With just 13 games to go, and with the Dodgers' magic number inexorably clicking down, their hopes for a pennant had been dashed.

The heat in St. Louis was a sometimes-overlooked factor in pennant chases. "It was unbelievable," related Bob Friend, who said he's heard of temperatures on the field of up to 120 degrees. "We had fans in the dugout, and the air was so hot. It was St. Louis, Midwest heat. And those double-headers in Sportsman's Park on Sunday afternoons, they were tough." The heat, he felt, just *had* to take a lot out of the Cardinals, playing so often under such conditions. Players took relief any way they could back then, including wetting down towels and placing them under their caps. Some pitchers would go "two or three innings then they change[d] wool uniforms because they got so wet—it weighed you down," said Friend.

Ultimately Brooklyn, who had ridden atop the league since July 6, clinched their title on September 22 by five lengths over the second-place Cards. The players, while glum, still took some solace in their formidable resiliency after their dreary play early on.

Musial wound up hitting .312, a very respectable average, but 53 points lower than what he had hit in 1946. That represented the 11th-worst one-year decline by a reigning National League batting champ. In his estimation, it was not one of his shining seasons.

In November Sam Breadon sold the Cardinals to Fred Saigh and Robert Hannegan. Breadon's initial investment in the club, which he owned since 1920, was a minuscule $200. He sold the team for $3 million. The new owners vowed they would keep the franchise in St. Louis. Unlike franchises such as the Athletics, which drifted from city to city like tumbleweed, the Cardinals organization was anchored in St. Louis.

Enormously popular, Musial continued to come across as almost too good to be true. Always open to the media and his fans, Musial's life was scandal free. If he played today, the media would find him relatively uninteresting, perhaps even bordering on colorless, quite the opposite of an egomaniacal, brash Barry Bonds or a volatile, narcissistic Albert Belle.

Writer James N. Giglio called him "the antithesis of today's superstars, many of whom have not only succumbed to drugs, alcoholism, crime, or infidelity but have also exhibited an unbelievable selfishness in spurning young autograph seekers, reporters, and charitable institutions." Pitcher Bob Cain said of his era—a comment which is probably indicative of any era of baseball, "Women were all over the place. They were available to players in every town." Musial never strayed and once rebuked a bartender for trying to help an interested female make contact with him.

Erskine commented, "What Stan has done that's made him remembered as he is: he had a good lifestyle. You never heard of Musial in any kind of big confrontations."

Still, like any human being, he had a few minor flaws and foibles. He would drink a few beers and was a cigarette and cigar smoker at times, but normally he smoked in moderation.

While Musial did some endorsements for cigarettes, he later avoided being seen smoking or drinking as he came to realize he was a role model to the youth he so genuinely enjoyed. In 1948 a writer chastised Musial for his affiliation with Chesterfield because kids would emulate their hero, and he soon quit endorsing cigarettes. He also forbade photographers to snap pictures when he was in a state of undress in the clubhouse. In general, he worked diligently to keep up his good image, feeling an obligation to kids, fans in general, to his team, and to his community.

Steve Russell, son of major-leaguer Jimmy Russell, said, "Stan would only, and this is something my dad said about Stan that I'll never forget, have a couple of drinks because he was always worried about his body— keeping that body in tune right for what he had to do.

"When he became the [national physical] fitness director [under President Lyndon Johnson], that all made sense. I'm surprised, though, that Stan smoked cigarettes up until 1956. He was very concerned about his image and very concerned about his health."

Musial, like most baseball stars, did supplement his income by lending his name to a slew of products. He was featured in a 1956 print-media ad for Wheaties, which included four pictures—one of Stan as a magician, a "Wheaties champion," pulling a scarf out of a top hat. The caption read in part, "A good magician, Stan also knows about the magic of wheat!" Three years earlier, a Chesterfield cigarettes ad touted, "Chesterfield *Best* For You." It featured a picture of Musial, cigarette in hand, and his signed endorsement, "I've smoked Chesterfield for 7 years. I know they're best for me. Try a pack yourself." He also backed Winthrop Shoes because, as the ad read, he insisted "on comfort off the field" and compared the shoes to a "four-bagger." Among other baseball-related products, he also endorsed Rawlings gloves.

Musial would utter an occasional oath but, unlike most ballplayers, did not casually drop swear words into his speech. Russell said, "I met Stan at the country club where my dad belonged, the Feather Sound Country Club in Clearwater, Florida, around spring-training time in 1983. They had been golfing, and they came into the bar to have a drink. He just always had a nice demeanor; he always came off very well, he was never ignorant, he did not use bad language."

Additionally, Musial found some of his roommates to be "unsuitable because of their affinity for alcohol or the night life." He once laughed, "Sure, I like beer, all right. But I don't want to drink it all night." As a rule, Musial's idea of nightlife was a meal at his hotel and a movie or musical show followed by a return to his room.

A controversial issue, one Musial did take a firm stand on, was baseball's reserve clause, one Brady Snyder wrote of as "antithetical to a capitalist, free-market system. The players believed the owners' rhetoric that the game could not survive without the reserve clause." In 1948 Musial, among other stars such as Bob Feller, spoke out in favor of the clause. Given such behavior, Curt Flood would later come to consider Musial a company man.

In March 1948 a critic told Musial he felt the Cardinals would improve, counting on the fact that Musial didn't "figure to have another lousy year like last season." Musial winced inwardly but said nothing. The next day, after doing some research, the man approached Musial again, saying, "Either I owe you an apology or you should thank me for the compliment, calling it a lousy year when a fellow hits .312." Why, he wondered, hadn't Musial corrected him? Musial replied, "For me, it was a lousy year." That would certainly not be the case in 1948, his greatest season ever.

Healthy now, with his inflamed appendix and his tonsils having been removed in October and his strength-sapping low-grade infections gone, Musial was ready to get back into his groove. Spring training was a joy once he found he could again swing the bat freely.

He was also relieved when he ended a holdout that had begun when he refused a contract offering no raise for 1948. New owner Bob Hannegan's cavalier treatment of the team's star stung, so Musial cut off communication with him. Finally a friend of the owner coaxed him to make amends with Musial. Eventually the friend said, "Look, do you want to fight him until you break him down and he comes in begging your favor and resenting it? Or do you want to have a guy on your side, satisfied and ready to hustle as he always hustled?"

Hannegan relented, phoned Musial, palliated the potentially volatile situation, and convinced him to sign a $31,000 pact. Musial stated in his autobiography that he signed after being assured that if he enjoyed a big year the club "would adjust my contract during the season." His 1948 salary would become, in light of what he would go on to accomplish, a steal of a deal for the organization.

Milestone hit number 1,000, a triple off Cliff Chambers in Chicago, came on April 24, 1948. When sportswriter friend Bob Broeg goaded him to shoot for 3,000, Musial said that goal was too far off to consider but told Broeg to keep reminding him about it. "This is a team game," said Musial, "and I play to win, but a fella has to have little incentives."

Over his next swing into Brooklyn for a three-game set covering May 18–20, Musial was as hot as a funeral pyre. He tagged Dodgers pitchers, going 11-for-15, including a record-setting nine hits over a two-day stretch, with six of his hits going for extra bases. In the game on May 19 he went 5-for-5 with each hit coming with two strikes on him.

Former pitcher Bob Friend said, "I remember when I was a kid working out with major-league teams, a scout took me up to Brooklyn and they had a doubleheader with the Cardinals. Musial, as usual, had one of those great days in Brooklyn. The scout was trying to sell me on the Dodgers [so] he said, 'This Cardinals team, they're all old.'" What Friend observed that day, though, was Musial ripping four doubles and driving home six runs. "He just peppered the ball. That was a good park for him." So good, Musial would hit .522 there that year with 24 hits over 11 games. Stunningly, he would hit 13 points higher there in 1949 with six homers and 19 runs scored in 12 games.

Musial said that if he could have hit for the entire 1948 season at Ebbets, the Polo Grounds, or, for that matter, on the road, where he hit .415, he could have hit .400 and "ripped the record book apart." Famed sportswriter Stan Isaacs reminisced, "Dodger fans and Giants fans were in awe of him, and they tended to be critical, they liked to find a weakness in opposing players, but Musial transcended that. There was awe about him."

At season's break he was the leading All-Star vote-getter in the National League with over 1.5 million votes. On July 13, 1948, he hit his first All-Star Game home run, doing so as a "visitor" in Sportsman's Park as the Browns, not the Cards, hosted the game. It was, according to Musial, during the break that he received a new contract calling for a $5,000 raise.

Two days later he upped his average to .415 and whispers of a .400 season began.

That year the Cardinals lost nine of their 11 games in Pittsburgh, and Musial's chances for .400 diminished when he hit a mere .255 in Forbes Field. Teammate Carl Warwick said, "He didn't like to hit in Forbes Field; a lot of us didn't. I can remember him saying, if he'd get a base hit there, 'Well, that's one more I worked on to get.' There's not a big, green background to look to like you do in other ballparks—you're kinda looking out into the sky because the fence was only about eight or so feet high at that point. It's kind of an odd-shaped field.

"You have certain feelings about certain ballparks," Warwick continued. "He loved Wrigley Field." Often the winds there bullwhipped the flags about and boosted balls over the fence. He may have loved the park and its then-existing day-games-only policy (lifetime he hit .340 during day games as opposed to .320 under the lights) but, oddly, he hit only .308 there, 23 points below his lifetime average.

To offset his lower averages in some parks, he naturally hit higher elsewhere. He trampled over Boston, pitching at .353 lifetime, better than any other club, followed by .349 off New York Giants pitching and .344 versus Brooklyn.

Musial's September 17 injury, which occurred when he banged up his wrists making a circus catch, also hurt his pursuit of .400. Still, on September 22, the second-place Cardinals visited Boston to face the first-place Braves. The wind was blowing out to an inviting target, the right-field stands. With wrists heavily taped by trainer Doc Weaver, Musial took to the field. Then, unhappy with his recent hitting, he ripped the tape off. He decided to make a concession to his physical condition; he would swing only sparingly but certainly not gingerly.

On just five cuts, he heroically lashed five hits. His binge began with a bloop single and a sharply hit double over the left fielder's head coming off a fastball from ace Warren Spahn. Then, facing Red Barrett, Musial worked the count to 2–0, correctly guessed a change-up would follow, and pounded it for a homer into the right-field bullpen with the resounding authority of a judge's gavel bang for a homer, swinging, as Musial recounted, "from the heels." In the sixth inning, his wrists now afire, he guided a seeing-eye single that scooted past Alvin Dark and through the infield against Clyde Shoun. His final trip to the plate resulted in a single that shot through the hole between first and second off an outside 2–0 pitch from Al Lyons, the fourth pitcher he faced. That hit tied Ty Cobb's 1922 record for four five-hit games in a season.

*Stan with his 10th-grade homeroom. He's standing in the top row, fourth from the left. Musial was popular, convivial, and modest, qualities he maintained throughout his life.* Photo courtesy of the Donora Historical Society.

*Musial, the fifth person in from the left in the bottom row, was not only believed to be good enough to play college ball, but many locals felt basketball was his best sport. His 1937–38 team went 11–1, and he was named to the All-Section and All–Western Pennsylvania teams.* Photo courtesy of the Donora Historical Society.

*Musial, wearing No. 16, was a fine ball handler and passer who possessed a deadly hook shot.* Photo courtesy of the Jimmy Russell Collection.

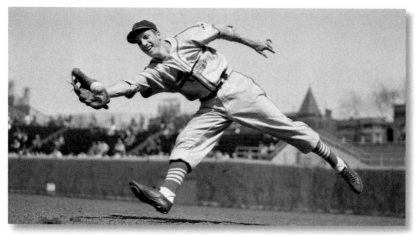

*Stan Musial, starting his first full year in the major leagues, practices on April 23, 1942.* Photo courtesy of AP Images.

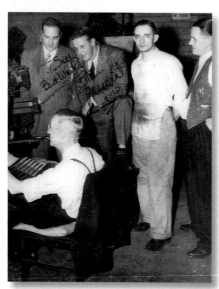

*Musial often made trips back to his hometown. Here he drops in on the local newspaper in 1943. He is flanked by two relatives and a worker.* Photo from the collection of Rose Cousino.

*Ensign Gerry O'Brien (right) welcomes Stan Musial to the Bainbridge Naval Training Center in Providence, Rhode Island, after Musial's induction into the navy on January 23, 1945.* Photo courtesy of AP Images.

*Musial's batting stance once prompted Ted Lyons to comment that it looked "like a small boy looking around a corner to see if the cops are coming." Here Musial demonstrates said stance at spring training in 1946.* Photo courtesy of AP Images.

*Musial demonstrates his batting stance for his wife Lil, son Dickie (6), and his daughter Geraldine (2) at their home in Donora, Pennsylvania, on November 22, 1946.* Photo courtesy of AP Images.

*Musial tells his father, Lucasz, that his left leg, sprained recently in a league game, is in good shape for the opening World Series game on October 5, 1943, against the New York Yankees at Yankee Stadium. Musial visits with his father October 4, 1943, in the New Yorker Hotel in New York.* Photo courtesy of AP Images.

*Stan Musial is flanked by his mother, Mary (left), and his wife, Lil, at a testimonial dinner in his honor at the Chase Hotel on January 24, 1957, in St. Louis.* Photo courtesy of AP Images.

*Stan Musial has always been approachable by fans. Here he signs an autograph for Bob Slater of Chicago at Wrigley Field on August 17, 1948, just before the Cubs-Cardinals game.* Photo courtesy of AP Images.

*Milwaukee Braves outfielder Hank Aaron (center) jokes with St. Louis Cardinals players Wally Moon (left) and Stan Musial before the start of the Cardinals-Braves game at Busch Stadium on August 15, 1956. Aaron was leading the National League in hitting at the time with .340; Moon was second with an average of .327; and Musial, a six-time winner of the honor, was third with .312.* Photo courtesy of AP Images.

*Stan and Lil circa 1957. By this point Stan had come a long way since his days as a boy growing up in poverty amid the Depression.* Photo courtesy of Laurel Grimes.

*The Musial children circa 1957. From left to right: Janet, Richard (better known as Dick), and Geraldine (Gerry). Another daughter, Jean, came along in 1958.* Photo courtesy of Laurel Grimes.

*Musial, 42, gropes for the right words as he announces his retirement from baseball on August 13, 1963, in St. Louis. Musial played 22 years with the Cardinals. "Baseball has been my life," said Musial, who three times won the National League Most Valuable Player Award, seven times led the league in hitting, and broke numerous career records.* Photo courtesy of AP Images.

*Musial stands near his statue, a tribute to "the Man" and a fixture just outside the Cardinals' ballpark in St. Louis that frequently serves as a meeting place for fans.* Photo courtesy of Rose Cousino.

*Lil and Stan together in 1990. The two have been together since high school and celebrated their 70th anniversary on November 21, 2009, which was also Stan's 89th birthday.* Photo courtesy of Rose Cousino.

*Stan Musial holds up the ceremonial first-pitch ball before the MLB All-Star Game in St. Louis on July 14, 2009.* Photo courtesy of AP Images.

Despite coming up short of the Braves in 1948, experts concurred this was easily Musial's finest season and one of the greatest hitting displays ever. He became the first player in NL history to take home three MVP trophies. The Baseball Writers Association of America somehow did not give him his 1948 honor unanimously—Boston's 24-game winner Johnny Sain and Dark stole six first-place votes from him.

Musial had dominated the MVP Award in the 1940s, though, winning the coveted trophy three times and finishing second and fourth as well over a six-year period. In addition, over a nine-year span from 1943 to 1952, he would finish in the top five vote-getters for the MVP Award an eye-popping eight times. Even when he was 41, he would still be among the top 10 vote recipients.

Musial had, in fact, hoisted the team on his shoulders, sweeping virtually every offensive department in the league—leading, while also setting personal highs, for batting average (.376), runs (135), runs driven in (131), hits (230), on-base percentage (.450), extra-base hits (103), total bases (429), and slugging (.702). He also led the NL in doubles and triples. The only thing he did not do was collect and wash the teams' uniforms.

In 1946 Musial's .365 batting average had been 109 points higher than the National League's composite average. In 1948 he widened the gap, hitting 115 points over the league average of .261, good for the fourth-widest margin of batting superiority in NL history. He also hit 43 points higher than the second-best NL hitter, Richie Ashburn, the seventh-biggest gap for the leader over his runner-up in big-league history. Plus, only one NL hitter, Tony Gwynn, would exceed Musial's .376 mark for the rest of the century, when he hit .394 in 1994.

Likewise, Musial's 230 hits—only 20 men had ever totaled that many—was 40 more than the No. 2 man, Tommy Holmes. That gap represented the third-biggest difference ever in that category, topped by only Nap Lajoie, who collected 232 hits for the 1901 A's—42 more than the long-forgotten John Anderson—and by Musial himself, when his 228 safeties towered over Dixie Walker by 44 in 1946. That was the all-time record until 2004, when Ichiro Suzuki's season-long rampage resulted in a new record 262 hits, some 46 more than Michael Young.

Musial even hit more homers (a personal high of 39) than he had strike-outs (34). Had he lofted just one additional home run, he would have become the only man ever to top his league in batting average, hits, doubles, triples, homers, runs driven in, and slugging in a single season.

The tale of 1948 has an intriguing wrinkle. Musial should have won the Triple Crown, but rain cost him a home run on, researchers believe, August 3 in the Polo Grounds. Musial recalled a lost homer, telling sportswriter John Kuenster, "I can't remember who we played, but if that homer had counted I would've been the first Triple Crown winner in the league since Joe Medwick [in 1937]."

Kuenster stated, "A lot of people were critical of that comment because they couldn't find the home run. And the reason, I'm quite sure, was they didn't even post a box score because the game was rained out. He probably hit the home run in the first inning, maybe they played only three innings, and the game was washed out, but those are his words."

With that extra home run, Musial would have hit 40, which would have tied him for league leadership with Johnny Mize and Ralph Kiner, men who hit with stampede-like power. Kuenster summarized, "Even by today's standards, Musial's work on offense in 1948 ranks close to being the greatest in the history of the game."

The season was, without doubt, his breakthrough year for clout. He had never hit as many as 20 homers in a big-league season, and he had more than doubled his 1947 power output of 19 shots. From 1948 through 1955 he would average nearly 32 round-trippers per season.

Musial, once said to be too scrawny for pro baseball, had filled out and could sock 'em out with regularity. He had developed big arms and big shoulders and was no longer a wispy boy incapable of slugging 30 or more homers. Still, for his career, 13 percent of his hits went for homers, 7 percent fewer than what most pure power hitters turned in.

Musial later declared he had hit his "athletic peak" in 1948 and attributed his power increase to his discovery that his bat felt feather-light, permitting him to drop his hands down about an inch from a position of choking the bat to resting entirely on the knob. "Gripping the bat at the end, I could still control my swing," he said.

Musial's power surge fit in with the times. "Baseball boomed in the late forties, but this kind of baseball would drive a purist nuts," wrote Bill James. "At its worst it was station-to-station baseball," with the offense relying heavily on the longball.

His 429 total bases, a whopping 113 more than his closest competitor, were the second-most since Rogers Hornsby set the National League record with 450 in 1922. His 103 extra-base hits had been matched or bettered by only Babe Ruth, Lou Gehrig, Chuck Klein, and Hank Greenberg and were just four fewer than Klein's NL-best set in 1930, a season replete with tainted stats due to the introduction of the juiced-up "rabbit ball." And his .702 slugging percentage was the highest mark since Hack Wilson's .723, also set in 1930. No NL hitter surpassed Musial in slugging until 1994, when Jeff Bagwell posted a .750 slugging percentage.

It was little wonder that Carl Erskine said neither he nor any of the Dodgers pitchers had "what you'd call a book on Musial, like he's got a weakness here or something. No. You had to throw a variety of pitches to Stan and, as I said, I had better success with him—I had a very good off-speed pitch, a straight change we called it—and you had to show him a fast-ball and so forth, but my best chance to get him out was to pull the string and give him an off-speed pitch. But you didn't have a book on Musial and say, 'Here's the way to get him out.'"

As good as Musial was, there was one pitcher who dominated him. Erskine related, "A pitcher on my team was named Clem Labine. I don't know if this is a record or not, but I can tell you the stats I know. Labine had a sinking fastball; he had excellent luck with Musial. He got Stan out [49] straight times, and that's just unheard of for hitters as good as Musial." Erskine was repeating an oft-told story, but the truth is Musial was a disappointing lifetime 10-for-42 against Labine (.238).

Erskine said that despite such futility, Musial never displayed a sign of frustration. Erskine joked that since Labine had a crooked finger due to its once being broken, "we [the Dodgers pitching staff] considered breaking that finger" if that's what it took to nullify Musial's skills.

Erskine's big overhand curve was so lethal, it should have been the original Dead Man's Curve. Erskine spoke of how Musial acknowledged his curve was tremendous, adding, "and neither one of us can figure out how it works."

Now a rare pitch, at least a handful of pitchers possessed the swooping overhand breaking ball in Musial's era. The Man would have had to factor that pitch into his hitting strategy when he faced Labine, who, according to Erskine, "had a good overhand curve and [Johnny] Podres on our team threw a fairly straight overhand curve. Spahn, of course, was a straight over-hand pitcher, but he never developed a real big curveball."

Some classic battles between pitchers such as Spahn and Labine and hitters such as Musial developed during this era of the game. Erskine said,

"When you faced St. Louis, now, remember, we [Musial and Erskine] were in the league together at least 10 years, 12 years maybe, you faced each team 22 times in those days because there were eight teams in each league [thus making up the then-existing 154-game schedule]—11 at home, 11 on the road. So, I don't know how many times I faced Musial, but I had 30 decisions or more against the Cardinals." A player *had* to be a student of his opponents if he was to adjust to the men they would face year in and year out, and they grew to know each other's strengths and weaknesses quite well.

By the end of 1948, the Cardinals' front office recognized their problems were running rampant. Their minor-league teams were "no longer churning out great players," while other clubs had caught up and passed the Cardinals in the important realm of player development. The team had also refused to sign black players, and such short-sightedness would also come into play. The Cards were coming off two solid years (finishing second both seasons), but it would soon be apparent that the dynasty was about to crumble.

Shortly after his 1948 season drew to a conclusion, terrible news came out of Musial's hometown. Long ago, men who worked on the rivers referred to Donora as "Hell's Bend" or "Hell's Bottom" due to the heavy fogs that gathered by the curve in the Monongahela River there, making it a dangerous spot.

That fog, in a deadly combination with the smoky pollution cranked out by Donora's steel industry, resulted in a tragedy that began on October 26, 1948, and lasted the rest of the month.

Mate the word "fog" with "smoke," and the union of their unholy marriage is the blended word "smog," a word that took on oppressive, deadly connotations in Donora when debilitating sickness and death swooped down on the town in the form of that smog.

The town was accustomed to abundant smokestacks piercing its modest skyline, standing straight and tall like ballpark light stanchions, each cranking out pollutants, but this time things were different. The smoggy conditions claimed 20 lives in one weekend—normally the town's death rate would be around 30 for an entire year—and nearly 6,000 took sick, about 43 percent of the town's population.

The technical explanation for the smog was "toxic emissions" from the Zinc Works, which "spewed out sulfuric acidic fumes, carbon dioxide and heavy metal dust that mixed with fog that hung low in the town and lingered [trapped there] because of a common, though unusually long, temperature inversion." In 2008 Dr. Devra L. Davis, director of the Center for Environmental Oncology at the University of Pittsburgh, stated that new evidence shows "fluoride gas [similar to the gas used as a lethal weapon in World War I and II] produced by the zinc smelting process...was responsible for the deaths." She added that an autopsy of one victim revealed "fluoride levels 10 to 20 times normal, well into the lethal range."

Townsfolk caught up in the poisonous event cared little for such explanations; they wanted quick relief, but none was forthcoming.

Drugstores remained open 24 hours and physicians labored around the clock and were aided by nurses and other volunteers, including policemen and firemen who went door to door administering oxygen, and even they had trouble locating homes due to the cloud of smog enveloping the town.

A Halloween parade scheduled for Friday, October 29 (precisely 19 years after the stock market's Black Tuesday) was nearly canceled due to the monstrous, suffocating smog, and spectators complained they could barely make out the participants. The home high school football game against Monongahela the following afternoon was played under conditions with even worse visibility as the Zinc Works continued to belch out still more billowing, smothering toxins into the air. After all, with around half of the townspeople working in the mills, few had the courage to speak out against their industry.

Paul Brown of Donora said he attended the game and, although he sat in the fourth row of the stands, he could hear the impact on the football when it was punted or kicked, but the ball "would disappear into the cloud." Another spectator, Sam Jackson, observed the smog "was like a big cloud of mist hanging over the players."

During the worst of the smog, "It was very difficult to breathe, even inside," said Donoran John Benyo Jr. "I can remember my throat burning, and I couldn't understand why my mother wouldn't let me go out to play."

The Donora Hotel was used as a makeshift hospital, and its basement became a temporary morgue. One funeral home ran out of caskets and another was packed with eight bodies, forcing the mortician to lay one victim out in his living room. Hundreds of locals were evacuated. To an outside observer, it must have looked like Godzilla had been spotted, as the town was abuzz with emergency workers racing around.

Those who lived through the hellish experience have never forgotten it. Joe Barbao Jr. worked in the Zinc Works during the disaster and remembered that if "you got up on top of the hill, it was clear up there and you could see, like you were looking down in clouds, all the way down [into the thick smog] over the whole valley. It just sat there. That was nasty.

"Downtown, even with headlights on, you couldn't see. I drove to Monongahela and I got on the wrong side of the road, all of a sudden a telephone pole that was supposed to be on my left was on my right—that's how little you could see."

On Halloween, steel mill officials shut down all of the Zinc Works smelters at 6:00 AM and, when rain mercifully followed a few hours later, the smog finally dispersed.

Monday found the furnaces up and running once more.

Years earlier, the pollution had killed vegetation and grass on the hills of a neighboring village, Webster, across the Monongahela River. Barbao Jr. noted, "The hills were bare from the sulphur that would go across [the river on] primarily a west wind. People over in Webster were raising all kinds of hell about it." Now it had killed humans as well.

Barbao pointed out an ironic situation, in that eventually "they shut the place [mill] down. They've got all kind of green grass over there now, but they've got no jobs." One positive note that came out of the tragedy was it made the government aware of the virulent pollution problem. The smog provided the impetus for the Clean Air Act of 1963 and ultimately the creation of the Environmental Protection Agency.

On December 17, 1948, Stan's 58-year-old father, whom he called Pop, slipped into a coma after suffering a stroke. While he had had several strokes before, this one proved to be fatal. He died in Stan's six-room ranch home in southwest St. Louis two days later and was transported by rail to Donora. Funeral services were held at St. Mary's on the day before Christmas. Many Cardinals came to Donora to pay their respects to the bereaved Stan. The realization that he had lost his father hit a forlorn Stan with a sudden, savage impact.

Studies made around 10 years after the disaster took place revealed Donora's mortality rate still "remained significantly higher than that of neighboring communities." Stan traced Lukasz's death back to the smog his father had just suffered through.

His father's health—he had suffered lung problems from around 1946 on—was a key reason that Stan had decided to move his parents to St. Louis shortly after the smog had enveloped his hometown. Shortly after her husband's demise, Mary insisted on returning to Donora.

Local doctor William Rongaus told reporters that as far as he was concerned, the victims of the smog had been murdered. Officially, though, on death certificates, the causes of the deaths were listed as either heart failure or pneumonia. Rongaus also estimated that had the smog lingered for just one more evening the death toll would have exceeded 1,000.

Ultimately, although the U.S. Public Health Service called the smog an act of God, there were more than 130 lawsuits filed against U.S. Steel's American Steel and Wire Divison. Damages of $1 million were sought and, after an April 1951 out-of-court settlement, the company dished out in excess of $270,000 in damages. The firm, however, steadfastly denied any responsibility for the disaster.

By 1949 a friendship between Musial and Julius "Biggie" Garagnani, an elementary school dropout, was cemented, and Musial was offered a partnership in Garagnani's restaurant for $25,000. The magnanimous Garagnani allowed Musial to pay him that sum out of his share of future profits. Musial readily agreed, making a move that would, in time, help turn him into a millionaire. By the early 1950s his income from the enterprise would reach around $40,000, and by 1954 they would own four dining establishments.

Musial said he was well aware that ballplayers were one injury away from being washed up and so he constantly strove to ensure his family's security. Musial once said that Mike Gonzalez, a former St. Louis coach, used to tell him that if he could hit like Musial, he'd play for nothing. To that, Musial replied, "Not me. But I wouldn't play for the money without the fun."

In a game against the Reds, Musial was struck out by Ewell Blackwell but scampered all the way to second base when the ball eluded catcher Dixie Howell. Cincinnati manager Bucky Walters later muttered, "That guy Musial is so good that even when he fans, a team is lucky to hold him to two bases."

Musial's speed and base-running savvy—the Hall of Fame website calls him "a strong aggressive runner"—could turn a long double into a triple (or a strikeout into a double). Joe Barbao Jr. reminisced, "I used to love to watch him down at old Forbes Field. One game I remember [in the late 1940s], Bob Chesnes was pitching. Stan had a double and a triple, and I think one of the most beautiful sights I ever saw was him making for that triple. He hit the ball hard and it bounced off the fence. It looked like his left shoulder was almost going to touch the ground coming around that bend, gliding around second. They [the grounds crew] had just come in around the [fifth] inning and they raked the infield, and Stan's were the only fresh footprints out there—long strides."

When Musial finally hit a ball harmlessly in his last at-bat, a nubber back to the mound, Chesnes ran the ball all the way to first "just to [make sure] he finally got him out."

When Musial played at Forbes Field, he would sometimes catch a ride home with Jimmy Russell, a Pittsburgh Pirate from 1942 to 1947. Musial would ask Russell, who commuted daily to the ballpark either by trolley or by automobile, "Jim, you going up to the Valley?" and, said Russell's son Steve, "My dad would bring him home so Stan could visit his family. All of those games back then in the '40s started at about 3:30 in the afternoon," so Musial could be with family by early evening.

Musial was always a strong family man—even strangers often felt he was like family—not so much the allegorical Everyman, but the prototypical Every Uncle. "Every time he used to come in [to Donora]," said nephew Ron Nagy, "he used to tell the family different jokes and show us magic tricks. He was a very good uncle. I can't say enough about him."

Honey's son Ed Stanley Musial commented, "We had a good time with him and joked [around]. He was a normal type of a guy, and he didn't have an air about him or anything like that. He just had a good time, had a couple drinks, that's all, just like a normal person, just like you or me. He'd sit down, you'd just talk to him, have a beer with him, and that's it. He would listen [attentively] to the stories that people would tell him. He was a normal guy, I'm sure you've heard that before, and that is the truth. He was pretty much a down-home type of a guy, family guy, and my aunt [Lil] said they must have 60 grandkids or great-grandkids."

As a husband, Musial was the portrait of small-town fidelity as opposed to the stereotypical view of celebrities who constantly carouse. Throughout his retirement, Lil was almost omnipresent in his many travels, at his side from Poland to Cooperstown and beyond. Theirs was a marriage as rock-solid as Stan's lethal bat.

When the 1949 season began, Musial struggled, hurting his productivity by trying to pull everything. Instead of driving long homers, he harmlessly grounded out or popped up. He blamed his woes in part on the difficult winter he had endured. "I had a lot of things on my mind," he remarked, alluding in part to the death of his father and the tending to his mother for some time when she had moved into the Musials' new house.

The team, in seventh place on May 22 with Musial hitting around .250, rebounded and scrapped their way into the race. By June 7 they had slipped into second.

On June 5, 1949, Happy Chandler lifted the ban on all the ballplayers who had jumped to the Mexican League, extending amnesty to them. Each of the players received a letter instructing them to state in writing that they were officially applying to be reinstated and that the "approval would be automatic."

At the July 10 All-Star break, the Cardinals trailed the Dodgers by a half-game. Another dogfight was in place between the rivals. Musial made good in the contest, hitting his second All-Star home run.

The Cardinals added three players—Lou Klein, Max Lanier, and Fred Martin—after they were permitted to return to their former big-league club, having served their time and having paid their figurative penance for signing with the Mexican League. Lanier had fled from Mexico several years earlier when he learned his salary had been slashed in half, the lucrative promises of the pasquel unkept. Now Lanier made a salary demand to the Cardinals of $15,000. Musial snorted, "Those fellows ought to be tickled to death just to get back."

Musial visited Ebbets Field for a four-game clash on July 22 and went ballistic. In the first game, his home run was a key to a 3–1 victory over Preacher Roe. A ninth-inning comeback gave the Cards a win in the next contest with Musial's monster performance stealing the headlines. He was a perfect 4-for-4, hitting for the cycle for the only time in his career. After another win, a 14–1 blowout, the finale ended in a tie, and the very satisfied Cardinals left town having usurped first place.

In August, however, St. Louis suffered a disappointing loss to the Giants, one Musial felt may have cost them the pennant. The Cardinals took what seemed to be the early lead when Nippy Jones homered with one aboard in the first inning, but the third-base umpire called a balk, which, under the rules of the day, negated the home run. Two runs were erased from the scoreboard, and the Giants went on to win the game, costing St. Louis ground in the standings.

The already tight pennant race—from May 27 on the Cards never trailed by more than three and a half or led by more than two and a half—grew tenser. Brooklyn made a September 21 visit to St. Louis, now behind the Cardinals by one and a half games. Lanier notched the win in the series opener versus big Don Newcombe, thanks to a Joe Garagiola single good for the game's only run. In the next contest, it was Brooklyn's turn to rack up a shutout, 5–0 behind Roe. The rubber match went to the Dodgers 19–6, shaving the Cardinals' lead to a half-game. Fans ricocheted back and forth between delirium and depression.

In Pittsburgh the Pirates, still fuming over a hard Enos Slaughter slide earlier in the season, relished the role of spoiler. On September 27, Pittsburgh's obscure rookie Tom Saffell hit a grand slam, grazing the foul pole for just his second home run of the season and one of his six lifetime homers over an undistinguished four-year career. His homer sealed the 6–4 St. Louis loss. Then, two days later, when the Dodgers swept a twin bill versus the Braves and the Pirates' Murry Dickson topped St. Louis, the Cardinals dropped out of first.

After games versus the Pirates, Musial said he would often "hang around with [professional boxers] Billy Conn, Fritzie Zivic, and [Pittsburgh Steelers owner] Art Rooney" at a restaurant "where the sports guys hung out."

This year, though, Musial was glad to leave town. Still, despite setbacks there, he retained pennant hopes. Moving on to Chicago for the season's final series, the Cardinals lost two games in a row to the last-place Cubs, but the Dodgers struggled a bit against the Phillies, giving St. Louis their last glimmer of hope. The Redbirds finally took one from the Cubs 13–5 on October 2, with Musial belting two homers and Pollet winning his 20th of the year. But on that same day, the season's finale, the Dodgers topped the Phillies in an excruciating 10-inning contest to capture the National League flag. The league's pennant would be won on the final day of the season three years running: in 1949, 1950, and 1951 as well, but 1949 represented the first time both pennant races were decided on the last day.

Still, it had been an incredible decade for the Cardinals. They had won four pennants and three world championships, finished second on five other occasions, and were a very respectable third-place club in their worst year of the 1940s. With the exception of 1940, the Cards were viable contenders for the pennant every season over that decade, a period in which they won 960 times (31 wins better than their closest competitor, the Yankees) versus 580 losses and posted baseball's best win-loss percentage of .623—the rest of the league was mere rabble. Their average season in the 1940s produced a record of 96–58. One writer called them "the Yankees of the National League."

Musial was no slouch, either. He hit 20 of his 36 homers during the second half of the season and led the league in hits, doubles, and triples.

Bobby Del Greco said, "Every day he just hits and hits and hits—left-handers, right-handers, it doesn't make any difference." In fact, in 1949 Musial set a record for the most homers by a left-hander off southpaws (21), and 155 of his lifetime homers (nearly one-third) came off portsiders—with 17 coming off Spahn.

Just as Ted Williams had led all American League players for the decade at .356, Musial dominated the National League, hitting .346, and he would have hit higher but inexplicably hit just .159 in Pittsburgh. Donora native Joe Patch said, "Sometimes it seemed like Stan couldn't buy a hit at Forbes Field, especially on 'Donora days.'" Actually, he hit .337 there lifetime, but early in his career he did call it a "hex park." He hit 46 of his 75 homers from 1948 to 1949 on the road, but not one came in Pittsburgh.

Musial kept busy in the off-season. Among other things, he traveled to New York to attend Joe Garagiola's wedding. Their friendship would last for years and years before a bitter feud ended their association.

Soon New Year's Day staggered in, and the decade came to a close. The Cardinals organization of the 1940s was a mighty armada, and Musial was its flagship. The new decade would not be so rosy. As a matter of fact, on the funereal train ride back to St. Louis the day the Cardinals lost their bid for the 1949 pennant, writer Bob Broeg said to Dyer, "When will we get this close again?" "That," replied Dyer dramatically, as he glanced at his wife, "is just what I finished saying to [her]."

In the 1950s umpires were instructed to enforce a no-fraternization rule. One ump would sit in the stands during pregame activities to monitor players. The atmosphere then was unlike the fraternity-like mood of today where opponents openly and delightedly hug and/or shake hands with each other around the batting cage. Bob Friend said, "They had a couple of meetings about stuff like that. It was a new rule they put in and [they told us], 'You're going to get fined.' I don't know anybody who got fined, but I do know we were warned about fraternization. It looks like you're taking away from the rivalry if you go in and pal around. It doesn't look good to the fans." If, for example, the Cubs and Cards met and spectators witnessed players chumming around, it angered them. "This is their big rivalry, you're not supposed to like them, you're supposed to beat them," Friend said.

Friend also said it was a time when players were more fierce, and therefore bone-jarring slides and ominous brushback pitches were prevalent. "I think they let it go more in my era than they do today. Players expected to be brushed back, and that's the way baseball was played in our time. Those big brawls on the field were never condoned at all, but we had some. They have some today, but I never saw pitchers warned as they are today about pitching tight."

Friend also believes the players of Musial's era were hungrier than today's players. "You didn't have a players' union, there was no leverage for the players to say, 'Well, I'm not going to spring training unless I get this [salary].' Branch Rickey used to say, 'Okay then, we've got a lot of players who want to play—just stay home.' The players knew there wasn't any way to get more money. I mean, the highest-paid players were making [around] $120, $125,000—that would be Musial and Ted Williams and Joe DiMaggio [going into the 1960s]. One hundred grand was kind of the standard for the highest-paid players."

Things would change, of course, as was foreshadowed in 1950 when Yogi Berra reportedly became the first player to have an agent.

The brand of baseball played in the 1950s was a powerful one but was, as writer Bill James put it, "one-dimensional, uniform, [and] predictable." The home run was king, and teams held to the concept of getting runners aboard and then blasting them around on the long ball.

The length of games in the 1950s stretched on and on, with the average time of play elevating by 15 minutes from 1951 to 1960. Perhaps even more alarming, the number of games completed in less than two hours shrank from 166 to 41. Still, even longer games would eventually unfold.

The 1950s were also still marked by the insignificant number of black players on the scene, only about 8 percent of all major-leaguers. Bill James wrote that Polish players were probably more represented in the game than blacks, with stars such as Musial, Ted Kluszewski, Tony Kubek, and Bill Mazeroski. Further, caucasians never roomed with African American teammates.

In 1950 Rickey, now with the Pirates, hired African American Sam Bankhead—former player-manager of the Homestead Grays—to manage and play for a Pittsburgh farm team in Farnham, Quebec, the following season. Organized baseball would not see its next black manager until Gene Baker came along to guide another minor-league team 10 years later, and the majors added only one new black player in 1950, Sam Jethroe of the Braves. Progress would continue to be torturously slow. In 1951 eight more black players arrived in the majors, and six more came in 1952, but the majority of those men were stuffed onto the rosters of six of the most far-sighted teams and not spread out evenly throughout big-league baseball.

By 1950 it was apparent that the Cardinals organization was racially myopic, acutely so. They no longer had the talent edge on most of the other major-league clubs. Better farm systems had sprung up throughout the game, and several other teams were not as reluctant as the Cardinals to sign black talent *and* to quickly move them up the ladder into the majors. The most noticeable beneficiary of employing black baseball players was, of course, Brooklyn, with men such as Robinson, Newcombe, and Roy Campanella leading their cause. The Giants were not too far behind; by the early 1950s their roster was rich with stars such as Willie Mays, Hank Thompson, and Monte Irvin.

From 1947 through August 1952, of the first 26 black players in the majors, a fraternity of men bound by their battle against racism, eight played for Cleveland, tops in the majors. Brooklyn followed with five, the Giants and Braves had four each, the White Sox had three, and the Browns had signed two. The crosstown Cardinals had none.

The Cardinals had lost some vital players, too. Kurowski quit in 1949, unable to throw after 13 operations. His teams had never finished worse than second place during his time in the majors.

Players new to the Cardinals in 1950 would not be able to stake such a claim. The team was headed for mediocrity and, in some years, destined for the skids. For the next 13 years they would never finish better than eight games out of first place, they would conclude nearly one-third of those seasons at 20 or more games off the pace, and they would trail the pennant winner by 12 ½ games or more in 10 of those 13 years. A team in turmoil, they would employ seven managers throughout the 1950s. Their dynasty quickly became unhinged.

George Shuba, a Brooklyn outfielder from 1948 to 1955, commented, "They had a decline; they didn't have the pitching, that's what kept them down in the standings." Musial, he said, could not carry the load himself, and the big-name pitchers Max Lanier and Harry Brecheen were fading.

Alex Grammas agreed, "To win, the first thing you've got to have is pitching. It's always great when you can have guys like Stan Musial and Red Schoendienst and those kinds of ballplayers. You need somebody to produce runs, there's no question about that, but you also have to have a team with pitching. It takes pitching—that's exactly what it takes to win baseball games."

Friend thinks that at the same time the Cardinals lost some key players, the Dodgers pretty much "took over the scene in the '50s. It was mostly the Dodgers and the New York Giants [dominating] in the early 1950s. Then the Braves came along with Hank Aaron, Eddie Mathews, and Joe Adcock."

Shuba even felt there was a residual effect on the Cardinals due to the defection of Rickey years earlier. "During the war he sent his scout out all over the country and signed up all the 18-year-old kids. Then after the war was over, he had all the good ballplayers; the other clubs sat back, and they figured, 'Well, we won't send our scouts out until after the war is over.' So Rickey beat them to the punch." Of course, that approach to signing talent, in part reflecting Rickey's genius, helped the Dodgers then, not the Cardinals, as he quickly signed on boys such as Shuba (at a tryout camp) and Duke Snider. Because he had crafted many a successful Cardinals team using such savvy tactics, his departure deeply impacted them.

Of course, even as the Cards plummeted in the standings, Musial continued to shine brightly.

By the 1950s most big-league teams were telecasting some of their contests, at first usually allowing only a handful of road games to be shown. The Cardinals took the plunge into TV with a few games, hoping that it would attract new fans, but they did not televise too many games. Radio was still king for this Midwest team, which also pulled in fans from the South and even out West, such was the influence and power of their exhaustive radio network. Powerful flagship station KMOX beamed Cardinals broadcasts virtually everywhere (sometimes, under proper conditions, to about 46 states).

In any event, much like the broadcasts of their games, baseball teams also took to the air more and more. The game was in the infant stage of air travel, and some ballplayers, accustomed to bus and train transportation, feared flight. Jackie Jensen, who retired prematurely due to his phobia, is an obvious example. And Musial's former teammate Ed Pado said he heard of many others with serious trepidations. "They'd get airsick. They didn't want to go by plane, they had to get used to it. There were a lot of them who had the rosaries out all the time."

Donora native Ted Musial remembered another incident that illustrated how the Stan Musial era was so different than that of today. "We went down to see Stan play a doubleheader. Before game time, we would always go early to get some foul balls. My buddies were antagonizing me when Stan was taking batting practice, 'I'll bet you're afraid to go out and get Stan's autograph.' So I leaped the fence and went out to the batting cage, and I said, 'Stan, I'm Ted Musial. Frank is my father. That was my tie-in. My dad was his instructor at the Polish Falcons when Stan used to come down on weekends to work out with the guys. Stan says, 'Oh, yeah, how's Frank doing?' Just then I felt an arm on my shoulder. It was a police officer. Stan says, 'No, no, he's okay.'" Musial then signed a ball, and the officer gruffly escorted Ted back into the stands.

Just before the 1950 season began, Musial confidently told George Kell that he would hit in the .315–.340 range that year. Musial explained he had been around "long enough to know exactly what he could do." Musial was incorrect; he would end up at .346.

Pitcher Jim Brosnan said Musial's belief in his hitting ability was "arrogant" and that Musial had told him that in his greatest season, "he hit the ball hard three out of four times every game" and that he "couldn't understand why he didn't hit .500." Even though Musial realistically knew he couldn't hit the ball solidly every at-bat, "he believed he could."

Musial himself once said, though more modestly than what Brosnan indicated, that in his younger days "there wasn't a pitcher born who could throw a fastball past me. I murdered those fastball pitchers."

Outfielder Bobby Del Greco recalled a game in Pittsburgh when the Pirates "brought a really good left-hander up. Everybody was coming to Stan like, 'Boy, this guy's going to probably get you out.' He said, 'Never in his wildest dreams will he get me out,' and he hit one out over the center-field fence in Forbes Field."

Westlake remembered another time Musial displayed an exuberant example of his confidence when the Cards took on the Phillies in a double-header in St. Louis. "If you remember the old ballpark, it was pretty deep in center field, and they were pitching the ball out and away from Stan. He hit a couple of balls about 400-and-some feet out there. He came in and sat down, and he knew that he wasn't picking his pitches right. I'll never forget his words—he said, 'Next time up I'll take care of that.' That's all he said.

"So his next time at bat they put that ball out over the plate again and he hit a screaming bullet into those left-field seats. You had to get your canon to it; you [especially a left-handed hitter] didn't hit pop flies out of there, not to dead left field."

In April Musial began his charge much like a world-class sprinter responding to a starter pistol. Despite a late-April knee injury that would bother him for the rest of his playing days, going into June his average stood at .422, and the Redbirds were perched in first place.

This season also featured Musial's longest hitting streak, a gratifying romp that stretched over a 30-game span and represented the third-best NL run of the modern era—topped only by Rogers Hornsby and Tommy Holmes.

Musial's onslaught ran from June 27, when he hit successfully in both games of a doubleheader, through July 26. The following day, Dodgers pitcher Chris Van Cuyk retired Musial his first three times to the plate, and Billy Loes got him out in his final at-bat. The Cardinals won a laugher 13–3. Over the course of his streak, Musial went 47-for-127, good for a sterling .370 average, and smacked 12 doubles and seven home runs.

This was also the year Eddie Dyer decided to have Musial split time between the outfield (77 games) and first base (69). For his career, Musial would play 325-plus games in each outfield position, a rarity. Harry "the Glove Doctor" Latina worked for Rawlings and devised a glove with six fingers, enabling Musial to use it in the outfield and at first, like a mitt, with no need to switch gloves.

The Cards were still atop the league on July 22, but their collapse was sudden. By September 1 they were in fifth place, where they would remain. The once-proud franchise must have felt like they were slumming it with their poor showing.

With the league's ever-increasing emphasis on offense, the Cardinals tried but failed to produce enough punch to win. They ended the year with a 78–75 record, their worst finish since 1938. The Reds were the only NL team with fewer than 100 homers, but the Cardinals' total of 102 was next to last. Dyer, who had guided the Cardinals to a world championship in his first year, was summarily fired.

A great clutch hitter, Musial hit .344 lifetime during games played in September and .438 in regular-season games held in October. His stellar hitting in 1950, .346, propelled him to his fourth batting title, and he led the league in slugging despite frequently playing hurt. By his own admission, in his early days in the majors he had hit quite well but "didn't know what [he] was doing." Now, he had it down pat.

Vernon Law, who broke into the majors at the age of 20 in 1950 and won the 1960 Cy Young Award, said, "Early on I knew guys were picking up my pitches, and I'm sure Musial [a smart hitter] was one of them who could pick them up. So the only time I got him out was on a line drive to somebody.

"Instead of being a pitcher, I was a thrower, so I had quite of bit a difficulty getting Stan out. Then, later on, after I kind of learned how to pitch and change speeds, it became a heckuva lot easier for me to get him out—at least I could challenge him and pitch to his weaknesses, [but] as far as I was concerned, he was one of those guys that really didn't have any weaknesses.

"You just had to move the ball around in the strike zone, change speeds, try to get him off balance, and get him out in front. That way, at least you've got a fighting chance." He then added with a chuckle, "After Stan retired, I pitched quite well against the Cardinals."

By 1951 Musial had clearly established his reputation as one of the greats of the game, well on his way to becoming one of the best ever. Back home, a new organization, the Mid Mon Valley All Sports Hall of Fame, began honoring local athletes by inducting Musial and pro football star Bert Rechichar from Belle Vernon.

The 1950s and 1960s were decades when clubhouse conditions were abysmal, especially when contrasted with those of today. Crosley Field in Cincinnati, for instance, was perpetually hot and steamy, and the bathroom there had only one proper toilet and a trough for a communal urinal; there was no semblance of privacy. As Joe Garagiola put it, "Being on the one-seater was a performance in front of a pack of hecklers." Philadelphia's Connie Mack Stadium had a clubhouse for visitors that was narrow and hot, and the Polo Grounds locker room greeted Musial and teammates with an unspeakable odor.

Sportsman's Park had cramped accommodations for visitors. Shuba recalled, "They didn't have a big shower, and we always had to take turns to go in and take a shower."

Musial's home park was not the greatest place to play. For one thing, the summers there were agonizingly hot. Westlake also noted that with two teams playing on the same field, there was little chance to water and groom it properly. "Come July that [surface] was almost like playing on concrete. But Musial, he'd almost stand up on his toes to hit a big hopper because when he did, nobody was going to throw him out; the ball bounced so damn high. Come July it was a terrible park to play in—the infield dirt area was just like a brick. It was just like a rock, playing on that thing, with those balls bouncing every which way," Westlake said.

While the outfield grass didn't die, it was most surely in critical condition, and that influenced the way Westlake, Musial, and others had to play defense at times. Said Westlake, "There were some balls you wouldn't challenge because once you flubbed them, they'd go by you—like a line drive hit at you and it's going to be [played] on a short hop, you kind of back off of it. If it gets by you, it's three bases. You had to be careful on that hard turf."

It was also a period in which all uniforms were either home white or road gray; the gray for away games was a tradition rooted in common sense—gray uniforms camouflaged dirt, which translated into less laundry being done while away from home.

But this was also an era of camaraderie, a time when players took the team bus from their hotels two and a half hours before game time. When players' salaries soared in the next few decades and when train travel became extinct—the Yankees were the first team to fly with any degree of regularity, beginning back on May 13, 1946, and other teams soon followed suit—the close ties players had began to dissipate. By the 1990s and into the 21st century the quote, "Twenty-five taxis for 25 players," became prevalent in baseball, indicating that players (much wealthier and more independent than their predecessors) rode to ballparks alone without the same esprit de corps they once had.

On the field most of the game's big stars were not, says Westlake, "rah-rah guys—they let their game do all the talking. You don't find many cheer-leaders in the major leagues." The leader on the 1951 Cardinals, he said, was probably Enos Slaughter. "He was a hard-nosed cookie, that guy." Musial fit into the classic superstar category of being a leader by example. "He just showed you how to play. Play hard, play good baseball. Don't get on the base paths and get dumb," Westlake added.

Among other things, the 1951 season marked the first time players had the chance to gaze at their likenesses on a new product, Topps baseball cards.

Marty Marion took over as the team's skipper at the tender age of 33, and when he did, he quickly decided he did not want to handle the job of player-manager, so Solly Hemus became the starting shortstop. Marion said there was no problem with him managing his friend and teammate Musial. "Well, if you're a manager, you manage," he said succinctly. Marion would return to St. Louis as an active player in 1952 but with the Browns, not the Cardinals.

"He liked to win," said Bill Virdon. "He could play anywhere and every-where, and he liked to do it."

"He came to play," said Westlake. "When he walked out there between those lines, he came to kick your butt." Westlake's overall take on Marion wasn't favorable. He felt Marion was like "most great players—[they] never made great, quality managers. You look at the great managers of the game, you'll find that most of them were lousy players going clear back to Miller Huggins [and on up to] Walter Alston and Tony La Russa, who could play a little bit."

Bob Friend, who broke in with the 1951 Pirates, related, "The Cardinals that I had to face as I came up as a rookie were terrific. They had Slaughter and Musial and Schoendienst. They were good athletes, and they were smart hitters, they knew what they had to do to win the game."

Prior to rookie Willie Mays' first game versus the Cardinals, his manager, Leo Durocher, was going over the St. Louis lineup, instructing his team on how they were to play the various hitters. He covered the leadoff and No. 2 hitters, skipped the No. 3 spot, and jumped to the Cardinals' cleanup hitter. Mays interrupted, asking, "What about the three hitter?" Durocher replied, "The third hitter is Stan Musial. There is no advice I can give you about him."

At the All-Star break, the Cards were nine and a half games behind Brooklyn. Ed Lopat of the Yankees was chatting with Brooklyn pitcher Preacher Roe before the start of the All-Star Game. Lopat declared that he had discovered a way to pitch to the Man. In the fourth inning, Lopat faced Musial. One pitch later, Musial was circling the bases on a home run. Roe shouted out from his perch in the dugout, "I see, I see. Hell, I know how to pitch him that way."

On August 19 the Cardinals were on the road, but Sportsman's Park was in for a treat. Outlandishly colorful Bill Veeck owned the Browns and the ballpark. A sideshow barker at heart, Veeck's wonderful promotions and his "Hurry, hurry, hurry! Step right up" approach kept spectators wondering what he would do next. What he did that day was send 3'7" Eddie Gaedel, wearing jersey number "⅛" to the plate, upsetting umpires but entertaining the fans. Carrying a toy bat to the batter's box, Gaedel crouched, shrinking his strike zone to one-and-a-half inches, drew a walk, and later commented that for just a moment he felt like Babe Ruth.

The 1951 Cards could have used some of Veeck's pizzazz. Though they had sinker-ball pitcher Gerry Staley (19–13), who would average 18 wins a year from 1951 to 1953, and the ever-dependable Musial, Marion's team finished third, eight games over .500, but a distant 15½ games out of first. Marion was through.

Musial won his fifth batting crown, hitting .355, and was again selected as the Major League Player of the Year. Personal success, without success for his team, seemed hollow, but it was something Musial would have to grow accustomed to.

By 1952 Musial was firmly entrenched as a successful businessman who continued to expand on his business holdings. In January he and his business partner Biggie Garagnani bought Garavelli Restaurant in St. Louis; by 1954 they owned four restaurants. Musial's investments were said to augment his baseball salary by $40,000 per year. He was also by this time pulling down $85,000 from the Cardinals.

Joe Cunningham of the Cardinals stated, "He was very smart. He surrounded himself with smart businessmen, and I think he was a conservative guy."

Laurel Grimes, niece of Stan and Lil, stated that thanks to baseball, Stan "had business connections, and he's just a very affable person. He's not a great conversationalist, but he comes across as sincere and liking all people. You wouldn't characterize him as an intellectual, but just like his innate sense of timing and hand-eye coordination, I think he just has a good sense of people. He's a good friend to people."

Linda Ruth Tosetti, Babe Ruth's granddaughter, stated, "I never saw him say no to an autograph. I have always seen him take the time for fans. He is the one nicest Hall of Famers that I have met.

"We really need more of these ballplayers to be like Stan Musial. He is a true *gentleman* of the game. He not only was a great player but a great personality. Very unassuming. I love him and Lil dearly."

So, never aloof, Musial mingled with his customers and genuinely cared about his fans. Nephew Ed Musial stated, "He would listen to the stories that people would tell him. He was a businessman—baseball wasn't his only livelihood. He probably made more from being a businessman than baseball. He took advantage of what he had through baseball, and he put it to his favor. Baseball opened the doors for him, and he walked through them."

Charlie James said, "Most evenings he was there [at his restaurant] greeting fans. Of course that was good business, but a lot of big star players didn't do that kind of thing—mixing a lot with the fans—but he did that. He always had a stack of photographs that he would haul around with him when he was meeting people there, and he would just hand out autographs on the pictures."

George F. Will elaborated, "I think there was a shrewdness about him. That is, he knew that the fans were his customers, which I wish more ballplayers would bear in mind. I think he not only liked them, but he also knew it was good business to present to them a smiling, welcoming face. I'm not saying he was hypocritical, far from it. I'm saying that his natural inclinations coincided with his professional interests."

One website observed that Musial's main business "focuses were on real estate and Stan and Biggie's, the steak and seafood restaurant.... In essence, Garagnani ran the business while Stan made himself available to the patrons." The two men also were involved in the Redbird Lanes bowling alley and other real estate ventures including the Ivanhoe-by-the-Sea Hotel near Miami Beach.

"One of my favorite people in baseball," said veteran writer Jim O'Brien, "was a fellow named Frankie Gustine. He was an infielder for the Pirates in the late '30s and '40s, and he opened a restaurant two blocks from Forbes Field and operated it for over 30-some years. A lot of people own sports restaurants, but not too many last as long as Gustine or Stan Musial, who was in with Biggie for a long time.

"I asked Ralph Kiner, who was aware that I was such a big fan of Frankie Gustine, 'What was Stan Musial like?' And Kiner said, 'Frankie Gustine with a better batting average.'"

Later in life, when Musial was out in public, he took to passing out postcard-sized cards that featured his picture, statistics, and signature, an idea he got from his friend John Wayne in order to avoid having to sign items such as tiny matchbook covers or flimsy napkins.

In 1952 *Life* magazine paid Ty Cobb $25,000 to write two articles revealing his view on the modern game. Cobb, a spine-tingling player but a curmudgeon at best and a near-sociopath at worst, contended (predictably) the quality of play in the sport had declined since the late 1920s. Cobb's tale, titled "They Don't Play Baseball Any More," declared that "only two players today can be mentioned in the same breath with the old-time greats," Yankees shortstop Phil Rizzuto and Musial.

Cobb lauded Musial for doing things such as scoring from first on a single. "He plays as hard when his club is out front as he does when they're just a run or two behind. He'll go after a ball even in an exhibition game, diving for a shoestring catch, as if the World Series depended on it."

Musial signed his 1952 contract under unique, theatrical circumstances. On Valentine's Day team owner Fred Saigh called Musial into his office along with the press, offered him a blank contract, and instructed him to fill in his salary. Musial reportedly mulled it over and said he would accept the same salary he had earned in 1951. Broadcaster Harry Caray told Saigh that he "must be a helluva fine crap player." Saigh countered that he had merely gambled on Musial's character. The cagey Saigh was also aware that the government's Wage Stabilization Board had created a salary ceiling, so when he told Musial to jot down any figure "short of your owning the club," his risk wasn't all that great.

The Cardinals had acquired Eddie "the Brat" Stanky in late 1951, giving him the player-manager job. As pesky as a hangnail, he was a Durocher protégé who possessed a fiery personality. Durocher once said of Stanky, "He can't hit, he can't run, he can't throw—all he can do is beat you." However, some of those who played for and against him found him as annoying as radio static.

As early as spring training, he verbally lashed those players he felt were slacking off. Wally Westlake recalled, "He called a clubhouse meeting, something we had never heard of—I made [it to] 10 of them [spring-training camps], and that's the first time I ever heard of anybody having a clubhouse meeting in spring training. Christ, you got 50, 60 guys in your clubhouse.... Come Opening Day, half of them are gone, back in the minor leagues.

"And for some reason he just gave us all a tongue lashing. It was about two weeks into the [exhibition season], and I came out of the clubhouse with Stan. That was the first time I ever saw him really upset. He was boiling a little bit, you bet. During the season, when you're putting the meat in the pot, that's another matter.

"I said, 'Stan, what was the hell was that about?' He didn't really answer me, but he wasn't happy, I'll tell you that."

Dick Schofield said the old-school Stanky had difficulty with veterans and expected his troops to conform to his ways blindly, loyally.

Ben Wade contended Stanky knew his baseball but was the worst manager he had played under, incapable of treating his players well. Wade believed Stanky suffered from "the little-man complex." Certainly at times the Cards did play like a team simmering with at least some degree of discontent—they were destined to finish in third place.

Stanky, however, praised Musial, saying he made his job as manager easier "by being on time, not taking extra swings in batting practice, not flying ahead of the club to the next town on a road trip. In other words, not seeking the extra privileges often demanded by top stars, sometimes to the detriment of team morale."

On June 30 the Cardinals embarked on their longest winning spree (10 games) of the year. An eight-game winning tear in August left the team optimistic and lifted them to second place behind Brooklyn, a team one writer described as the "knock-'em-down, step on-'em Dodgers."

Musial still had his blazing speed and utilized it often. Pirates rookie shortstop Dick Groat, who said Musial "frightened [him] because he could flat-out hit," recounted a story about Musial's speed. He was in the field when Musial came up to bat. He recounted, "[Musial] hit a ground ball past the pitcher's mound, and I came up with it. By the time I came back to throw, he had already crossed first base—he could *fly* out of that batter's box. That's why, when he was young, so many years he led the National League in triples." Groat felt Musial got down the line to first "in a class with Mantle, before Mickey hurt his knee. He was that quick."

George Shuba recalled another game. He said, "Musial was playing first base and I hit a line drive by him. As I got down to first base he started rubbing himself up against me. I said, 'Hey, what's going on here?' He said, 'I just want to get some of that good hitting stuff rubbed off on me.'"

On September 9 in Philadelphia Musial collected his 2,000th hit off Curt Simmons, becoming the 91st man to reach that level. He would climb over virtually all of the men ahead of him before he was through.

Then, on September 28, the host Cardinals and the Cubs set up a season-ending stunt, allowing Frankie Baumholtz to face Musial. They ranked No. 1 and No. 2 in the race for the batting crown with Musial comfortably ahead, .336 to .326.

The game began with Cardinals starter Harvey Haddix issuing a walk to Tommy Brown. At that point the machinations for the stunt began. Musial trotted in from his center-field spot and took the ball from Haddix, who moved to the outfield.

Matters took another zany turn when Baumholtz, usually a left-handed batter, turned around in the box and hit righty against the southpaw Musial. On Musial's only big-league pitch, basically a lob, Baumholtz sent a sizzling grounder to third baseman Solly Hemus, playing there for just the seventh time in his major-league career; he bobbled the ball for an error. "It was hit pretty well, there's no doubt about that," said Hemus. "I just booted it, I didn't play it real cleanly. I'd say it was a hit."

That was it. Musial resumed the game in center, Haddix took over on the hill. When Musial returned to the dugout, he phoned the press box, scolding the scoring decision. "If I ever saw a base hit in my life," he said, "that was a base hit." Many felt that even if Musial had been in the middle of scraping for the batting title, he still would have made the call, defending his rival. It was immaterial, though, because Musial went 1-for-3 on the day, maintaining his .336 batting average, while Baumholtz took a 1-for-4, finishing the year at .325. For the record, the Cubs blanked the Cardinals 3–0 in a meaningless game. The classy Musial, however, called his mound stint a "box-office circus" and a "cheap gag," one he was not proud of at all.

Team-wise, water ultimately found its own level, and St. Louis wound up in third place, going 88–66, four games behind the Giants and eight and a half behind Brooklyn. St. Louis also tapered off at the turnstiles with their attendance of just over 913,000 representing the third straight season their gate receipts dropped and their first sub-1,000,000 season since 1945.

Still, Musial enjoyed another standout season with yet another long hitting streak, this one covering 24 games. He won his third consecutive batting title, his fourth over a five-year span, and also led the National League in slugging, hits, doubles, and runs.

Distinguished writer Bill James picked Musial as the best player in the majors in 1944, 1948, 1949, 1951, and 1952, a whopping five times over eight years. Even as the Cardinals slid a little in the rankings, the Man remained a true phenomenon.

## CHAPTER SIX

# More Glory, More Golden Years

In January 1953 Fred Saigh was convicted of tax evasion. He was ordered to pay more than $500,000 in back taxes and was given a 15-month prison sentence. The Cardinals front office was in further turmoil due to the drought taking place in their farm system. No longer could they lose or trade a player and then reach down into their minor leagues to pluck a talented Joe Medwick, Dizzy Dean, or a Stan Musial for a replacement.

Across town Veeck and his Browns were scrambling, too. Always the maverick, Veeck fully realized the AL brass wanted him out. He knew the conservative powers that be considered him a pariah. Veeck once stated that other team "owners have looked at me as though I were a little boy trying to run fast so the propeller on my beanie would spin."

With his team's finances in dire straits, it wasn't long before he was forced to scrap the Browns. When Veeck had purchased the team, sportswriter John Lardner sarcastically wrote, "Many critics were surprised to know that the St. Louis Browns could be bought, because they didn't know that the Browns were owned."

The team was often so pathetic, Veeck once joked that many times they basically "played to some intimate acquaintances and the groundskeepers." He first attempted to salvage his team, though, by getting permission to move the franchise, but the big boys of the league blocked his way. Only when he agreed to sell the team did the AL allow the team to be uprooted and shifted to Baltimore, where they became the Orioles of 1954.

In 1953 the Boston Braves became the Milwaukee Braves. The move was the first franchise shift in 50 years. The age of baseball carpetbagging had begun, and the face of baseball would continue to change forever.

At one point Saigh had considered selling the Cardinals to Milwaukee businessmen. Such a transaction would have resulted in the team moving to Milwaukee, so for a time there was a very real chance that St. Louis could rapidly lose both of its big-league clubs. Anheuser-Busch stepped in, though, and when the brewery company offered $3,750,000 for the club, Saigh snatched up the offer, and the deal was consummated on February 20, 1953. Beer magnate August "Gussie" Busch took over as the head of the team and vowed to keep the team in town, where his headquarters were located.

He had the wherewithal to do so. In a 1957 article, he stated his brewery grossed $250,000,000 per year, while his investment in his team was only $4,500,000. Once, in 1956, when he offered to buy Ernie Banks from the Cubs for $500,000, he was informed by his general manager, Frank Lane, to forget it, that "Mr. Wrigley needs a half-million dollars as much as you do." Money was no object at all for such owners.

Sportsman's Park had its name changed. It became Busch Stadium in 1953, when Busch bought the property, and kept the name through its final game on May 8, 1966. Originally, Busch's intention was to rename the park Budweiser Stadium for publicity purposes, but he caved in to pressure from National League officials. Busch did, however, give his players a free case of his beer each week. "That," said Del Ennis, "is when I started to drink beer."

It was a rickety, ancient ballpark that had been the home of the hapless St. Louis Browns since 1902. When that joke of a team played its final game there, they did so in front of a ludicrously sparse crowd of 3,174 spectators. It was also, dating back to 1920, a park that saw some marvelous Cardinals baseball games unfold.

On April 9, 1953, with the country phobic over the Communist scare, Cincinnati general manager Gabe Paul declared the team nickname had to be changed—no longer would the team be called the Reds due to the connotations of that word. The team would be known as the Redlegs.

Meantime, even though Jackie Robinson had been around since 1947, Dick Schofield said the Cardinals continued to "holler a lot of racist stuff" at him, yet they didn't pick on other black Dodgers "any more than they would white opponents."

Musial's early play was erratic until player-manager Stanky noticed his stride, normally about a foot long, had almost doubled in length. He had fallen into a bad habit that had kept him bogged down so badly he could only hoist his batting average to .251 by mid-June. Then came a patented Musial binge—over a period of a dozen games, he collected two dozen hits, including a 19-for-27 week, and his average stood at .303.

Stanky usually didn't bother Musial, knowing the veteran could handle himself. "You just penciled him in third on the lineup card," recalled teammate Dick Schofield, "and left it at that."

Down the stretch, Musial hit safely in his last 15 games (.437) and nearly made up enough ground to win his fourth straight crown. He entered the season finale with 198 hits. He came up with two more, giving him his sixth and final season of 200-plus safeties. Like the boast of many a radio station, the hits just kept on coming.

The Cardinals finished tied for third place but 22 games behind Brooklyn. Musial had churned out another quality season, achieving something that had only been done five times before: he amassed 30 or more home runs (hitting 30 on the nose) with 50-plus doubles (he had 53). He also drew 105 walks to lead the league in that department for the only time in his career.

In 1954 the Cardinals were, for the first time since 1901, the only show in town, and with the Browns gone, they had a ballpark exclusively for their use for the first time since 1919. The team was no longer overflowing with dependable veterans; only a few men such as Schoendienst and Musial, as reliable as an atomic clock, remained as stars from the halcyon days.

Outfielder Wally Moon reported to "the wrong spring-training base," remembered Joe Cunningham. "He was playing winter ball, and he was supposed to go to, I think, Daytona Beach for Triple A. He went to Al Lang Field. They didn't check him out, they gave him uniform No. 20, he went out, starting playing, started hitting the devil out of the ball, and they traded Enos Slaughter to the Yankees" for Bill Virdon in order to make room for Moon.

Two days after the swap, the season began with Moon homering in his very first big-league at-bat. He would go on to hit .304 on his way to winning the Rookie of the Year Award over Ernie Banks, Gene Conley— who also played in the National Basketball Association—and Hank Aaron. Predictably, and way off the mark, writers began calling Moon "the next Stan Musial." Virdon, by the way, would win the Rookie of the

Year Award the following year, giving the Cards a two-year stranglehold on the trophy.

In the meantime, the team took a different direction when it finally brought up a talented black ballplayer, power pitcher Brooks Lawrence, to help their cause. Big and strong, he went 15–6 as a rookie.

Actually, the first African American to play in the Cardinals uniform came along on April 13, 1954, a few months before Lawrence. He was Tom Alston, an outfielder and a classic good-glove, no-stick man, who would last four years with the team but compile only 271 at-bats over his career.

Alex Grammas stated, "I was with St. Louis when they got their first black player. He was a good guy, he just didn't hit like they thought he would. If he had, he'd have been there for a long time." As for teammates' reactions to Alston, "Not one bit of trouble," said Grammas.

Alston's initial game with the Cardinals allowed them to avoid, by a mere five days, being the next-to-last National League club to play an African American man. In the NL only the Reds and Phillies were more tardy in that area, and only four American League teams took longer to integrate—the Senators, Yankees, Tigers, and Red Sox. Alston, incidentally, suffered a nervous breakdown caused, it was reported, at least in part, by racist abuse.

On April 18, 1954, in just the fourth game of the year, an event occurred that typified Musial as a man. Paul Minner of the Cubs was in command on the hill, having retired 18 straight after giving up a game-opening single. Then, with one man out in the seventh and the Cubs up 3–0, Moon singled to center. Schoendienst flew out, bringing Musial to the plate. He laced a double to the corner in right to score Moon. When third sacker Randy Jackson bobbled the relay throw and then made a wild throw, Musial crossed home, presumably completing his round trip for a Little League–like "home run."

That's when the insanity began. First-base umpire Lee Ballanfant finally called attention to the fact he had called Musial's hit foul. The Cardinals were apoplectic over the terrible call. Soon Augie Donatelli, working the plate, ejected the vociferous Solly Hemus and Eddie Stanky. Musial ambled over to Donatelli for further clarification. When told he had just lost his double, he genially replied, "Well, there's nothing you can do about it."

There was, however, something Musial could do about it—he connected again, this time for a double to right, which Hank Sauer couldn't hang on to as he leaped near the right-field vines. Moon crossed home, Musial soon followed, and a six-run rally had been ignited; St. Louis held on to win 6–4.

While there are other, incorrect (urban legend–like) accounts of this scene, what really matters is two-fold: Musial did come through in the clutch (twice) and the story's theme of his gentility and benevolence, the crux of the tale, remain unadulterated.

On May 2, 1954, Musial, for the first time serving as his team's most veteran player, once again indelibly wrote his name into the record books with a barrage of five home runs during a home doubleheader. In the stands that day was a young Nate Colbert, who would himself—in an incredible what-are-the-odds scenario—go on to blast five homers in a twin bill (driving in 13 runs), tying Musial's record some 18 years later for the San Diego Padres.

Solly Hemus said, "There were a lot of other big games that he was very instrumental in helping win. That was everyday stuff for him, but when you look back and see what he's accomplished, you got to realize he was one of the greatest stars of all time." Thus, it wasn't too shocking that Musial was "more nonchalant than anything" in the dugout the day he hit his five homers. "He acted like he did it every day. That's just the way he was, very nonchalant about his accomplishments," said Hemus.

Unlike the silent treatment a pitcher gets from teammates when he's working on a no-hitter, teammate Alex Grammas said, "We were all just laughing and having a good time with it. I mean, those things just don't happen, but he made it happen."

Despite Musial's brilliant performance, the Cardinals managed only a split against the Giants. In the opening game, a 10–6 victory, Musial connected twice off Johnny Antonelli, a solo homer in the third and a two-run shot in the fifth, both banging off the right-field roof. Three innings later he torched Jim Hearn for a three-run poke. Between games he fueled up on milk and a ham-and-cheese sandwich.

In the second game Musial pulverized a ball 410 feet—which was hauled in by Willie Mays—and twice took Hoyt Wilhelm downtown out onto Grand Avenue (the second blow coming off a knuckleball, hardly Musial's favorite pitch). Musial confessed that on his final opportunity to hit a sixth home run that day he uncharacteristically *tried* to kill the ball. Instead, he popped up weakly. Counting rain delays, the games stretched to nearly seven hours, but few fans departed until they watched Musial's final at-bat.

On that day, Musial amassed 21 total bases—good for another new record—nine runs driven in, and tied the standard for the most homers over a two-game span.

Musial was fond of relating what his son said to him when he returned home: "Gee, Dad, they must have been throwing you some fat pitches today."

The next night, pitchers gave him *no* pitches—at least none that were juicy enough. He was walked four times.

Through the first 50 contests, Musial connected for 20 homers, on pace to break Babe Ruth's record 60 home runs. Musial, quite naturally, could not sustain his output and finished with 35. The sizzling summer—one day the thermometer hit a city-record 113 degrees—sapped Musial. One player said between wearing flannel uniforms and the St. Louis heat, a player could drop as many as 14 pounds during the course of a game. Still, Musial led the NL in doubles for the eighth and last time and topped the league in runs for the fifth and final time.

The Cardinals finished the year at 72–82, their first sub-.500 season since 1938. They even lost a game by a rare forfeit in the nightcap of a doubleheader versus the Phillies. Manager Eddie Stanky pulled out every tactic he could summon to stall with Philadelphia ahead. Pitcher Cot Deal was ordered to throw pitch after pitch out of the strike zone. A fight between the two clubs ate up more time. Eventually, the umpires forfeited the game to the Phillies.

Preacher Roe of the Dodgers retired after the season. Once, when asked how he pitched to Musial, he quipped, "I throw four wide ones, and then I try to pick him off first."

Years after Musial retired, he spoke of his era as a rough one. For most of his career, batters didn't wear protective helmets at the plate—this practice began in the National League in 1955 and the following season in the Junior Circuit. "We were knocked down and hit by pitches and thought nothing of it," said the steel-tempered Musial. In those days, he said, players realized "a pitcher had to throw inside, because if the batter knew you were going to pitch away every time, he'd have a great advantage." Further, most experts agree players were hungrier and therefore more aggressive than nowadays. Beanballs and savage slides to take out defenders were more prevalent.

Musial's time period was one in which, according to Erskine, even the craft of pitching was different. It "was really power—power pitching and big curveballs."

The year 1955 also saw a team made up of all black players from Charleston, South Carolina, integrate Little League baseball. Just as had been the case in the majors when some white players threatened to boycott

Jackie Robinson, there was a vociferous protest against the young All-Stars playing in the Little League World Series. In their case, however, the boycott worked. The boys felt the same sting of malicious segregation and its ugly ramifications that Robinson had suffered. Eventually the Charleston stars were banned from the playing field, forced to watch the Little League World Series as "guests."

It was against this backdrop that Stan Musial went about his business, playing in a league that now featured black stars such as Newcombe, Banks, and a young Hank Aaron.

The Cardinals decided to tailor Sportsman's Park to favor their left-handed hitters and to cash in on Musial's power to right and right-center. Since 1930 a screen had extended 21½ feet above the 11½-foot concrete wall there. Musial was said to have peppered the screen approximately 15 to 20 times per season.

Vernon Law recalled, "He loved that screen. That was to his great advantage. Balls he hit there were home runs a lot of the time, where they were just big outs in our ballpark in Forbes Field," a larger park and one that had a much higher screen, 30 to 35 feet high, in right that prevented cheap homers down the line.

Now the Cardinals removed their wiring, expecting that many a ball that had gone for a double off the screen would now become homers. This move proved to be a one-year experiment as the Cardinals' pitching staff gave up 42 homers more than their offense could muster, and Musial's home-run total actually declined by two from the previous year, even though he did swat seven into the pavilion.

The club was composed of too many kids hurried into the majors, basically no better than Triple A players. The Cards would strike a team record 143 homers, led by Musial's 33, but they were not a good ballclub.

In 1954 Cunningham had played well at first base, but all it got him was a demotion to the minors. The move upset Cunningham, but, he said, "Then they bring in the greatest ballplayer who has ever played for the Cardinals to play first—it was Stanky's decision; that left me out in the wind.

"Competition was very strong in those days because you had 32, 33 farm clubs and, boy, I tell you one thing—if you were hurt at all, you didn't want to get out of that lineup, you played hurt because there were 30-some first basemen looking for your job. Now, we have six farm clubs.

"Stan did not like the idea of moving to first base because there's an awful lot of work to do at first if you're going to be a good first baseman—a lot of action [there]. Left field is a little easier. In the infield, you're moving all the time. When he ended his career, he [was back] in left field. In those days you just did what the manager said, that was it, even if you were a superstar."

Alex Grammas commented, "We had a lot of guys that didn't take to Eddie Stanky, but I liked him. He was the kind of guy who was all business, and as long as you tried as hard as you could, you wouldn't have any problems with him. I like it when a guy's all business like that. Some guys got irritated with him, but he was one of my favorite managers."

Moving Musial to the infield was one of Stanky's final managerial moves with the Cardinals. After a mediocre 17–19 start to the season, he was replaced by Harry "the Hat" Walker, who earned his nickname for his propensity to fidget with his hat while at the plate—he was said to go through as many as 20 caps in a season.

The Cardinals promptly went out and played worse after the managerial change, winding up at 68–86, having sunk near the cellar (groveling in seventh place) with a sickening thud, a miserable 30½ games out. No Cardinals team since this 1955 club has won fewer games over a full season. Some called the team "the best seventh-place club in history."

"By now, the Cardinals were playing a game called musical managers," observed one writer, and Walker was out while Fred Hutchinson, the team's fifth skipper of the decade, would be hired for 1956.

On the plus side for Musial was his performance on July 12, 1955, in the All-Star Game in Milwaukee's County Stadium. Played on the day of the funeral of Arch Ward, a Chicago sports editor who had originated the midsummer showcase in 1933, this game was a classic. The game's starting time had, in fact, been shoved back from 1:30 to 2:00 PM to allow time for people to attend Ward's services.

The AL led 5–0 through the mid-innings but then unraveled. The NL tallied twice in the seventh, then put a three-spot on the board the next inning. That forced just the second extra-inning All-Star Game ever.

The game labored on until the twelfth inning, when Musial led off. Many of the 45,643 fans present at the start of the contest were long gone. As Musial wearily dug in at the plate, he turned to catcher Yogi Berra and said, "How ya doing, Yog?" After Berra complained that his feet were killing him, Musial replied, "Don't worry. I'll get us outta here in a hurry."

Then, swinging at Frank Sullivan's first pitch, he hoisted it into the right-field bleachers for a most satisfying walk-off homer, mercifully ending the marathon. The NL had won a remarkable comeback 6–5. Due to either fatigue or elation (Musial had played every inning of the three-hour-and-17-minute contest), he uncharacteristically jogged slowly out of the box, gazing at the ball sailing toward the fence, before going into a quicker home-run trot.

His home run was his fourth in All-Star play, which vaulted him ahead of Ralph Kiner and Ted Williams for the most All-Star homers. Interestingly, the only other extra-inning All-Star Game, held in 1950, was also broken up by a homer, that one a fourteenth-inning belt by Red Schoendienst, Musial's roomie.

When asked if he remembered what Musial said to him before hitting the game-winning home run, Hank Aaron replied, "I sure do. I will always remember. A lot of people—I don't know whether they believe it or not, but it was certainly the truth—I remember him standing up and saying, 'They don't pay us to play overtime,' and he went up and hit a home run. I heard that myself." In effect, then, he called his shot. "I know a lot say Babe Ruth pointed, but I know Stan called his."

On August 10 Musial collected his 1,000[th] lifetime extra-base hit, but by season's end he failed to lead the NL in any offensive department.

Another bright spot was the play of rookie Ken Boyer, who had originally been signed as a pitcher. At third base Boyer possessed superb range to his left and a strong, true arm. Those qualities would help him earn five Gold Gloves.

Over their shared time with the Cardinals, Boyer and Musial would combine for 401 home runs—183 by Musial—placing them among the NL's most powerful one-two punches by teammates.

Still, in 1955 the team had little pitching potency and ranked last in team ERA. Their top winner, Harvey "the Kitten" Haddix, won just 12 times.

Bobby Del Greco praised Haddix's stuff: "He had a slow curve that stayed up there for a while and then another one that just dropped. He had a good rising fastball, too." On May 26, 1959, Haddix would pitch a perfect game that stretched over 13 innings—he remained perfect over the first 12 frames—yet the outcome of his gem was a Haddix defeat, 1–0 (later his fantastic, unprecedented performance was ruled *not* to be a perfect game when a baseball commissioner decreed any perfecto had to end without a single runner having ever reached base).

Overall, this was a year of ignominy, one better left forgotten, a cobweb-ridden tome sitting on a dusty shelf of the team's archives. After all, who wants to wallow in the memory of a season in which the Cardinals were so abysmal? The last time they had played more poorly was 1924, when they won just 65 times—nor had they finished as low in the standings since 1919. "Hell," one writer grumbled, "even the Cubs passed the Cards in the standings."

In 1956 the Musials built a nine-room, red-brick ranch house for $75,000 in an upper-middle-class suburb called St. Louis Hills. The home, said niece Laurel Grimes, is more modest than palatial. "It's meant for entertaining— it has a big open patio in the back that can accommodate 100 people, 200 people easily if you wanted to do that. It's not ostentatious, but it is a very nice house."

This was also the year Pennsylvania representative John P. Saylor read a tribute to Musial in the Congressional record: "We salute Stan Musial not only for his greatness as a ballplayer but also because he has remained the quiet, modest, humble, dignified, religious, refined, and sympathetic person that he was in the days of his boyhood...." He cited Musial as an example of a person "who made it in a competitive system because of hard work, diligence, and sobriety."

Everyone who has been around Musial has a favorite anecdote to tell. Teammate Joe Cunningham called Musial "a regular guy" but added "super-stars got a little more attention from our clubhouse guy, Butch Yatkeman. I remember Solly Hemus used to put his spikes in Musial's locker because he always got a better shine." Hemus said, "Anybody who hit what he hit, they should [take better care of]."

Likewise, Carl Erskine narrated his favorite Musial story from around this time period. "I was pitching a night game in St. Louis and I got the Cardinals beat in the last inning, I think 2–1, and it comes down to the last out of the game with Musial at the plate and a man on base. So I'm pitching to Stan, and I get two strikes and a ball on him, and [Roy] Campanella gives me the curveball sign. Well, I threw a real hard curve, a 'drop,' we used to call it. To make that pitch effective, it's gotta be real low, you gotta break it right down into the dirt because my curveball was big. Well, I threw him one of the best curveballs that I ever threw. I mean, it was right in the right spot, it broke plenty, and Musial hit it on the pavilion that night and beat me on a home run 3–2.

"I couldn't believe he hit it, and Campanella couldn't believe he hit it. The game was over, and Campy was standing back of the plate. In a high-pitched, excited voice, [he said], 'There ain't no man gonna hit that pitch. They can't hit that.' Well, he did hit it.

"And I was so disappointed in losing that game to the Cardinals that I waited outside the clubhouse door at old Sportsman's Park in the lobby. The two clubhouses kind of came into a little lobby before they exited out onto Grand Avenue, and I waited for Musial. I knew him, but I wasn't a personal friend or anything. I was frustrated, and when he came out I said, 'Stan, I always heard that outstanding hitters like you never guess. Now, I can't believe you hit that pitch unless you [were] looking for it.'

"He said, 'Well, Carl, let's put it this way. You have an outstanding curveball, and when it came down to the last pitch of the game, I said to myself, "He's not going to let me beat him on anything but his best pitch," so if that's guessing, I guess I did.'"

That night, inspired by the home-run heroics, Erskine wrote a song about Musial. "We were riding on the trains in those days, so I got on the train after the game, and I felt so bad about losing this game—I had this game won, within one pitch, and wins are tough to get in the big leagues. I pitched eight-and-two-thirds innings, and all I got to do is nail down this win and Musial hits this best pitch of mine on the pavilion. So I'm feeling down. I can't sleep on this train. I'm rattling around.

"So, what'd I do? I got out my harmonica and I started fooling around and I started playing the blues, and I wrote a little tune, just in my head, and I call it 'The Stan Musial Blues.' Now I got a little group that I play with here in my hometown, and we play for benefits and for nursing homes. The guys always kid me and say, 'Tell that story about Musial hitting the home run and about "The Stan Musial Blues" you're getting ready to play.'" Clearly Erskine wasn't the only pitcher to belt out the blues because of Musial.

Entering spring training, the team was optimistic. "Everybody thinks they can win," said Virdon. "We thought we were going to be better." As the season was unveiled, the Cards struggled, and Musial became upset. "He wanted to win bad. Loved to win, but he always played hard. [Losing] didn't change his approach."

Pitcher Kirby Higbe once wrote that the greats of the game, from Warren Spahn to Joe Medwick to Musial, were not good about accepting failure. They were, Higbe wrote, "all nice fellows off the field, but all of them were fierce competitors and none of them was a good loser on the field."

Stan's brother Honey recalled a time when Stan, who was the Zincs' starting pitcher that day, hit a ball deep into left-center and, instead of making a play on the ball, which came to rest near a fence, Honey, playing for a Monongahela team, cleverly kicked it under a hole beneath the fence, holding Stan to a ground-rule double. When he told Stan of his trick that robbed him of at least one base, Stan said little. However, on his next trip to the plate, said Honey, "his first pitch to me hit me right between the shoulder blades."

Joe Barbao Jr., whose father coached a young Musial in summer ball, added that despite Musial's intensity, he didn't squawk with umpires and never tried to show them up. Once, when a veteran big-league umpire called a pitch a strike, an upset Musial simply "turned and glanced at the umpire who [later] said he felt like the devil because it was a questionable call, it was *that* close. He called it a strike but then he said, 'I must have missed it if Stan did that because he never argued, he never said anything, and he knows the strike zone.'" Indeed, moments after his slight show of displeasure, Musial faced the pitcher, putting the call behind him, "ready to hit again."

Umpire Bill Stewart said the times Musial turned and looked at him to quietly question a call made him "feel bad. He never says anything. But there's a hurt look in his eyes that runs clear through."

Musial, in fact, was never ejected by a big-league ump, not once over the course of 3,026 regular-season contests, more games for one team than any man had ever played. Veteran umpire Tom Gorman once stated, "The bigger the guy, the less he argues. You never heard a word out of Stan Musial." Only once, in a Class D game, did Musial, then only 19, get the thumb.

It's safe to say that Musial never possessed the monomaniacal drive of a Ty Cobb or a Rogers Hornsby, who preceded him, or of a Pete Rose, who followed him, but he played sports with zeal. Julius Caesar did not trust men with a lean and hungry look, but for Musial, on the thin side and ravenous to win, it was a winning combination.

The season began well, but general manager Frank "Trader" Lane, so named for his propensity to peddle flesh—he traded players as if he was a kid swapping baseball trading cards—just couldn't stand pat. Cunningham said Del Greco impressed Lane by hitting "a couple of home runs off Harvey Haddix in spring training, I think it was." Lane figured Bill Virdon was expendable and that Del Greco was more valuable, so he completed a May 17, 1956, Virdon for Del Greco and Dick Littlefield swap. Del Greco lasted only 102 games for St. Louis before being traded away and Virdon went on to become a great center fielder for the Pirates.

Lane wasn't done. On June 14 he pulled off a nine-player blockbuster trade. The Cardinals acquired slick shortstop Alvin Dark, Ray Katt, Don

Liddle, and Whitey Lockman from the Giants in exchange for Jackie Brandt, Dick Littlefield, Bill Sarni, Red Schoendienst, and Gordon Jones. Thus the 1956 Cards had a slew of new faces, including their double-play combo in shortstop Dark and Walker Cooper's son-in-law, Don Blasingame.

On Easter Sunday in April 1960, Lane, serving as the Indians' general manager, would trade the team's most popular player, the reigning home-run champ Rocky Colavito, for returning batting champ Harvey Kuenn in a terrible swap. Four months later, Lane engineered a unique move when he swapped his manager, Joe Gordon, to the Tigers for *their* manager, Jimmy Dykes. Such were the machinations of Lane.

Often he contemplated or made trades that had "hang him in effigy" written all over them. A striking example took place when he wanted to swap Musial—who would own a lifetime .340 batting average by season's end, 27 points higher than the next best active National Leaguer, Richie Ashburn—to Philadelphia. Just prior to the then-trading deadline of June 15. Lane offered Musial for pitching great Robin Roberts. Fortuitously, Busch intervened, and fans in both cities were relieved.

Busch issued this statement: "At no time has a trade for Stan Musial been considered." Lane bristled, saying the statement should have come from him. Busch countered, "I don't give a damn who makes it, so long as it's made." He wanted it known that Musial "was, is, and will continue to be a St. Louis institution" and that he would stay with the organization then "and as long after he stops playing as he wants to."

When Musial first discovered the Cardinals were considering trading him, he was as apoplectic as he was indignant. Years later, Cardinals broadcaster Jack Buck noted, "If you were to mention it now to Musial about the fact that Frank Lane almost traded him, that's when you would see the eyes narrow." Buck added if someone crossed Musial once, he would never have another opportunity to do so.

Despite such chaos, on June 19 St. Louis was tied with the Reds for first. It would be the last day they could stake such a claim, though.

On July 7, 1956, baseball announced that Musial was selected as the first winner of the Player of the Decade Award (covering the 10-year span after the war) in a *Sporting News* poll of 260 players and members of the media. Joe DiMaggio and Ted Williams finished second and third, respectively.

Musial accepted the award with both wit and modesty, saying, "I can't hit like Williams, I can't field like DiMaggio, and I certainly can't throw like Feller. I can't figure out why I'm getting this."

Just prior to the July 10 All-Star Game, AL catcher Yogi Berra sat quietly in the clubhouse as his squad's manager went over National League hitters, discussing their tendencies and how the American League pitching staff should attack each hitter. When they came to Musial, Berra interrupted. "You guys are trying to stop Musial in 15 minutes when the National ain't stopped him in 15 years."

The NL was seeking their sixth win over the last seven contests. Thanks in part to Musial's homer, they won it by a score of 7–3. The loss dropped Casey Stengel's managerial record in All-Star play to 1–5.

In the sixth inning, Ted Williams and Mickey Mantle hit back-to-back homers off Warren Spahn for the only runs the AL scored. Williams' blow tied Musial for the most All-Star homers ever.

Mere moments later, in the top of the seventh, Musial stepped in to face Red Sox pitcher Tom Brewer. With one man out, he reclaimed his record quickly, crushing one to left-center, doing so in front of a sparse crowd of 28,843 in old Griffith Stadium in the nation's capital.

The year's longest losing skid began on August 26, 1956. Cunningham recounted, "We had a ballplayer named Jackie Brandt. He had the nickname 'Flaky.' Well, we had lost six in a row, and Hutchinson was calling for a chew-out meeting. And when Hutch chewed you out, you knew you were chewed out, believe me.

"Brandt was learning how to chew tobacco. Just before the meeting started, he came over to spit in one of those boxes the players had with the sand in there for the tobacco. Hutch had his foot on the sandbox and Brandt spit and missed, spit all over Hutch's leg and sanitary sock and shoe—I mean it was a gob. He looked at that and couldn't do anything but laugh and say, 'Meeting over with. Get out of here.'" The Redbirds lost that night, then broke out of the tailspin, winning seven of their next eight, but were relegated to a bleak fourth-place finish nevertheless.

Hutchinson, who never came to accept defeat casually, was widely known for his volatility. Del Greco recalled, "We'd lose, he'd really let us know about it. After one game in St. Louis [where] they had this walkway you'd walk across the people underneath [in the stands]. And we lost a tough game and we were going up the steps, and he threw a garbage can down the steps." Upturning clubhouse spreads after especially difficult losses was also typical of Hutchinson. A Garagiola line has it that Hutchinson was basically a happy guy, "but his face didn't show it." One sportswriter's take on

Hutch's demeanor was that he "always looks like his team has just hit into a game-ending triple play."

Cunningham, however, loved playing for Hutchinson. "He was just a great guy. All you had to do was hustle for Hutch."

"Ol' Hutch was a tough cookie," stated Law, "but everybody respected him. He was a good man; he was tough, but I'll tell you one thing—he protected his players. He was on top of the game and managed the players very well."

In this, Musial's 14th full season, he took over Mel Ott's NL record for extra-base hits when he passed Ott's total of 1,071. Musial shrugged off his new record modestly, saying, "Nice to have." With his 332nd homer, he also breezed by Hank Greenberg to take over sole ownership of the ninth slot on the all-time home-run list. Still, he said he believed he would play just two more seasons.

Ultimately, 1956 was a troubling year. Musial went through a significant hitting downward spiral—his peers were astonished to see the great hitter flail at pitches like a weather vane in a cyclone. On August 22, in a home game in which he committed two errors and went hitless, fans were unforgiving and for the first time in memory, he was booed when he came to bat. The following day 10 Cardinals fans, appalled by the heckling, paid for a newspaper ad apologizing for the mistreatment he had suffered. While he admitted it was the worst game he had ever played, the booing hurt; the apology was, to some extent, a palliative.

Having hit .319 in 1955 followed by .310 for 1956 (a solid average but his lowest one to date), Musial felt his game was off and that he had been hampered by fatigue. "When you're tired physically, you become mentally tired. That affects your hitting. I know when I was really in my prime I could concentrate on every pitch." While he had led the NL in RBIs for his second and final time, he remained vexed. Perhaps, he pondered, the end was indeed very near, but, maybe, just maybe, he *could* turn things around.

In January 1957 Gussie Busch announced Musial's uniform number would be retired when he left the game. Announcing such plans for a player who was still active is as rare as a two-dollar-bill sighting.

Musial's 1957 salary (some sources list $80,000) continued to place him among the highest-paid players in baseball. In spring training Garagiola dropped by the Cardinals' St. Petersburg camp. He teased Musial about his wealth. "I've gotten a lot of thrills out of baseball," he began, "but the big one will be when you invite me to open a joint bank account." Money would later be the source of the falling out between the two friends.

Money matters for most players, however, weren't as positive. The average ballplayer's salary was somewhere around $15,000, with approximately 75 percent of the players grossing between $10,000 and $25,000. About 10 percent of all players were earning $25,000 or better, and only 10 players had contracts for $50,000 or more.

This was also the first year the Boeing 707 jet transport was used by commercial airlines, allowing cross-country travel in approximately six hours, setting the stage for the Dodgers and Giants to move their teams to the West Coast for the 1958 season.

Musial always preferred road trips through Pittsburgh because the ballpark there was only about an hour's ride away from his mother's residence in Donora. Ted Musial said, "When he played the Pirates, he got permission to depart from the team and stay in Donora with his mother. She would prepare his favorite Polish dishes, 'hunky' foods, such as noodle soup, haluski, and pierogi.

"He would go to Frank Pizzica's Buick [dealership], and his good friend Frank gave him a Buick at his disposal to drive around. So all the kids knew: the Cardinals are in town, look for a new Buick and you might see Stan. If he would come up the street and you happened to notice and waved at him, he would toot the horn and wave back. If he knew you, he would stop and shake your hand.

"When he played a night game, he always would drive down McKean Avenue past Costa's Restaurant. There used to be guys hanging outside there, just talking, smoking, whatever. Stan knew the guys and he would always stop the car and chit-chat with them. When he'd get ready to leave, they'd say, 'Hey, Stash, how about 4-for-4 tonight?' Stan would always say, 'Hey, guys, you know I kinda struggle at Forbes Field.'"

The Cardinals again (naturally, with Lane in charge) featured a ton of new players, including Del Ennis. Additionally, Lane engineered an eight-man transaction that put "Sad" Sam Jones (famous for chewing on a toothpick even during pitching stints and for having perhaps the best, sharpest curve in the majors), Jim Davis, Hobie Landrith, and Eddie Miksis in Cardinals uniforms.

Determined to focus better than he had the previous two seasons, Musial was back in form. He later said that, "When I was at the plate, I wasn't going to swing at a ball that I didn't have a reason for swinging at." He also strove to lay off good pitches when he didn't feel he had them timed perfectly.

He believed he could match his lifetime batting average that season. "That used to mean .350. Now it means .340," he quipped. Musial, his bat always Jack-in-the-box quick, was once more wrong with his prediction. He wound up sitting atop the NL with his .351 batting average (the fifth time he surpassed the .350 plateau), hauling home his seventh and final batting crown like a Hollywood star loaded down with so much corporate swag. Six of his titles had come over an incredible stretch of nine seasons. For him, a hitless game no more annoying than a stubbed toe.

In the traditional Opening Day in Cincinnati, Musial got off to a rousing start, going 4-for-4. On the debit side, he tore some back muscles and had to be taped up in order to continue staying in the lineup for future games. The injury left him in as much pain as a victim of a pistol whipping. Soon the team began to suffer as well, and by May 23 they sank into sixth place.

On July 9, Musial played in the All-Star Game, this one held on his home field, Sportsman's Park. This was the year fans from Cincinnati stuffed the ballot box, resulting in a player from the Reds at virtually every starting position. *The Sporting News* reported, "Those nutty, fervent Cincinnati voters were up to their old tricks again, this time voting their whole team (except George Crowe [first baseman] and the batboy) onto the National League's starting lineup." Gus Bell won the starting spot in center field and Wally Post the right field job until commissioner Ford Frick stepped in and replaced them with Willie Mays and Hank Aaron. Bell made the team anyway, but Post did not.

Frick also ruled that from then on, under his watch, players, managers, and coaches, and not the fans, would determine who made up the All-Star roster (that decision was upheld until commissioner Bowie Kuhn reversed it in 1970).

Before the game began, Musial spoke with Yogi Berra. "I hope you'll be kind to me, Yog," Musial told Berra. "I'm getting old and not going good. Since we're such old friends, I expect you to tell me what pitches to expect." Berra jokingly assured Musial that he would, but the skeptical Cardinals star retorted, "I'm not sure I can trust you." Batting in the third hole, Musial went 1-for-3 and scored a run in a lost cause.

Musial may have been joking, but he was making some concessions to age. From around 1956 he had been getting his legs massaged, becoming quite familiar with the redolent scent of oil of wintergreen. "When you start to get older, you look for ways to save yourself," he explained. "I can get loosened up here [in the trainer's room]. And it saves me a lot of running out there [on the field] before the game."

As late as August 4, 1957, the resilient Cardinals led the pack in a five-team dash for the pennant. Two days later, a nine-game losing skid began, causing them to slip out of first. They fought on against the first-place Braves, taking three out of four in Milwaukee in mid-August, then faded shortly thereafter when an injury to Musial hurt their cause.

The injury took place on August 23rd when he chipped a bone in his left shoulder blade and tore some muscles while swinging at a high pitch, well outside the strike zone, trying to pull the ball to protect Wally Moon on a hit-and-run play. Thus, his NL record for the most consecutive games played—895—73 more than Gus Suhr's old mark established decades earlier, officially ended on August 24, 1957.

Earlier in the season, Musial had been hurt badly enough to miss a game, but his streak was kept alive by a rainout. He commented that he didn't especially care about the record. Twice in 1955 the streak had been artificially extended by a then-existing technicality. Manager Harry Walker had listed Musial on his lineup card on August 30 and 31, only to pinch-hit for him in the top of the first inning. From then on, Musial saw his record as "tainted."

When the streak snapped, Musial said, with no trace of rationalization, "Having it end may have been a blessing in disguise." In some years, such as 1956, he believed the continuation of the streak had worn him down. By 1958 he would concede he was glad to take an occasional day off, especially nightcaps of doubleheaders on hot days.

Cardinals trainer Bob Bauman praised Musial's "great recuperative powers," adding that despite his shoulder problems, he was out only briefly and "came back to win the batting title." Bauman noted Musial could tolerate pain "that would make most men fold up." After partially recovering from his injury, he enjoyed a 16-for-30 tear during which, he said, "I just punched the ball."

Hank Aaron hit a two-run homer versus the Cards in the last of the eleventh inning on September 23, 1957, to ensure the pennant for the Braves. After coming as close as two and a half games out in September, the Cards had faded a bit and would ultimately settle for second place, eight out, but with their best win-loss percentage (.565) since 1952.

The day after the Cards were mathematically eliminated from the pennant chase was another sad one for Musial, as the Dodgers closed the gates on Ebbets Field for the final time. The old ballpark, which had opened in 1913 and which had been built for $750,000, would never again host a big-league ballgame, and the Dodgers would open in Los Angeles the following season. A sparse crowd of 6,702 spectators turned out for their farewell to the old ballpark.

Musial modestly conceded his hitting in Ebbets had been "phenomenal," adding, "There was always excitement in Brooklyn. My adrenalin was always flowing in Brooklyn. The tension, the atmosphere, the fights, you knew something was going to happen."

Earlier, Musial said good-bye to the Polo Grounds, homering against the Giants on August 21. That smash gave him a home run in each of his final three games at that venue before the Giants moved to San Francisco.

Musial's .351, aided, he felt, by frequently having Ennis hitting behind him, complemented his 29 homers. While batting with 171 men in scoring position, he drove in 102 runs (including himself when he homered).

The 1957 campaign was also the season in which Musial strung together his last of four hitting streaks of 20 or more games. At that time only Ty Cobb, Tris Speaker, and Dale Mitchell had ever racked up more hitting skeins of 20-plus games. The final Musial streak ran precisely 20 games and, considering it came when Musial was 36, may have been the most difficult one to achieve.

Soon after season's end, another St. Louis personnel move involving Lane took place. This time it was he who left the team, a victim of too many arguments with Gussie Busch over his multiple moves. Lane was livid that Busch had questioned his ability and his trades, especially in 1956, and remained upset that Busch vetoed trades such as his Musial-for-Roberts deal. Lane moved on to Cleveland, while Bing Devine took over in the Cardinals' front office.

Musial, his hair now thinning somewhat, was presented the Lou Gehrig Memorial Award. The honor, established by Gehrig's fraternity at Columbia, Phi Delta Theta, is bestowed yearly upon the player who, through his deeds on and off the playing field, most typifies the character of Gehrig. Musial also took home the Sportsman of the Year award given out by *Sports Illustrated*. Still, his most pressing issue was this: He ended the year just 43 hits shy of 3,000.

## CHAPTER SEVEN

# *All Good Things Must...*

With technological advances and the expansion of baseball to the West Coast, the game of baseball had been quickly and drastically revamped by 1958.

Cunningham recalled such changes. "[Formerly] we traveled by train, got that midnight train. Then, when the Dodgers [and Giants] moved out there [to the West Coast], you flew by [chartered] jet. After the ballgame, you got on the bus, you went to the airport, got on the plane, and then you landed, got on the bus. You didn't really pay that much attention to [your environment], the hotels, or even the [novelty of] the planes." The pace of the game and of the world in general had sped up considerably.

The first live coast-to-coast broadcast of a baseball game hadn't taken place until October 1, 1951, during the first game of the Giants-Dodgers playoffs. Before long, though, the country was hooked on televised baseball.

Revenue from television, the medium that initially hurt baseball attendance, led to another change in baseball. Erskine remembered, "TV money was brand new in the early '50s, and Stan was there in the National League player-reps group. Stan and I and all the player reps of that era were somewhat specifically involved in getting a pension that we now know as one of the best in any industry.

"We were able to get the owners—and we didn't have a union, players of our era were not in favor of a union, but we did have representation—through negotiation, on a handshake basis, to commit 60 percent of the newfound television revenues from the World Series and All-Star Game to restructure a players' pension that really has become one of the best. And Musial was in on the early years of the formation of what's now baseball's pension plan."

Musial's active, assertive role in this political realm refutes claims that he was perpetually too docile or apathetic to get involved in any pivotal issues. Erskine continued, "He was there at a key, critical time and, like so many things in life that we enjoy or we inherit, we don't bother to find out how they came into being. He did work to make it happen.

"Well, I can tell you that in the case of players today who are drawing pensions from baseball, they can thank Stan Musial and player reps of that era for getting the plan structured and for getting the owners to agree to use TV revenues to fund it."

Still, Musial and many other stars—including Robin Roberts, Ted Williams, and Mickey Mantle—testified in July 1958 at the Senate Subcommittee on Antitrust and Monopoly hearings, saying they were content with the way they had been treated and that they saw no reason to modify the reserve clause. Williams went so far as to state, "Personally, I don't see how baseball could operate without the reserve clause and preserve its dignity."

Meanwhile, this was the season when the Cardinals finally employed what could be called their first true regular black player, Curt Flood. One year earlier, Charlie Peete stood a good chance of claiming that role, but he died in a plane crash en route to the States after playing winter ball.

Coming over from Cincinnati, Flood would eventually prove to be a fine acquisition for the Cardinals. "Curt could go deep in the count," wrote Tim McCarver, "hit behind the runner, and steal a base," and he wound up hitting .293 lifetime. Defensively, he played a shallow center field and ended up winning seven Gold Gloves over just 12 full big-league seasons. Vernon Law stated, "He threw well. He chased down a lot of base hits. He rated right up there with most outfielders in the league at that time. As a matter of fact, Carl Warwick asserted, "Curt Flood was a better center fielder than Willie Mays. He did it all right: he never missed a cutoff man, he never made a bad throw. And his personality was fantastic, too. I don't think he got enough credit for his ability.

"Flood was quiet, and he didn't demand any attention. He was a fine gentleman; everybody on the ballclub liked him. It's unfortunate that he didn't get to play any more after he broke that reserve clause."

After asking general manager Bing Devine to make him the highest-paid player in the league, Musial verbally agreed to a contract for $91,000, a symbolic $1,000 more than Ralph Kiner's salary. However, in a stunning move, Gussie Busch ponied up an additional $9,000, lifting the salary to $100,000. Devine said when Musial was handed the contract he began to sign it without reading it. Not until someone pointed out the salary did Musial realize he'd made NL history.

Only two other players had ever reached the $100K level, Ted Williams and Joe DiMaggio. In this era the average baseball player's salary was still well under $20,000 per year.

Busch appreciated players who, like Musial and Schoendienst, would "glad-hand with his cronies" and "weren't terribly pushy on pay, aware that lifetime employment awaited 'good boys.'" It was a paternalistic attitude, one that would soon die out in baseball.

Musial's salary was still chump change compared to what today's players rake in, but considering Hall of Famer Robin Roberts said he earned $530,000 over his 18-year career, an average of a meager $29,444 per year, Musial wasn't complaining.

Musial missed out on one of sports' earliest and most lucrative gold rushes—not long after his retirement, sports salaries shot up in the brief period from the late 1960s to the mid-1970s. In the NBA, for example, during that period salaries went up some 700 percent.

Alex Grammas said that at one time when he was a teammate of Musial's, "I think that the whole salary of the St. Louis Cardinals—25 players, four coaches, a manager, was less than a million—I'd say $850,000, and Stan had $100,000 of that.

"I made $6,000 and [other guys] made $7,000, $7,500, $10,000. That's the way it was. You had to play hard to get up to $10,000. So you didn't [worry] about who the manager was or 'I got to worry because my contract's going to run out.' Ours ran out every year."

Those who feel Musial played in a more glittering, wonderful time period, certainly in a more innocent era, also assert that the coming of the big money did not make players happier. Further, those who played in the pre-big-bucks era argue that today's players find the game to be more toil and less fun than men who had preceded them and that the modern players lack a sense of community, a loyalty to something besides money.

At any rate, Musial's 1958 contract settled, he spoke of how much he wanted to reach his 3,000th hit: "It takes so many years of hard playing and so much luck in avoiding serious injuries." Just six years earlier, he had reached the 2,000-hit mark. Back then he began to doubt that he would be able to stick around long enough to attain 3,000. Now, he confessed, he wanted to get the hits he needed quickly so he could finally "stop worrying about it."

In the spring, the Cardinals' prospects were looking good. That is, until Del Ennis and Musial tapered off and so did the Cardinals. Ennis would see his power numbers plummet from 24 homers in 1957 to just three, and his RBIs crash from 105 to 47. Musial would experience what was his weakest full season to date with a personal low of 62 RBIs with only 159 hits and 17 homers.

In the spring, after dropping about four pounds in camp, Musial reached his playing weight of 182 pounds, only seven pounds more than what he weighed as a rookie, so he was still trim and fit. He said that he didn't suffer the aches most players his age complained of. Why, then, he wondered all year long, were his power numbers down?

One theory held that Musial's statistics took a nosedive because, for the first time in his career, he was not afforded the chance to hit in New York. Both the Giants and Dodgers had evacuated the city, and Musial absolutely *loved* hitting in the Polo Grounds and in Ebbets Field, both destined to be razed eventually.

In fact, although Musial was famous for his nitro-like hitting in Ebbets Field, he absolutely lit up the Polo Grounds like Bill Veeck's exploding scoreboard.

Musial hit more home runs at Ebbets than any other visiting player—37—seven more than the No. 2 man on that list (Ralph Kiner), but he walloped 49 (21 more than the next-highest total) in the Polo Grounds, a park that featured inviting home-run porches of just a bit over 257 feet down the right-field line and about 279 feet to dead left field (although it was a country mile to straight-away center—some years as far as 505 feet from home plate). Brooklyn fans dubbed him "the Man," but Giants fans realized he was a veritable giant killer as well.

For the record, Musial ranked third for the most home runs hit by a visitor in Boston's Braves Field (18) and fifth in Cincinnati's Crosley Field (34). When it came to total homers hit in Sportsman's Park, nobody topped his 252, a sum nearly double the second-best total by Ken Williams.

On April 17, 1958, Musial connected for a home run versus the Cubs. That hit pushed his lifetime total bases figure to 5,045, moving past slugger Mel Ott. Musial had entered 1958 with 2,957 hits and quickly upped the figure after hitting safely in 20 of his first 22 games.

During a doubleheader of May 11, 1958, Musial had five hits, leaving him two shy of 3,000. That night, a private party was held in his restaurant in anticipation of his historic hit. Then it was on to Chicago, where he doubled the next day.

Musial entered the game on May 13 hitting a lusty .483. Not expected to play in the game, Musial, wearing his gray away uniform, had been soaking up the May sun in the Cardinals bullpen.

When he was called upon to pinch-hit in a tight spot, he hit a 2–2 curve from fellow Pole Moe Drabowsky with authority, sending the ball into the left-field corner, well beyond the range of outfielder Walt Moryn, who conceded the double. Musial had reached 3,000 hits quicker than any other player, doing so early in his 16th season.

After the game, a Cards 5–3 victory, Musial was bombarded by the media, required to answer the same old questions ("How does it feel to get that big hit?") with a pat answer, "Great," and stand still for photographers' myriad contrived poses (e.g., Musial kissing his bat or pointing to the spot where ball met bat).

Joe Cunningham noted that the media back then did "play it up fairly big—maybe not as big as they would now." Typically, Musial had "3,000" drawn in red on his souvenir ball.

The *New York Times* quoted Musial as saying his 3,000th hit was his most gratifying feat because he realized "how many really great hitters didn't reach [that strata]" and he was cognizant, too, of "the many games and hits—big and little—that it took to get here."

Aboard the Illinois Central to St. Louis, on the final train trip the club would ever make, Musial plopped into a chair on a private club car, let out a sigh, and said, "I'm glad it's finally over." But it wasn't.

When the train steamed into Clinton, Illinois, darkness setting in, he heard the chant, "We want Musial," rising staccato-like from the station platform. He went to the rear of the car and greeted about 50 people, shaking hands and signing autographs. Fifty minutes later at the next stop, Springfield, the scene was repeated with a crowd of around 100 fans on hand. In this innocent era, the crowd spontaneously broke out into "For He's a Jolly Good Fellow" just before the train departed. Lil said the crowds greeting them were like a whistle-stopping "presidential campaign." The pocketa-pocketa of the train finally lulled Musial asleep. He dozed the last half-hour of the trip.

When the Cardinals' train hissed to a halt in St. Louis' Union Station around midnight, Musial shared his happiness with a throng of his fans. A group of 800-plus, some who had waited for two hours, was on hand. Disembarking the train, dressed in a suit and tie, he joined the crowd, holding his talismanic baseball aloft.

Musial peered over the crowd and joked, "Now I know how Lindbergh felt. Hey, kids, no school tomorrow." Writer Robert Falkoff pointed out that while Lindbergh had flown the airplane called the *Spirit of St. Louis*, "Musial *was* the spirit of St. Louis."

Once more the press swarmed all over the superstar. One member of the media offered to help Musial slip away, but he insisted, "I wouldn't do that. If all these people thought enough of me to come down here to the station, the least I can do is stay around and sign autographs."

It was nearly an hour later before he finally headed to his restaurant. There was no respite there because he was soon signing menus. It would not be until 3:00 AM that he went to bed, his 24-hour whirlwind over.

The next day, Musial was greeted by a standing ovation at the ballpark and responded by homering in his first at-bat back home. He continued to sizzle, and as late as June 11 his batting average stood at .406. However, a victim of baseball's law of gravity, he could not sustain such a clip. By season's end his apogee of .406 took a nosedive of nearly 70 points. Still, his .337 finish trailed only Richie Ashburn and Willie Mays among major-league hitters, and he was the only man in the game to sport a state license plate that read "3,000," presented to him shortly after his historic hit.

Dismal play by the Cardinals in 1958 eventually led to the dismissal of manager Fred Hutchinson, despite his revivalist act one year earlier. With two weeks to go in the season, he was replaced by Stan Hack, and the team limped to a sixth-place finish on a poor 72–82 record.

The team toured Japan that fall, and a pregnant Lil accompanied a worn-out Stan, who somehow managed two homers. During an interview he stated he was in the restaurant business back home. A writer asked, "Are you then a waiter?" That, laughed Musial, was a gross misinterpretation.

In February 1959 daughter Jeanie, the last of his four children, was born and Musial received permission to report late to spring-training camp. Consequently, when the season began, he was not in top shape. His weight was up to around 187 pounds and he felt it through his hips and waist.

Solly Hemus was now the Cardinals manager, calling his being named their skipper the highlight of his career. He had no prior big-league managerial experience but believed Busch probably hired him because he had faith in him as a person and as a St. Louis player from 1949 through early 1956.

Hemus was destined to suffer more than his immediate predecessors had, despite running a team with some promise.

Curt Flood, not quite ready to shine, had one year of experience, and Bill White, who would hit .302, was picked up in exchange for an aging Sam Jones. Ken Boyer, who would enjoy a 29-game hitting spree in 1959, was a solid four-year veteran. Things didn't sit too well with Musial, though, when Hemus, several years Musial's junior, declared he would rest the team's favorite player more often to save his strength.

Charlie James felt Hemus had the toughest job of any manager Musial played, having to handle the aging, revered star as delicately as possible: "He had to make some choices as to who was going to play and who was going to be Stan's replacement."

Pitching woes plagued the Cardinals, although this season featured Bob Gibson's debut. In addition to that, Musial, handicapped by a terrible start, wound up with a humiliating .255 average, 76 points lower than his eventual lifetime average. He had never hit lower than .310 until now, at the age of 38. He hit an anemic 14 home runs and drove in just 44 runs. It was, simply put, a sepulchral season.

There were the inevitable rumblings that Musial's days as a viable offensive force were over. Musial claimed his poor showing was due to fatigue and being out of shape. He played in only 115 games, his lowest total ever, and his Cardinals went 71–83, mired in seventh place. More alarming, their 776–763 log over the decade was their worst showing since the 1910s.

There were a few bright moments for Musial. On May 7 his 400th home run defeated the Cubs in the ninth inning. His 652nd double on June 21 established a new NL record. On August 7 his two-run homer in the ninth sent the Cardinals home a winner over the Phillies. Finally, on September 20 he racked up lifetime hit 3,200 in a win over Chicago.

Musial was involved in one of baseball's screwiest plays ever on June 30, 1959. The Cardinals took on the Cubs with Musial at the plate when Chicago pitcher Bob Anderson chucked a wild payoff pitch, high and tight. Cubs catcher Sammy Taylor saw the ball soar toward the brick wall behind the plate but believed it had been foul-tipped. Home-plate umpire Vic Delmore had, in the meantime, signaled ball four, triggering an argument by the Cubs' battery mates. Musial unhesitatingly took off for first via the base on balls. Taylor asked for, and received, a new baseball from Delmore, which he then tossed to Anderson.

That's when the insanity broke out. Cubs third baseman Alvin Dark darted to the backstop to retrieve the original baseball while Musial's teammates were shouting for him to take second base. Al Barlick, who was umpiring the bases that day, picked up the account, "Dark and Anderson both throw out to second base. Dark's throw is low and is fielded by Ernie Banks, then playing shortstop.... Anderson's throw is high and sails over the head of Tony Taylor, the Cubs' second baseman. Musial slides into second." When Musial saw a baseball fly by him and into the outfield, he headed for third, where Banks tagged him out with the ball Dark had just thrown.

The Cubs contended Musial was clearly out, while the Cardinals pled that, due to the second wild throw, the one that eluded Taylor, Musial was entitled to third base. The umpires finally cleared the issue up by declaring Musial out because he had been tagged by the original ball.

It was later discovered the bizarre play had another wrinkle. When the ball first bounced to the backstop, it was touched by the on-the-field public-address announcer. He then surrendered the ball to Dark after he had demanded the ball be handed over. Therefore, the correct ruling should have been Musial was permitted to take first due to the walk, and he should have been frozen there when the ball was touched by the P.A. announcer.

When the season ended, Musial was mortified by his hit total, 87. He insisted he would know when it was time to retire, but, understandably, the question persisted—*was he washed up?*

Also, trade rumors had surfaced in *The Sporting News* in August, rumors that had Musial going to the Yankees for catcher Yogi Berra. Both teams emphatically denied talks between the two clubs had taken place.

It is, of course, impossible to know what ramifications would have followed the trading of Musial, but it is unfathomable to picture him in any uniform other than the one featuring two cardinals perched on opposite ends of a baseball bat.

One thing is certain—Musial did not feel his career was through. Determined to whip himself into tip-top shape for the 1960 campaign, Musial signed up for a physical-education program at St. Louis University, taking part in routine exercises but with a focus on tumbling, a sport Musial had shined in as a youth.

At decade's end, among the galaxy of great hitters from the 1940s and 1950s, Ted Williams and Musial shone the brightest. Nolan Ryan, Williams, and Musial are the only men to lead their league in a category for an entire decade more than once. Musial led the NL in total bases for the 1940s and again in the 1950s. He had also led the league in the 1950s for doubles just as he had led his league in triples throughout the 1940s. He went on from there to lead the league in three-base hits a record five times.

Musial also ranked fourth for the most homers hit in the decade by a National Leaguer with 266, trailing only two Dodgers, Duke Snider (326) and Gil Hodges (310), and Eddie Mathews of the Braves (299). Musial was also named to the All-Decade team for the second decade running.

By that point Musial had a legion of fans, none more devoted than family and friends back home. John Benyo Jr. grew up in Musial's hometown and recalled, "There was an insurance agency in Donora, and in the window they had a board and they always had Musial's current batting average and hit [total] for that season. Whatever he was doing, you knew it."

For that matter, townsfolk also kept track of Stan's mother. When she would walk through town, those who recognized her would point her out to younger residents, "There goes Stan Musial's mother," they'd say, as if passing down the town's lore.

By the 1950s and into the 1960s she was, said Benyo Jr., the very picture of "one of the old folks of the parish. She was the typical, old, if you'll excuse the expression, hunky lady—carrying the purse and with a babushka on her head. She just looked like anybody else's grandma. *Stara baba* [studda bubba]."

Said Joe Kostolansky Jr., "She was a feisty, older lady, kind of husky, and very independent—her needs were modest.

"I remember one time when Stan's son, Richard, who went to Notre Dame and was on the track team, and my father and I took Mrs. Musial down to the track meet between Pitt and Notre Dame. When people found out she was there, they would congregate around her, and she would kind of hold court. She liked the attention very much."

For Christmas of 1957 Stan had had a house built for his mother, who, like many elderly widows, insisted on staying in the town she was most familiar with. It was a pleasant, modern, yet unimposing one-story brick-and-siding ranch-style house that sat at 21 Second Street Extension, an upscale part of town. It was "modest by today's standards," said Benyo Jr., but that section of town was where "the up-and-coming people moved. It was away from the mill and away from the smoke. Her home had brick pillars on either side of the driveway and there was a concrete insert that said 'Musial' almost like a tombstone effect in one of those brick entryways." Musial also ordered a statue of the Blessed Mother, which they placed in the middle of her yard.

Emma Jene Lelik, who wrote for the local newspaper, added, "It was not a huge, luxurious home, but it was fine for her, quite adequate for a person living alone, and I think he felt good about building that for her so that she was in a nice, safe area." She refused to move to St. Louis but visited her son quite often, just as he came into town frequently to be with her.

While sitting in her favorite chair, Mary would gaze down through a picture window at the high school field where her son had played baseball as a youth.

Before the 1960 season began, Musial, in a virtually unheard-of show of integrity, walked into the Cardinals' executive offices and requested his salary be slashed by the maximum amount contractually allowable, down to $80,000, a 20 percent cut from his $100,000 deal for 1959. Dismayed by his stats the previous year, he felt he could not, in good conscience, accept another 100 grand for the upcoming season. His honorable move, he said, "made him feel hungry again."

He said he had no gripes about the cut. "In fact," he stated, "I'm glad to sign this contract. Because a couple of times in the past the Cards have had me sign for more than we agreed upon orally. This year I thought I'd be kind to them."

When it came to negotiating a new contract, Musial's normal philosophy was, he said, "Don't tell them what you did in the past; tell them what you are going to do in the future." Despite all the promises of future accomplishments that he could have made, he wasn't usually a hard-nosed negotiator, and, according to a friend of Musial's, "Stan never really had an agent until late in life."

By way of contrast, contemporary ballplayers are more akin to the materialistic cartoon character Sally Brown who, in the *Peanuts* Christmas special, crassly said she only wanted what was coming to her, greedily demanding her fair share.

Still, the Cardinals needed Musial to hit better in 1960 than he had the previous season if the team was to avoid their first string of three sub-.500 seasons since 1918 to 1920. Could he bounce back, or would his career crumble like the walls of Ebbets Field?

Pitcher Vinegar Bend Mizell once joked, "Stan hasn't done so much. He's just been on a 20-year hitting streak." In the 1950s, astoundingly for the second decade running, Williams had the best batting average in AL play (.336) and Musial topped the NL (.330) among men who played in at least seven seasons of that span. Both, however, were coming off the first season in their big-league careers in which they failed to hit .300. The end of the line for the greats could be avoided, but it was not too far off; it was inevitable.

Vowing to get in top shape, Musial and Schoendienst began working out together six weeks prior to spring training, going to a St. Louis gym following Walter Eberhardt's regimen, which stressed "strength, stamina, suppleness." Soon their winter flab was toned into muscle, and when Musial reported to camp his manager permitted him to work out at his own pace.

Writer Roger Kahn once stated that aging ballplayers are paradoxical in that they are "old but not grey; tired but not short of breath; slow but not fat." Musial clearly fit the description as spring training opened.

McCarver recounted the first time he met Musial when he was an 18-year-old rookie catcher in camp and was impressed when he squatted behind Musial for his first spring batting session. Musial took the first three pitches and, as they blew by, made a comment. "No, that's outside.... No, that's not a strike...." McCarver wrote, "Here he was 39 years old, he hadn't stepped in a batter's box in five months, yet his eyes were tuned to midseason form."

Like Ted Williams, who claimed he could see his bat meet the ball at the exact moment of contact, tales of Musial's great eyesight exist. Once Joe Cunningham came to the plate after Musial had just made an out. Cunningham recalled, "As he was running back I asked, 'What was that pitch?' and he said, 'The fastball. The seams were running in.' I said, 'Oh, the seams, huh?' Well I went up to hit; I never saw any seams, I just saw a white flash. That showed me he had excellent eyes when he could tell the seams, the spin of the baseball."

When exhibition games rolled around, Musial's hitting was fine and seemed to foreshadow a comeback as he hovered around the .300 level late into April. His fielding at first base, observers noted, was poor, but there seemed to be nowhere else to station the aging star. Things got worse when his hitting performance began to match his glove work and his batting average dipped.

Musial's diminished fielding skills also hurt his pride. He knew he had been a fine outfielder in his youth, and he was pleased that he was good enough to play center field in nearly 300 games. "I had great speed," he declared, "and was a good outfielder." No Gold Glove Awards were issued until 1957, but using an elaborate formula, statistical expert Bill James determined Musial would have been a multiple winner of that trophy. Overall, he led his league in fielding three times.

For much of his career, he disliked playing first base. "First of all," he critiqued, "it's a lot of work, whereas in the outfield, if the ball is hit to someone else, all you do is watch. At first base, you're jumping off on every pitch…. You're in on every play, more or less." He also disliked handling hot grounders, an occupational hazard at first, much more so than in the outfield.

Musial said that when he initially played first base in 1946, he did enjoy it, but when he reached the age where he *had* to play that position, he did not like it much at all. For one thing, he said, in the outfield he had more opportunity to think about his hitting. Still, by the late 1950s and into the 1960s, he grew more comfortable with the first-base position because playing there lengthened his career.

The 1960 season was the last one in which Musial saw some action at first base. Michael E. Kelley, who grew up not too from Donora, stated, "The Cardinals were in Forbes Field, and he was playing first. There was a routine ground out and the ball was thrown to him, but somehow the ball got through him. And it wasn't where he had to dig it out of the dirt, it just went right through him. He was so embarrassed, [and a lot of] his hometown people were there. His face turned the most beet red of anybody's I've ever seen. You could see that [from the stands]. I felt bad for him because here was a man who was a living legend in baseball, and I'm sure he felt this was tarnishing his image. He had a lot of pride, and that hurt him personally. It's not that a person is above making an error, it's just that this was so routine, 'And I'm Stan Musial—this isn't supposed to be happening to me.'"

To many observers, Musial, at 39, seemed to be just about through. Yet he maintained every intention of ending his career with dignity and good hitting. The season was a trying one, one of "agony and pride." His poor play early on was an ordeal for Musial, but he refused to quit.

Nor did he moan or make concessions to age. Teammate Alex Grammas said that even when Musial's productivity was fading, he never expressed any pessimism. "He wouldn't express anything about, 'Well, I'm slipping,' or anything like that. In fact, when I was with him, he looked like he was still hitting the ball good. Of course, everybody's going to get a little bit slower as they get older, but he had such a great swing, you had to make some great pitches on him to keep him from hitting it solid."

On May 6, after whiffing twice and with his average at a quiet .268, Hemus decided not to start him again. "I sat him on the bench," recalled Hemus, "which I caught hell for doing and probably wished I never did it, but you can't look back. But he took it like a man."

Grammas commented, "I'm sure he felt, I don't know if strange is the word, felt disappointed, maybe that's a better word, that he wasn't playing, but Stan is a very smart guy and a proud man. Here's a guy who set major-league records and all of a sudden he's sitting there—just talking about it, I could sense how he felt. I'm sure it wasn't easy for him to take something like that, but I never heard him say anything derogatory to anyone."

Musial sat until the eleventh, when he started against southpaw Warren Spahn and went 3-for-5 in a loss. By the 14th game the club had dropped eight straight to plunge into seventh place and Musial had gone 1-for-11 after his success against Spahn. The team had lost all 12 of their road games going into a May 15 doubleheader in Wrigley Field. Hemus told Musial he'd sit out the first game but probably start in the nightcap, but, after the Cardinals won the opener, Hemus went with the same lineup. Musial later wrote this was the first time in his career that he "questioned a manager's judgment." According to Musial, he told Hemus, "You were just kidding about playing me, Solly." Another source has Musial a bit more forceful, chastising Hemus to never again toy with him. Hemus agreed but remained determined to go with a young lineup.

Hemus' account of the situation was this: "What happened was we played a doubleheader in Chicago, and I told Musial I that I was going to play [Leon Wagner] in the first game and that he'd play in the second game.

"Well, after we won the first game, I just said, 'It'll be the same lineup.' He didn't react at all. A day or so later Musial came up to me and said, 'Yeah, I knew that if we [won] that first game that I'd not be in the second game.' I told him I didn't know if I thought that far ahead or not, but it was probably the truth. He was very observant about anything in the game. He always had his head in the game."

Hemus noted that Musial was used to only playing one game of double-headers anyway. "He was getting up there [in age], so that didn't bother him at all, but when he didn't play [the second game of the twin bill] that kinda dug into him because I had been a friend of his all these years—I broke in when he was playing and I played with him—so he just took me at full trust that I was going to play him, and I didn't play him. I can see where he was upset. He never did carry a grudge—he's not that type of person."

On May 27, with Musial hitting .250 after getting some at-bats, Hemus once more relegated Musial to the bench and occasional pinch-hit duties. Musial began to atrophy in the dugout. Local sportswriters contended Hemus had been mishandling Musial, often playing him against the game's top lefties and then, illogically, sitting him versus some righties that Musial normally owned. Whatever the case, Musial's pride was badly ruffled.

Hemus informed the media that Musial surely would be back in the starting lineup but appeared vague when asked for a time frame. A crushed Musial simply commented, "I'll play whenever they want me to." Privately, though, he was caged-tiger antsy and famished-lion angry with his passive role on the squad. It got to the point where he told some friends that he would almost welcome a trade to a club that still saw him as an every-day player. He also told Roger Kahn, "Don't let anyone tell you they were resting me. I was benched."

Hemus, described as a combative man, broke into the majors with the Cardinals in 1949 and played in 125-plus games in a season only twice. Musial had been kind to a young Hemus, giving him some batting tips, and Hemus readily admitted he admired the St. Louis star. Naturally, then, benching him was highly awkward. Hemus contended that his duty as the manager was not a matter of friendship. "My obligation is to the organization that hired me and to 25 ballplayers. I have to win." He felt Musial was hurting the team: "I had to do it [bench Musial]."

Hemus pointed out the problem was with Musial's hitting, not his glove work. "I don't think his defense was any different from the time he first went out there until the last time I took him out," said Hemus, calling his defense, even as he got older, "adequate, very adequate."

Still, at least one teammate downplayed the issue. Charlie James felt the situation between Musial and Hemus was "kind of hyped up a little bit" by the press, who tried to "make it a little more controversial than it really was." In the clubhouse, he recalled, the matter didn't seem at all volatile.

The Pirates came to town on June 10, shortly before the trading deadline. Their manager, Danny Murtaugh, learned from Musial's friend, sportswriter Bob Broeg, that Musial might be interested in joining the Pirates as a way to prove he could still play and help a pennant contender. When Broeg told Musial that Murtaugh wanted him and asked if he would consider leaving the Cardinals, Musial replied, "I never thought I'd say this, but yes." Murtaugh then notified his general manager, Joe L. Brown, who also wanted Musial but said making a trade for him was, for numerous reasons, not feasible.

In mid-June Musial, then hitting about 90 points below his lifetime batting average, was taking batting practice in Milwaukee with the non-starters. A player asked Musial if he was aware that Preacher Roe used to throw him spitballs. Musial, who once joked that he never fretted or com-plained about pitchers loading one up, that he simply "hit the dry side," replied that he knew all about Roe's tactics.

Once Terry Moore, then coaching third base, semaphored a signal to Musial, warning him of an impending spitter. Roe, said Musial, realized the Cardinals star knew what was coming but had already started his windup, so all he could do was change his pitch to "a lollipop," a pitch with nothing on it. Musial promptly teed off on it, sending it into the stands. "I laughed all the way around the bases," said Musial. Seconds later, in a sad contrast to his past exploits, Musial took three B.P. cuts, which produced three grounders, none traveling farther than the mound. Braves fans jeered, some booing and others taunting.

After May 26 Musial did not start a game for nearly a month, pinch-hitting sparingly (1-for-9). On June 21, a rusty Musial saw his average hit a nadir of .238. *This*, people everywhere thought, *has to be it for Musial; he's done.*

Hemus said that all the while Musial sat he never approached his manager, never bellyached: "Nor did I talk to him. I should have talked to him, but I didn't. I never tried to lay any [placatory] garbage on him, I respected him too much. I'm just sorry it happened because of the type of person he was, and I know what he meant to a ballclub when he [was] in there, but he just wasn't hitting, that's all. I had to have another right-handed hitter in there, and I could move some of my other hitters around. The move was all right; it was just who were you moving, the franchise."

So the media continued to get on Hemus for tampering with the man who could be called the king of the club—"Rightfully so," conceded Hemus, who said the situation was tough for him. "Yeah, it was. I thought long and hard over that thing. It did bother me."

However, when left fielder Bob Nieman got hurt and replacements didn't pan out, Hemus reinserted Musial into his outfield. He started on June 24 and went 1-for-4 versus the Phillies. After taking an "oh-fer" the next day, he caught fire, becoming a proverbial one-man wrecking crew when he went 20-for-40 in games that he started over a 15-day stretch.

"It was like a lightbulb," said Hemus. "He had to prove a point. And he proved a point," Hemus laughed. "He was working out all the time in between—like a rookie, very, very determined."

His torrid stretch, a fabulous resuscitation act, prompted Musial to observe, "Just say I never been away."

This season was one of several in which two All-Star Games were held. On July 11, Musial came off the All-Star bench, singling amid 100-plus-degree conditions in Kansas City. Two days later, in Yankee Stadium,

Musial, shaking off any spiderwebs of old age, came up big, clubbing an upper-deck pinch homer in the seventh inning to provide the NL with an insurance run in a 6–0 win. It was his first at-bat in the ballpark since the 1943 World Series. With his sixth All-Star homer, he extended his own record for lifetime homers in the showcase game and he became the only man to collect two All-Star pinch-hits in one year. After the second game, he noted, perhaps reassuring himself, "I can hit. I can still hit."

Elroy Face, a Pittsburgh Pirate who just one year earlier had posted an incredible 18–1 record pitching out of the bullpen, understated that at any stage of Musial's career, "You had to be careful with him. I just went along with whatever the catcher called and tried to keep it out of his power. I remember him hitting a home run to beat me in a ballgame one time [August 27, 1960]. I came in in the seventh inning of a tie ballgame in St. Louis, and he came up in the bottom of the ninth—it was [still] a tie score. The second or third pitch I threw he hit on the roof in right field. It was a forkball, down and away, and he pulled it. He may have been looking for it and reached out and got it, adjusting to where the pitch was. There was no place he *couldn't* hit."

By the tail end of the 1960 season Musial casually hinted that he would be coming back for yet another season. This time, people wondered if it was another case of an older ballplayer simply not knowing when to hang up the cleats once and for all. Many suspected his assessment, "Maybe my wheels are gone, but I'll be able to hit like hell for a long time," was delusional.

The Cards managed to put up a decent fight down the wire against the Pirates and Braves. After an August 12 win in Pittsburgh, the Cardinals trailed the Pirates by only three games. St. Louis dropped the final three contests of the five-game set, though, and their last serious chance to make up ground was gone. Hemus said, "We were going along pretty good. We had a doubleheader with Pittsburgh [on August 14], and they beat us both ballgames. They just played a little bit better ball than we did." The club had been "headed in the right direction, but we just didn't quite turn them, I guess." When asked if it was a case, then, of the Pirates being a slightly better club that year, Hemus mused, "I don't know if they were any better, but I think that we made a run for it, but that was about it."

Still, five times in August the Cardinals played spoiler in beating the Bucs; in three of the games a Musial homer was the game-winner.

Tim McCarver called Musial "the greatest low-ball hitter" ever. One shred of evidence to support his claim came on August 11 when the Cardinals and Pirates were locked up in a 12-inning affair that Musial brought to a startling and sudden conclusion by smashing a Bob Friend curveball deep into the seats of Forbes Field. McCarver marveled that the next afternoon players standing around the batting cage "were still talking about it. It was the first time I ever heard anybody say, 'He hit it with a shovel.'"

Despite Ernie Broglio's league-leading 21 victories, St. Louis finished nine games off the Pirates' pace and two games behind the second-place Braves. It was, nevertheless, a huge rebound from their seventh-place 1959 finish. Musial managed to salvage his season somewhat after his dreary days early on, hitting .275 with 63 RBIs in only 331 at-bats over his second-lowest total of games played, 116, just one more than in 1959.

Busch was reportedly ready to fire Hemus after the season ended, but he first spoke with Musial. Despite Hemus' having benched him, Musial told Busch to give him a break: "I probably could have ended Solly's career at that time...but I gave Solly a vote of confidence."

On November 17 his hometown feted Musial, with everyone having the sense that his big-league days were rapidly nearing a conclusion. Typically Musial, who pleased the crowd by saying he rooted for the World Series–winning Pirates "just as I did when I was a kid," remained noncommittal and deflected the issue by employing humor. "With all these banquets, I'm starting to get the notion that everybody wants to see me retire," he said. Hemus commented that Musial was a positive "influence on the younger players" and said he selfishly hoped Musial would return in 1961.

Certainly by 1960, at the very latest, (in 1955 *Life* magazine ran the Ogden Nash poem, "The Tycoon," which joked about Musial's business savvy) Musial was "wealthy, independent of the game" and a friend of his believed that he earned around $200,000 per year with "no more than half" coming from his baseball contract.

Carl Warwick said when he discovered he had been traded from the Cardinals, Musial approached him. "He said, 'Let me tell you something now, Carl. Just for advice, you're going to a new town with a new team and you may end up living in that town. If somebody comes to you and asks you to make a speech to Little League kids or a Lions Club, make every one of them you can because if you're going to stay in that town, that's where your business people are going to be.' I did that and consequently got into the real-estate business [with] a bunch of those people I had met at those luncheons or baseball clinics. A lot of those people turned out to be investors for me."

Warwick ran into Musial years later and told him how his advice to make appearances "and not try to get money out of [groups] like some players did" had paid off. Musial responded, "That's how I built my restaurant up."

Although Musial knew little, perhaps nothing, about the restaurant business from the outset, Warwick believed "he was smart enough that he found out about how the business was to be run, and he was pretty good at keeping up with what was going on, but his part of the deal in the partnership was to be out front with people, and that's what he did—going around to tables, say[ing] hello, how you doing, stuff like that."

Musial, a baseball version of Horatio Alger, certainly has prospered—like an alchemist, he turned his relatively small salaries into a glistening, lucrative business kingdom. He went from being the son of an immigrant to becoming a polished man who, with an air of confidence, swapped smiles and stories with presidents while somehow remaining modest—although he once candidly admitted that he did get a kick out of "the fact that so many people have made such a fuss over me."

Joe Ravasio, former football coach at Ringgold and a current phys ed teacher in that school district, said Musial's office is adorned with pictures "of every sitting president from the time he played in the minor leagues." When Ravasio said how impressed he was, Musial replied, "Come here, I'm going to show you my favorite picture." It was one he took standing with President Kennedy and his wife. It was natural that Musial, a Catholic, would be drawn to Kennedy, the first elected Catholic president in the nation's history, and the two men developed a solid relationship.

James Michener wrote that he had come to know 60 athletes over his years of reporting and only one, Musial, was a Democrat. Athletes tend to live in a conservative world, Michener stated. He may not have taken into account the fact that Musial's ties to the Democratic party were deeply rooted, dating all the way back to his days in Donora, a staunchly Democratic community.

Michener also wrote that he first became acquainted with "the peculiar life a great athlete lives" when Kennedy was running for the presidency in the fall of 1960. In an effort to gain some publicity in Republican strongholds, an entourage of famous movie stars, intellectuals, Musial, and a few of the Kennedy girls were flown into 11 states, with the sole purpose of drumming up headlines. The one person in the group who "accounted for most of our success" was Musial. "I lived with him for the better part of two weeks and witnessed the awe and love in which he was held," Michener wrote.

Michener recalled one "windy night as we landed at a small Nebraska airport well after dusk. In the shadows we saw several hundred silent ranchers awaiting us....." One by one the celebrities were announced to the crowd: actors Jeff Chandler and Angie Dickinson, Pulitzer Prize–winning historian Arthur Schlesinger, and Ethel Kennedy. None produced applause from the Republican spectators. Then, when Musial appeared, even before his name was announced, "a low rumble arose from the crowd, and men pressed forward, dragging their boys with them." Musial made his way toward the gathering, "a tall, straight man...an authentic American folk hero...the men fell back to let him pass."

Fay Vincent, former baseball commissioner, said that Musial grew to become comfortable even among "powerful luminaries" such as Stephen Jay Gould, Tom Brokaw, and Bucky Bush, the brother of George H.W. Bush. Fay described Musial's demeanor as being "gentlemanly, gracious, comfortable with himself."

The most famous story relating to Musial and Kennedy involves the time the two first met in 1959. The 42-year-old presidential hopeful said, "They tell me you're too old to play baseball and I'm too young to be president, but maybe we'll fool them."

When Musial saw Kennedy after he had won the 1960 election, Musial flashed his incandescent smile and said, "I guess, Mr. President, we fooled them."

By 1961 it was apparent that the game of baseball may not have undergone a radical face lift, but television had certainly changed its appearance. Television was gradually, yet inexorably, changing all sports. For one thing, David Halberstam stated that even in the early days, television created "new pressures" that caused baseball officials to become "less able and less willing to make distinctions between what was good for the sport and what was good for them personally." The power of the networks that feed mountains of money to Major League Baseball today is enormous. Musial, many contend, was fortunate to have played when the games were, for the most part, more pure and at least somewhat less infiltrated by greed.

Halberstam also saw the negative impact of outside "commercial interests," such as television. Men such as Musial soon found the direction baseball was taking to be lamentable. Halberstam said that by 1980 in our nation's sports scene "there was no God but Madison Avenue and A.C. Nielsen was His prophet."

Broadcasters such as Harry Caray carried clout. When Warwick joined the Cardinals in 1961, he soon noticed, "Harry made a lot of bad comments about players on the radio. I think he might have been a little critical at times. Of course, to him, he probably thought he was telling the truth, and that's the way he saw it. But Harry Caray was not a Jack Buck. Jack was really a nice guy. He mixed with the players. He was just a super guy—everybody was crazy about Jack Buck."

Charlie James added, "I wouldn't say that he liked certain players more than others, but you kind of got that feeling a little bit. Some players he was always giving a hard time over the radio—like Boyer. He always did like Stan."

Vernon Law also knew of Caray's propensity for getting on Boyer in particular. It got so bad, Boyer's wife, Kathleen, once came to the park, sat in the wives' section and was promptly booed. Law said of Caray, "He'd say, 'Here's Boyer. There's a fly ball; oh-for-four.' And he didn't give some of the guys the credit that they deserved. That always bothered me. He was a little bit negative back then. He was a real competitor. He wanted the Cardinals to win every game, and when somebody was in a slump, he'd get down on him, and rightly so, I guess."

At any rate, as the Cardinals' spring-training camp opened in St. Petersburg, Florida, there was trouble brewing. A handful of white veterans were not housed in the team hotel near a yacht club. Musial and his family stayed in a private condo. Black players such as Curt Flood were forced to dwell in a boarding house in the city's black section, a place about five miles from camp and one he felt was not fit for his wife, who remained up north. Flood once stated, "I am pleased that God made my skin black, but I wish he had made it thicker."

Flood, irate with the Cardinals' housing, discussed the matter with owner Gussie Busch, who responded, "You mean to tell me that you're not staying here at the hotel with the rest of the fellas?" Busch was oblivious to the matter of the team's segregation, but soon he finally began to take serious steps to rectify the situation.

The Cards became the first big-league team to "house all their players under the same roof in spring training," but it took some time and effort.

On the last day of July, Bill White and Bill Bruton of the Detroit Tigers spoke to the Players Association reps in Boston about the housing issue during the second All-Star break. The association supported a resolution, asking team owners to treat black players the same as white ones in spring-training sites. The Cardinals' ownership, fearful of a black boycott of Anheuser-Busch beer products, promised the team no longer would stay at the Vinoy Park Hotel. In 1962 they would stay at two motels that bordered one another, with all the players mixed together.

The Cards got off to a 33–41 start, which prompted Hemus' firing. One of his coaches, Johnny Keane, took over. The mild, soft-spoken Keane never played a single day in the majors but had been in the Cardinals system for an eon and had been a manager in the minors for 20-plus seasons. He fared better than Hemus, going 47–33, laying the groundwork for the future, a future that held another world championship for the franchise but not for Musial.

Signs the club was heading for better days included the play of second baseman Julian Javier, a fine glove who made great plays so quickly that he earned the nickname "the Phantom." The native of the Dominican Republic had the outstanding range and quickness that enabled him to turn double plays with a hint of prestidigitation. "He had the magic glove at second base," said Warwick. "He was a great defensive ballplayer. He and Dick Groat were a great combination."

Boyer hammered 24 homers and drove in 95 to go with his .329 average. Like his brother Clete, he excelled on defense. Bob Gibson had a modest record of 13–12, but his ERA was 3.24, and he averaged just over seven strikeouts per nine innings of toil.

Always a fast worker, Gibson would, recalled Joe Cunningham, "pitch a ballgame in two hours. He didn't like to waste any time out there." He possessed feline grace and exuded athleticism. He had even played basketball for the Harlem Globetrotters.

Gibson, whose perpetual snarl and scowl advertised his burning competitive nature, took pride in every facet of his game, including his hitting. He once said of opposing pitchers, "They pitched to me as they would a hitter, not a pitcher." Years later, when asked his opinion of the split-finger fastball, he explained he never threw the pitch because he couldn't "spread my fingers that far apart so I didn't mess with it." Then he dismissively asserted, "I didn't need it." He added, "The day that I had my good stuff, I wasn't concerned too much about anybody."

"He was one of the fiercest competitors that I knew," said James. "You couldn't talk to him before the game because he would just shut himself off from almost everybody and all conversation, but after the game he was pretty relaxed, and you could talk to him and kid around—not so much after a loss."

He not only intimidated opposing players, he scared his own teammates. Gibson told of the time his catcher, McCarver, offered him advice during a tight spot in a game. "He'd come out to the mound, tell me, 'There's a guy on second base so watch him.' Well, shit, I knew he was there—I put him there.'"

As for Musial, his age was truly beginning to show. Not unlike an antique automobile, buffed to a shine but with underlying corrosion, Musial, said teammate Carl Warwick, "was usually on the training table, getting his shoulder worked on. When you're [that old] you're going to have some soreness."

Warwick speculated if Musial, muscles groaning and joints whimpering, was frustrated, it may have been because as he grew older and his stats tapered off, he had to decide if he should play another year or not. "I think he realized at that point that he could not play every day. And in those days we played more doubleheaders than they do now. He knew he couldn't play two games. I think the frustration was him trying to make the decision of 'What should I do, what do I want to do.'" Still, according to Warwick, Musial displayed no animus toward Keane, nor would he spout off to the media when he had to sit out games. Cunningham concurred, "If Stan was upset, he didn't show it."

Musial told writer James Michener that there were few days sadder than the one when he discovered his eyesight was slipping. It took until he had passed the age of 40 before, as he put it, "The ball looked so much smaller than it used to. First base seemed to be actually farther away." He said the team had specialists examine him "with the latest machines, and at the end they gave me the bad news. 'There's absolutely nothing wrong with your eyes.' I was just getting older, like everyone else."

Older, yes, but still capable. Of his 15 home runs in 1961, a phenomenal total for his age and a new record for a 40-year-old, his blast on June 23, 1961, made him the second-oldest player ever to connect for a grand slam. Musial, at 40 years and seven months, trailed only one other player from the modern era, Honus Wagner, who cracked his slam at the age of 41 years and five months.

Still, Musial's overall stats were disappointing, not up to his rigorous standards. On the final day of the season, as Musial was concluding his relatively fizzling season, his third disappointing one in a row—.288, 70 RBIs, and only 46 runs scored—elsewhere baseball history was being made.

In New York City, fans attending the October 1, 1961, Boston Red Sox game against the Yankees shied away from sitting in the left-field stands. By way of comparison, many of the 23,154 in attendance packed the right-field stands—Yankees announcer Phil Rizzuto said it was "hogged out there." After all, the fans reasoned, if Roger Maris, a pull hitter, homered, he would most likely deposit the ball there. He obliged. Maris, although fatigued, cracked his record-setting 61$^{st}$ home run to usurp Babe Ruth as the single-season home-run king. The ball flew over the head of outfielder Lu Clinton and flew into box 163D of section 33 in the sixth row of the lower deck in right field, a 360-foot poke. It was chaos as fans scrambled for the ball. A reward of $5,000, modest by today's standards for an act of baseball simony, was the bounty for the retrieval and return of the relic.

Maris, who would later help the Cardinals win a World Series, commented, "If I never hit another home run—this is the one they can never take away from me."

Musial continued to visit his mother in Donora. "Whenever St. Louis was in town, we would see him," said nephew Ed Musial "The last few years, now that he's older, he hasn't traveled as much, we just don't see as much of him."

When Ed saw his uncle in the early 1960s he was just a boy. "His time had passed when I was young," he said. Ed, consequently, had no idea back then how big of a star Stan was. "He was just my uncle, that's all. I knew he played baseball, and I knew he was a good baseball player, but he was my uncle, and when he came up and visited, everybody wanted something signed. Yet he signed everything. He was more than happy to sign. All I knew was he was my Uncle Stan, that's all."

In spring training of 1962 Musial and Boyer moved into the team motel, the Sheraton Outrigger. Thus, the Cardinals' black and white players stayed in the same facility for the first time ever. All the families intermingled, eating, playing, and swimming together.

The result was a wonderful feeling of camaraderie. The food at the motel was so bad players and their wives agreed to prepare their own food. Bill White and Bob Gibson were the main chefs, and Boyer and Larry Jackson were in charge of buying the meat and manning the grill. A total of 137 people stayed there, enjoying a weekly fried-chicken picnic, occasional fishing trips, kiddies' costume parties, and a cruise on team owner Gussie Busch's yacht.

Going into camp, Warwick said, the team felt good about their chances, an attitude typical of most players in spring training. Warwick said, "Keane was new [in his first full season as the manager] and everybody was getting used to him, and there were some trades made—Groat came in as our short-stop. We looked like a real good team leaving spring training."

Expansion hit the National League in 1962 as the league added the New York Mets and the Houston Colt 45's (later renamed the Astros). The last time the NL had increased their number of teams had been 70 years earlier, prior to the modern era. Playing against two weak sisters, especially the hapless Mets, seemed a sure way to pad players' stats. Musial had to salivate at that prospect. Plus, the Mets began their existence playing in the old Polo Grounds, a Musial favorite—he would hit .440 there in 1962.

Musial's prowess spawned many a quip. In 1962 Houston's Dick Farrell confessed he had thrown a spitball to Musial, which he hit safely. The pitcher ruminated, "I can't even get you out with an illegal pitch." Carl Erskine once joked, "I've had pretty good success with Stan. By throwing him my best pitch and backing up third."

Musial's skill somehow resuscitated, he embarked on what was arguably the greatest season ever for a 41-year-old hitter. The Cardinals baptized the Mets under fire, beating them 11–4 in the teams' season-opener on April 11, 1962, with Musial going 3-for-3. Ed Bouchee of the Mets stated, "What I thought made Musial so great was that he could hit the best curveball." He recalled the old baseball tale of a young prospect who had been invited to training camp only to write home soon, "Get my room ready, Mom. They started throwing the curveball." Bouchee concluded, "Musial never wrote that letter."

In May, a glum Musial slumped just when he was one hit shy of Honus Wagner's NL record for lifetime hits, needing six games to tie Wagner with a single against Juan Marichal. Oddly, Jim Tobin, who had served up Musial's first big-league hit, was in attendance that day. Musial's dry spell reached 1-for-25 proportions on May 19, 1962, before he connected off Ron Perranoski for a single to top Wagner's 3,430 hits. Throughout the long history of baseball, only Tris Speaker and Ty Cobb had accumulated more hits than Musial.

Another milestone toppled on June 22, 1962, when Musial surpassed Cobb's career total-bases record by rapping out two hits in an inning. Around that time, Stan and Lil attended their son's Notre Dame commencement exercises, which made Dick the first Musial to graduate college.

Soon Stan heated up, tattooing a late game-winning homer on July 7, 1962, against the Mets, then he began the next game with three straight homers in a 15–1 romp, making him the oldest player to hit three in a game. "I didn't believe in letting an inside pitch get away at the Polo Grounds," he beamed.

When President Kennedy attended the 1962 All-Star Game in Washington, D.C., on July 10, 1962, he spoke with Musial before the game. Later, Musial got a key hit, a line shot to right, and departed for a pinch-runner. As he trotted off the field, he noticed the president clapping for him.

At that moment, Musial's first thought was, *If only Lukasz Musial could see his son now.*

On July 25, 1962, Musial shattered Mel Ott's National League RBI record of 1,860 with a two-run homer versus Don Drysdale.

The Mets held a special night for Musial on August 18, which writer Bob Cutter noted as being "something almost unprecedented for an enemy player."

On September 26, 1962, Giants owner Horace Stoneham maintained his annual tradition of having Musial visit him. He reflected back to another get-together when he had asked Musial to "take it easy on us" and Musial responded with his five-home-run day. This time Musial joked, "Yeah, Horace, don't ask." The following day against San Francisco, he enjoyed his final 5-for-5 game, hoisting his average to .333.

As the season wound down, Musial had incredibly drawn a bead on yet another batting title. Keane showed confidence in his venerable veteran, playing him in 135 games. As had been expected, Musial, who arose phoenix-like in 1962, feasted (.468) on the Mets pitching. At season's end he wound up as the league's third-best hitter with a .330 average (the 17th year he hit .310 or higher), almost exactly what his final lifetime average would be. His sterling pinch-hitting also helped boost his average as he went 8-for-13 and reached base on 14 of his 19 pinch appearances.

Team trainer Bob Bauman had toiled painstakingly over Musial, and his rubdowns and work on Musial's sore shoulders had paid off. No 41-year-old has ever hit as high (nor, among players of the modern era, driven in as many runs (82)) as the resilient Musial. Also, only a handful of men at that age had a better on-base percentage, slugging percentage, hit and home run total, or more total bases than Musial did in 1962.

Warwick said Musial, still flexing some muscle, loved to hone in on the right-field stands at Sportsman's Park. "He had little hands, but he had a real quick bat and he would shoot the ball to the gaps a lot...he hit the ball all over, from foul line to foul line. I've never seen anybody be able to stay back and wait as long as he [did] before he [swung]. He was really quick at getting the bat out to the ball," even into the 1960s. Musial wound up with 19 homers and 82 ribbies, but the Cards finished a gloomy sixth, 17½ games out.

Hal Smith, who only half-jokingly nicknamed Musial, "Musical Hitter," said, "I remember one pitch he hit in Houston [in 1962] with a runner on first and second, and they were one run behind. He reached out, the ball was about two or three inches outside around his knees. I mean, down and away, a good fastball. He hit a line drive over the first baseman's head off of a fastball, a double. And I just shook my head, just like I did when Ted Williams was hitting, wow! If he'd have hit it over the third baseman's head I wouldn't have thought too much about it—he reached out, low and away, but he just reached out, and gave it a little flip, pulled that line drive, right down the right-field line.

"Stan was just a pure hitter. I pretty well knew what most hitters hit; I didn't know what he hit because he hit anything. We shoulda walked him.

"As a catcher, I sat behind Musial, Ted Williams, Mickey Mantle, Yogi Berra, Willie Mays, and everybody. I remember how Musial could always kinda do what he wanted to with the ball, according [to] what the situation was. If he needed a double, he'd pull one down the line or hit a 'tweener' [a ball finding a gap *between* outfielders]; if they needed a single, he'd hit one someplace, up the middle or over the shortstop's head; and if they needed a home run, he'd go for the fence."

Warwick said, "We had a mix of players—some older, some younger. The karma on the ballclub was fine; we all got along together. We didn't seem to gel as a team. We'd play some good games, then we'd go in a slump. We just never could put it all together in '62."

Looking to the following season, octogenarian Branch Rickey (who had a son nicknamed Twig), now back with the Cardinals as a senior consultant, advised it was time for Musial to retire. Musial's throwing and running abilities had waned, and Rickey thought it was time to gently pressure Musial into retiring honorably.

Both general manager Bing Devine and Musial recoiled at the recommendation. Musial, upon seeing a memo from Rickey with those views expressed, was insulted. Team owner Busch stepped into the fray and pronounced, "Since when do you ask a .330 hitter to retire?"

The year 1963 was, in many respects, a sad one. While it was the year Martin Luther King delivered his famous "I Have a Dream" speech in front of 200,000 spectators in the Washington Freedom March, it was also the year the bombing of a Birmingham, Alabama, church took the lives of four black children. It was the year the man Musial so admired, John F. Kennedy, was assassinated in Dallas. It was also the year that marked the demise of Musial as a player.

In January, baseball officials expanded the strike zone, redefining it from what had been the area from batters' armpits to the top of the knee to a more elongated zone—from the shoulders to the bottom of the knee.

Musial, as a respected, prominent player, would not be impacted much; perks come with the territory. Rogers Hornsby, a Cardinals star prior to Musial, knew that to be the case. A rookie pitcher once walked Hornsby, squawking over several close pitches. Veteran umpire Bill Klem glared at the upstart, then quieted him with a caustic, "Young man, when you pitch a strike, Mr. Hornsby will let you know."

Leo Durocher said stars such as Musial, those respected by umpires, "get a fourth strike. You're damn right they do. Especially in the clutch." Warwick commented, "Musial had such a good eye at the plate, if he didn't swing at it the umpire called it a ball most of the time."

Cubs pitcher Don Elston complained he seemingly could never retire Musial. He said, "One night I had him 2–2 in St. Louis. I threw a pitch that just covered the outside corner of the plate, and Jocko Conlan called it ball three. Next pitch Stan slapped one for a base hit." Classic Musial. The following game, Elston approached Musial by the batting cage and proclaimed, "Damn it, I finally had you." Musial, fully realizing the truth about baseball's star system, simply replied, "I know it." While many other players had a strike zone as large as a pair of Randy Johnson's hip boots, Musial's was the size of the cover of a copy of *The Sporting News*.

Stu Miller stated, "He never argued with an umpire, and consequently he got every pitch that was close. Although one time he got just a wee bit upset with the first-base umpire when he clearly had beat out a hit, but [that lasted] just two seconds. He was a mild-mannered guy. A lot of guys would have climbed all over the umpire."

Alex Grammas said that if today's umpires, many with generous strike zones, had worked the plate when Musial played, "they would have driven Stan crazy because he could take a pitch that was an inch outside for a ball and if they started calling them two or three inches outside as strikes, they'd have driven him nuts." That is to say, providing they didn't adjust their zones, compensating for superstars such as Musial.

The start of yet another spring-training session presented mixed feelings for Musial. The release from the icy grip of winter always brought a buoyant feeling, but the tedium of another exhibition season coupled with the passage of another year was unwelcome.

Breaking camp, the Cardinals, said outfielder Charlie James, felt "we were a first division team, and I remember [in 1960] getting a nice check around Christmas time for being in the first division." Being among the top half of the teams in the final standings back then was important to players; second-division finishers finished sans money, receiving no bonus for being among the teams in the top half of the league. Somehow, having finished third in 1960, despite faltering the next two seasons, "everybody felt like we could win it. We just felt good about our team," James said.

Even though Musial was 42, James stated when he was in the batter's box teammates always had the feeling that he'd come through. "He just exuded confidence even in his later years."

In this, Musial's final season, he again earned $100,000. Writer Maury Allen stated the Cardinals paid that amount but secretly wanted him to retire, paving the way to make "a run at the pennant." Former Cardinal Dick Groat, however, says he knew "absolutely nothing" about such machinations.

Musial's salary was especially large considering players' per diem money then was $8. Further, the Cardinals were hardly a generous club—if any player ate a meal on a team flight, he would be charged $4 of his meal money.

The Dodgers thrashed St. Louis on May 8, 1963, but a Musial homer gave him his 1,357th lifetime extra-base hit, propelling him past Babe Ruth's long-standing record. Eighteen days later he became the oldest modern-era player to appear in a doubleheader, and he scorched four hits to celebrate.

On June 1, 1963, Musial pulled a muscle, hindering his play for some time to come. Still, on July 9, he played in his 24th All-Star Game—matched later only by Hank Aaron and Willie Mays. He had made the All-Star squad, playing four different positions, 20 years in a row—not counting 1945, the year rosters were selected for the All-Star Game but no game was held due to wartime travel restrictions. That was also the year Musial was serving in the navy.

Musial also displayed versatility during regular-season competition and would go on to become the only player ever to appear in 1,000-plus games in the infield and in the outfield.

In his final All-Star at-bat he pinch-hit for Ed Bailey, lining out to Al Kaline against Jim Bunning. His lifetime line for All-Star play included a record 40 total bases and six homers, 20 hits, and a .317 batting average.

Hitting poorly into late July, Musial contemplated retirement. Coincidentally, he decided to call it quits right after his double beat old foe Warren Spahn on Senior Citizens Day. He breakfasted with Devine the following morning and announced, "After this year, Bing, I'll have had it."

On July 28, 1963, Dick Ellsworth whiffed Musial three straight times, a shocking and fully unprecedented occurrence.

On August 12 Musial formally made the announcement that he would hang up his jet-black, spit-shined spikes forever, effective after the Cardinals' last game of the season. Twenty-two seasons, after all, was a very long time to play the demanding sport of baseball at its highest level. His retirement would conclude the longest stretch of time for a major-leaguer playing for just one club to date.

Groat recalled the yearly family picnics held at Grant's Farm, owned by the Busch family and previously owned by Ulysses Grant. In 1963 the event fell on a particularly muggy St. Louis day. Players' children scampered around, many having their pictures snapped as they sat atop the trunk of an elephant. "The Cardinals' family picnics were really special," Groat said. "They had all kinds of wildlife and game out there. They had Clydesdales; it was a neat place. And then all of the sudden, the news media started coming in with the television trucks. Then you started realizing something was going to happen.

"That's when Stan announced his retirement. I knew nothing about it until Stan announced it that night at the picnic. I was disappointed. He was such a joy to play with. I really hadn't given any thought to his retirement because I thought he was having a heckuva year. Then he *really* turned it on after the retirement announcement."

When his mother received word of his impending retirement, she muttered dazedly, "I just couldn't believe it. Never to see Stan on the field again. Twenty-five years gone, just like that." She had been crocheting while listening, as she always did, to a Cardinals game, when she heard the announcer reveal the news. "I couldn't stop crying," she said.

A picture accompanying a UPI story about Stan's retirement featured Lil weeping openly in the background and Stan, left hand pressed to mouth, with a glassy-eyed look on his face. The story, which described Musial as a "lithe and slightly stooped slugger," stated his jersey number would be retired in the fall and that an executive job with the Cardinals awaited him.

"I've dreamed for a long time of playing in one more World Series," said Musial, who added that no matter his stats in his final year, "I just think I've had enough." The article went on: "Baseball has been my life," Stan told the shocked gathering of players, their wives and children, and a few newsmen. "I love baseball. I like nothing better to do than play baseball."

Making his plans public may have spurred him on to excel, motivated him. "Yeah," noted Groat, "and he motivated us with him. We just kept playing better and better and better. We won 19 out of 20 [from August 30 through September 15]."

Musial had already played in more games than any other NL player, and such toil had finally caught up to him (he would compile just 337 official at-bats that year). Long before the farewell tours of stars such as Cal Ripken Jr., Musial was honored in NL ballparks on the road when he made his last visit to those venues.

"There were times when Musial was in danger of being drowned in treacle.... Moist eyes blinked from coast to coast," wrote Theodore M. O'Leary. The first two whistle stops for Musial were Los Angeles and Houston. He received gifts such as a rocking chair painted in Cardinals red. He would discreetly give away some of the gifts that he had no need for.

Meanwhile, players such as shortstop Groat, acquired from the Pirates in November 1962 for Julio Gotay and Don Cardwell, kept the Cards in contention virtually all season long—they were never as many as eight games back.

Groat, who had won the 1960 NL MVP when he tied the record for the fewest home runs (two) by an MVP winner, fit in well with the Cardinals right away. "First of all, they treated me so great when I went to St. Louis. I'm very proud of the fact that in '63, hitting in front of Stan, I was second in the MVP voting to Sandy Koufax [who had won 25 games with a 1.88 ERA and 306 strikeouts]. Part of that was because I hit in front of Stan."

Bill James called the 1963–1964 Cardinals infield of Groat, Bill White at first, Julian Javier at second, and third baseman Ken Boyer the best of the 1960s. Groat said, "I was extremely proud to be part of the [first-ever starting] infield [made up of regular-season teammates] that ever started in the All-Star Game. And that was an infield that *players* voted for. You weren't elected [by the] public the way it is today, which is garbage. It means a lot more to all of us to be elected by your peers. We played good, solid defense.

"Kenny was just a magnificent third baseman. It must run in the family because Clete was a great one with the Yankees, too, but Kenny was marvelous. Javier really came along as a second baseman, and having played so many years with [Bill] Mazeroski, I really was fortunate to move from the greatest second baseman ever to play the game in Mazeroski to, without a doubt, the second-best second baseman in the National League. Bill White was just one of the greatest competitors I ever played with, just one of the great guys in baseball.

"That 1963 season was the greatest season I ever had in my life. Better than I had in '60 when I won the MVP. I hit in front of Musial all year, and I never had better balls to hit than I ever had in my life because nobody was going to walk Dick Groat to get to Stan Musial. Hitting in front of Musial was a privilege that I'll always thank the Lord for." Groat did, in fact, accomplish career highs in 1963 for hits, doubles, triples, runs, RBIs, on-base percentage, slugging percentage, and total bases.

"Believe it or not, once he announced his retirement, when we got red hot and got back in the pennant race, Stan got more big hits than you can imagine," continued Groat. "He was absolutely sensational. He led that team into a pennant race. At age 42, he was magnificent.

"He was so calm, and so nice, and so friendly, and so warm as a teammate. If you asked him for advice any time, he was always willing to help you. I can't say what a pleasure and what a privilege it was [to play with him]. I'm proud to say I played one season with Stan Musial."

August 26, 1963, found the team in San Francisco, where Mayor George Christopher made Musial the city's honorary mayor. Staying at the Palace Hotel, Musial dined with Schoendienst in the dim Tudor Room tucked away in a corner of the hotel. Often the hotel featured the music of Red Nichols and his band, one of Musial's favorites.

The team's next stop was Philadelphia, where Musial tried to get some rest at the Warwick Hotel, but demands on his time continued unabated.

After a brief four-day home stand, Musial made his final swing through Pittsburgh on September 6 to take part in Stan Musial Weekend. His final game in the ivy-walled Forbes Field took place on September 8, 1963. Prior to the contest, his mother, seated in her normal spot behind the Cards' dugout, stated, "I'll be crying, so I might hide somewhere so Stan won't see me. I know how this affects him. We're all sad about it."

Before one contest his mother, attired in a simple pink cotton dress, stood by his side at home plate and witnessed a mail truck easing its way onto the field to drop off a load of 16 sacks of mail, all addressed to her son as part of radio station KDKA's promotion to honor Musial. A win in the first game of a doubleheader gave St. Louis a nine-game winning streak, but Musial went hitless at Forbes Field and left town hitting .241 for 1963.

The Cardinals were then only three and a half games out, but a victory in their September 6 contest could have been devastating. In the first inning of the opener of a doubleheader, Pirates pitcher Don Cardwell broke one of Groat's ribs, causing him to be out of the lineup until September 10. The

Cards lost the second game of the doubleheader but rebounded the next day to begin a 10-game winning streak.

Groat chuckled, "The one thing I didn't do was run. I started [the next game] and doubled down the right-field line; that was the first time I had [really] run after I had the broken rib. I said, 'Wow, did that hurt.' And I'm holding myself in. I didn't even get a chance to move off second base and Musial hit a line shot into center field and I had to score. And I'm hurting all the way around."

Earlier, the first time Groat batted, he had singled and that time Musial made it easy on Groat. "I just got to first base and Stan hit a bullet right over the first baseman's head, and I'm running—I was never so happy to see an umpire put his fingers up [indicating] it was a home run. I didn't get a chance to relax; he hit the first pitch after I got on base both times. I wanted to laugh because I thought, *Only Musial could do that to me as sore as my rib was.*"

September 10 was the day of Musial's first plate appearance as a grandfather. With several fans bellowing, "Hit one for the baby," he celebrated by clubbing a home run off Chicago's Glen Hobbie, his 11th and his next-to-last one he'd hit as a baseball Methuselah.

After battling each other for 18 full seasons, Warren Spahn faced Musial for the last time on September 13, 1963. The crafty southpaw fired an outside, knee-high fastball, "what I thought was a perfect pitch," he said. Musial took it to left for a double, then scored the only run the Cardinals needed to defeat Spahn, crossing home on a Boyer homer in a 7–0 win.

Spahn stated Musial was "the only batter I intentionally walked with the bases loaded." Once, with two out and a full count on Musial, Spahn refused to give him a hittable pitch. He threw the ball way outside, forced in a run, and then went on to win 2–1. "If I had given Musial a good pitch, we'd probably have lost," he said. While he had always mixed things up on Musial, Spahn said the Cardinals star "seemed to know what kind of pitch I was going to give him even before I wound up."

When St. Louis swept a September 15 doubleheader from the Braves, they had rattled off 19 wins over 20 games and had drawn to within one game of Los Angeles.

The following day, the Dodgers trekked to Busch Stadium with, by all reckoning, the pennant at stake. The first game pitted Ernie Broglio against Johnny Podres and featured a game-tying solo homer, a thunderclap-loud poke in the seventh by Musial off Podres. It was to be his last home run ever. The Dodgers spoiled his heroics with a two-spot in the ninth to win 3–1. The next day Sandy Koufax topped Curt Simmons, twirling a nifty 4–0 shutout, losing his no-hit bid on a late Musial line single. "Podres and Koufax were untouchable," lamented Groat.

The losses did not negate the fact that Musial had always hit well in the clutch. Bob Friend observed, "I had my problems with him. I had good luck at times, but he was the kind of hitter that when the game was on the line he'd usually deliver, that's why he was so good. He'd break a pitcher's heart. You figure you made a great pitch and he could find the holes. It may be a high bounder over the mound, but it would get into center field or it would be just out of the reach of the shortstop. And then when he had to deliver a longball late in the game, he could do it. The guy was phenomenal doing that."

The September 18 series finale found the Cards up 5–1 as late as the end of seven innings only to drop a heartbreaker 6–5 in 13 frames, despite two hits by Musial. The most damaging blow came in the top of the ninth when Dick Nen lifted a pinch-homer to send the game into extra innings. The sweep was complete, and the fading Cardinals were four games out.

"Musial was as easygoing, as pleasant a man as I've ever known," said Groat. However, he added, "I was told he got upset in the locker room when we lost to the Dodgers in that game. I led off [the tenth inning] with a triple, and Stan would have been hitting behind me, but he was taken out for defense in the [top of the] eighth inning because we had a lead; and then they tied it up in the ninth."

Then Musial's replacement, 23-year-old Gary Kolb, came to the plate. Groat recounted, "They didn't send a pinch-hitter up for the kid, who didn't want to face [Ron] Perranoski, and he struck out on three pitches." Dodgers manager Walt Alston intentionally walked Ken Boyer and Bill White before Perranoski induced Curt Flood to hit into a fielder's choice, with Groat thrown out at the plate on a force play. Mike Shannon followed with a ground out to end the threat.

"They finally beat us, and I guess Stan got upset [in the locker room]. We didn't see it, but I heard later on he was unhappy because he hoped we were going to score after I led off with a triple," Groat said. While it was not like Musial to tear up the locker room, he was livid.

True to form, he did not, for example, rip manager Johnny Keane. Groat said there was never friction between the two. "I never heard him ever being in any kind of controversy; he got along with everybody."

Charlie James said that while the team did feel the white-hot pressure of the race, "Stan, more than anybody else, tried to keep everybody on an even keel and not get to feeling too much pressure. He wouldn't get up on a chair and make a speech, but he was a quiet leader."

Even with pennant hopes becoming moribund, Warwick noted, "He was such a good ballplayer, baseball was so easy for him, there was never any reason for him to get frustrated." Still, he continued to yearn for one more pennant, one more World Series ring.

On September 20, 1963, Musial, who was playing in his $22^{nd}$ of the Cardinals' last 24 games, dragged himself to the outfield and took a meaningless 1-for-4 in a 1–0 loss to the Reds. Musial was drained. So were the Cardinals, who would limp into Chicago on September 24, lose their sixth in a row, and get knocked out of the pennant race.

After one contest down this stretch, he sat almost motionless for 20 minutes in front of his locker, half out of his uniform, sipping a paper cup of beer. His exhaustion was oppressive. Indeed, after leaving the game on September 24 in the seventh inning after singling, he trudged into the clubhouse, created a makeshift pillow from towels, and napped on an equipment trunk.

Age had not mellowed Musial's desire to win one iota. Warwick pointed out that even in his waning seasons, "If he hit a ground ball, he ran it out, he hustled." Over the years, such hustle, along with his natural speed, had earned him many infield hits.

Groat added, "He was a great competitor. He couldn't have been the great Hall of Famer he was without being a great competitor. He was intense.

"We would have loved to put Stan in the World Series in his last year because when he announced his retirement, we were in [third] place [six games out], and it was almost like he lit all of us up and we made a great run."

St. Louis eventually tumbled, finishing second for their best showing since 1949. The Dodgers had neatly wrapped it up, just as Musial was wrapping up his career.

The morning of September 29 began for Musial at 7:45. He peered out a window to see dark, rain-soaked clouds. He dressed quickly in a conservative black suit, white shirt, black shoes, and dark tie, somehow suggestive of mourning, then attended the 9:00 Mass at St. Raphael's.

Later he gobbled down his breakfast and by 10:30 hopped into his blue Cadillac, steered it down his curved driveway, and made his way to Busch

Stadium one last time as an active ballplayer. He greeted a neighbor and, acknowledging the way his life had gone, mused, "You know? Everything breaks for me. It started out to be cloudy, and look at it now."

At the park he was greeted by the marquee, which sported the message: A FOND SO-LONG TO STAN. Inside, the park was bedecked with bunting in honor of the occasion. When he first spotted his manager, he joked, "Am I playing today?"

Pressure on Musial had built as his finale neared, with everyone hoping for him to exit the game with a flourish. He remained, as always, unflappable. He calmly stated that he planned on staying in the game until he hit safely but added, "If I don't get a hit, it's not going to worry me." During batting practice, taken under ever-clearing skies, the fans' intensity level swelled and the crowd went wild with every swing. He crushed two balls into the stands in right and blasted another off the screen.

Musial signed autographs for seven Reds players with a six-piece Dixieland band swinging away in the background. Finally, he retreated to the privacy of the men's room to compose and review his speech. At 1:30 he walked the ramp leading to the field.

Pregame ceremonies stretched for nearly an hour and featured friends, family, and dignitaries sitting on folding chairs set up near the mound. Teammates respectfully formed a queue along the third-base line, and the Reds did the same down the first-base line. Lil sat next to Stan wearing a hat that fittingly bore a resemblance to a crown and a coat with a regal-looking fur trim. Team captain Ken Boyer, representing Musial's teammates, presented him with their farewell gift, a ring adorned with Musial's jersey number—6—in diamonds. Crude homemade signs spangled the stands with heartfelt messages such as "Stan for Pres."

Standing in front of a phalanx of microphones, a rather uncomfortable Musial gave an emotional address to the crowd, a simple "it's been fun and thank you" type speech. The visibly nervous Musial stated, "As long as I live, this will be the day I'll remember most.... If my baseball career has taught me anything, it is this: the opportunity America offers any young man who wants to get to the top of his chosen career." At that point, wrote Theodore M. O'Leary, "The crowd shrieked itself hoarse." Musial then hopped into an open convertible for a turtle-paced tour around the border of the field, a farewell spin, and soon the game began.

Even though Groat was a teammate of Musial for just this one season, he was emotional about Musial's departure. "It wasn't an easy game, I know for me, because it was such a privilege to play with this man. I was upset that Stan was retiring that day."

In general, teammates "kind of stayed away from Stan that day because it was his day," said Groat.

When the 27,576 fans, including his mother, whom he had flown into town, finally settled down after the pregame festivities, they were in for a contest that would stretch to an interminable 14 innings. The contest began with two standout pitchers on the mound, Gibson and the hard-throwing Jim Maloney. Musial was in left field but would be long gone before the game's end three hours and 45 minutes later.

In the first inning, directly after the first pitch to Musial at 2:25 PM, the game came to a halt and the ball was taken out of play and presented to Sid Keener of the Hall of Fame. Musial later revealed that baseball official asked him not to swing at the first pitch so they could retrieve the ball for posterity.

Moments later, home-plate umpire Al Barlick, who had umped Musial's first big-league game 22 years earlier, rang Musial up on a nip-the-corner curveball, torn no doubt between his reluctance to punch out a class act in his final game and his own duty.

In the fourth, on a 1–1 fastball, Musial rifled a single into right-center field, past Reds second baseman Pete Rose, who would soon win the Rookie of the Year Award. At that point, given the chance to exit the game on a positive note, having just basked in a standing ovation, Musial elected to remain in the game. Perhaps he was hungry for just one more hit, much like a greedy game-show contestant salivating, "I'm going to play on."

In the sixth inning, as Musial stepped into the box, assuming his corkscrew stance, a contortionist's delight, for one final time, announcer Harry Caray admonished his listeners to "Take a good look, fans, take a good look. This might be [Musial's] last time at bat in the major leagues. Remember the stance and the swing."

It was a stance that, years later, caused commissioner Fay Vincent to ask Musial if anyone at all had ever tried to alter his appearance at the plate. Vincent related, "I think he was slightly bemused by the question. 'Commissioner,' he said, 'why would they do that? I was always hitting .500.'"

At precisely 3:47 PM, Musial's last at-bat produced a single on a Maloney 2–1 low, inside curve that he bounced sharply to right, driving in Curt Flood from second base for the game's first run. Defying the tacit rule prohibiting cheering in the press box, even reporters "stood and applauded" his final hit and run driven in. One writer, who realized Musial had bowed out as he had broken in—with a two-hit game—quipped, "He hasn't improved at all."

Musial later mused that "the odd thing about those two base hits is that I got them past Pete Rose.... He dove both times, and the balls went under his glove." He added that Rose banged out three hits that day, so on Musial's very last day as a player, Rose, who would end up with more career hits than anyone, "was gaining on me."

After Musial's third at-bat, he vanished from the game as an active player. A smattering of boos cascaded down when Keane inserted pinch-runner Gary Kolb, who trotted to first base, congratulated Musial, and watched as the Cardinals legend, showered with applause and love, jogged to his wife for a quick kiss and then disappeared into the dugout. Kolb would go on to hit .209 lifetime, becoming a mere footnote in the annals of the game.

Musial had managed to compile a perfectly symmetrical career-hit total, with 1,815 of his hits coming on the road and 1,815 coming at home. His home and away home-run totals were also balanced well—252 at home versus 223 on the road. Furthermore, only Ty Cobb, with 3,900 lifetime hits collected in a Tigers uniform, had more hits for one club than Musial. Through his final day, no National Leaguer had more hits, extra-base hits, runs, or RBIs than the Man.

George F. Will once observed, "Baseball's rich in wonderful statistics, but it's hard to find one more beautiful than Stan Musial's hitting record.... He didn't care where he was, he just hit."

Musial peeled off his shirt in the clubhouse, hung it up, patted his familiar No. 6 on the jersey and the letters spelling out his name. "Pal," he said, "you're all right, if I do say so myself."

The media swamped him once more, and Musial, sitting on a red stool in front of his locker, confessed that going into his final game he was apprehensive about the possibility of going hitless, but after pounding out his hits he "felt like making a comeback." He dressed and waited in the trainer's room for the game to end.

It labored on eight more innings, and the Cardinals prevailed 3–2, winning by the same score of Musial's first big-league game, but the outcome this time seemed inconsequential. Other than the game marking Musial's exodus, the 1963 season finale truly was a totally meaningless contest. The Cards had already been mathematically eliminated from the pennant race and wound up with 93 wins, their most since 1949, good for a second-place finish behind the Dodgers. Better things were in the near future for the Cardinals.

Later, Musial glanced back on the season. "I hadn't really made up my mind [initially] one way or the other whether I would play another year.... My RBI production was good, but my average wasn't. I was taking called third strikes, something I'd rarely done."

Musial stated that he was able to walk away from the game because he played approximately "four more years than I had any right to expect." Plus, he said, he never wanted to think of himself as "a liability to a ballclub." He had been steadily losing the ability to change his mind at the last split second and to swing crisply at a ball he initially felt would be out of the strike zone. Then, when told that by retiring he would miss out on breaking Ty Cobb's record for the most games played in the majors, Musial cracked, "What's wrong with being second to Ty Cobb?"

Butch Yatkeman, former Cardinals clubhouse manager, commented that none of the Cardinals he had dealt with in almost a half-century "loved baseball any more than Stan or hated to give up the uniform any more than Stan."

Former teammate Joe Cunningham said that for Musial, "every day going to the ballpark was a thrill for him. And he felt he was the luckiest guy in the world, being able to play ball." Musial ended the year at .255, tied for his worst batting average ever, and his 10 doubles and 86 hits were also career lows. Yet he went out as a baseball monolith.

Still with no trace of gray in his hair, Musial finished sixth on the all-time home-run list with 475, including 15 hit when he was 40, 19 as a 41-year-old, and a dozen more tossed in during his final season. Only Ted Williams, with 44, had ever before produced 40 or more homers while in his forties, and now Musial had topped him with 46. Musial also set records for the most home runs by a 40- and a 42-year-old player (Williams had hit 13 at the age of 40 for the former high-water mark, while no 42-year-old player had ever before topped five home runs). Musial had nothing left to prove.

It had been a remarkable quarter-century ride through professional baseball for a remarkable man and now, sadly, the Stan Musial era was over.

## CHAPTER EIGHT

# *Beyond the Field*

Certainly by 1964, Musial was financially set for life. Writer Tim Cohane said at the time that "He brought up his family comfortably, unostentatiously.... Instead of tossing away his money, he invested it wisely. As a result, no former star ever faced a sounder future."

He was emotionally sound, too. Roger Kahn called Musial one of a handful of great athletes who "are able to prevail in retirement. Their glory intact, they move from the ballpark to other arenas, still special heroes." Such rare men, he said, "learned how to transform obstacles into stepping-stones."

The lives of athletes are drastically different than the masses who toil for, say, 30 years before they can quit and draw a pension. George F. Will stated, "Great athletes compress life's trajectory unnaturally—rapid ascent, glamorous apogee, slow decline. Most great athletes live most of their life after their life, as it were. 'Didn't you used to be a ballplayer?'" For them, retirement can mean a loss of identity.

That was not the case with Musial. He once stated that he had been prepared for retirement: "The last two years it had become work. The ball was getting to look smaller and smaller, and it was hard to bounce back game after game."

Erskine pointed out Musial was not only successful outside the realm of baseball with his restaurant business, but "the Cardinals kept him on as an officer for years to do all the things he'd be naturally able to do with his personality and his willingness and his class reputation."

His front-office duties would entail, quite naturally, "public relations and [using] his popularity" to further the Cardinals' image and business. "In those days, with teams having superstars that were tied to them, it [their

195

relationship] lasted well after their playing days. You mention [Joe] DiMaggio, you say, 'Yankees.' When you mention Ted Williams, you say, 'Red Sox.' You mention Jackie Robinson, you say 'Dodgers.' When you say, Musial, it's absolutely 'Cardinals.' So that was valuable to the club years after he played."

Bobby Cox remembered, "The first time I met him was in Tulsa, Oklahoma. He was working for the Cardinals at that time, retired, going around watching the hitters. He sat in our dugout, the *visiting* team, and talked a little bit about hitting. It was a thrill for everybody on our team for him to do that."

So, from visiting the minors and working with young players to doing P.R. work, Musial was kept active, traveling frequently, especially with the 1964 club. Former outfielder Bob Skinner said Musial was often around the club and was always "more than willing to talk about hitting" but didn't formally give instruction to the Cards.

Erskine said, "I'm sure Stan, being a part of the organization, [was] used in [many] ways because, certainly, what kid in the minors wouldn't want Musial talking to him about how to make contact with certain pitches? Plus, I'm sure he did signings at the ballpark, and Stan's in the Hall of Fame, having that credential is really an attraction to the fans."

Charlie James recalled Musial's being around the Florida clubhouse in '64, soon to become a yearly harbinger of spring. "He was always around there—he loved to come to spring training." In short, he took to retirement quite well.

In February 1964 he also took on an unpaid job, traveling at his own expense as the adviser for the President's Council on Physical Fitness and Sports, a cause he deeply believed in. He would hold the job until 1967, when he took on the duties of Cardinals general manager.

Musial also continued to make appearances that star players typically made. For instance, in February, before the Cardinals started their training camp, Musial, along with Joe Garagiola and Yogi Berra, was on stage at the New York chapter of the Baseball Writers Association of America dinner.

When the Cardinals got off to a rough start in 1964, rumors flew like a redbird: manager Keane would be fired; general manager Bing Devine had not made enough moves going into the season, so he would be axed; and one story had Musial coming out of retirement to revive the team.

On August 17, with fourth-place St. Louis trailing the Phils by nine games, team president Branch Rickey did replace general manager Bing Devine with Bob Howsam.

On September 1, 1964, Musial got a scare when, overworked and torn in many directions, he collapsed at Busch Stadium and was hospitalized. But he quickly recovered from his bout with exhaustion and dehydration.

Dick Groat reportedly had "no baseball respect" for Keane and was convinced Red Schoendienst should be the manager, believing that he could lead them to the pennant. He would prove correct about Schoendienst, but not for a few more seasons.

The team stuck with Keane, who the other Cardinals appreciated, and, in a tremendously tight race, won the flag by a scant one game over the Phillies, who had folded down the wire. The Cards still trailed by 11 games on August 23 and were still in fourth place as late as September 3, 1964. The Phils were still up by six and a half games with a mere dozen games to go on their schedule. They had reduced their magic number to seven—clinching the pennant seemed inevitable. Even the Cardinals players felt they hadn't a prayer. The race was so tight that the Giants, who finished fourth, were not eliminated from the race until their 161st game. In addition, entering the final day of the season, the Phillies were just one game off the pace set by the Reds and Redbirds, now tied for first. Thus, four teams had entered the final weekend of the season with a chance to capture the NL pennant, and there remained a mathematical chance for baseball's first-ever three-way tie for first place at the end of the regular season.

The Cardinals secured the pennant on the last day of the season, with an 11–5 win over the Mets while the Reds absorbed a 10–0 pounding by the Phillies. The Cards went 28–11 down to the wire, while the Phillies folded.

In the middle of the Cards' typical champagne celebration in the locker room, a beaming Musial soaked up the joy of the occasion. When he stuck his head out of the clubhouse, a throng on hand cheered him. He beamed, waved, then pointed toward the clubhouse, saying, "They won it, not me."

A writer cornered Musial and commented that it was unfortunate he hadn't played just one more season so he could have been on another pennant winner. Musial, always graceful and modest, replied, "If I had played one more year, we wouldn't have won the pennant, because then we wouldn't have traded for Lou Brock."

Many factors led to the team's success, but their top-of-the-lineup catalysts were often singled out. "You had Curt Flood leading off and Lou Brock hitting second. I don't know of a combination any better than that in baseball," said Carl Warwick.

The World Series against New York came down to Game 7. A fatigued Bob Gibson had labored through 10 innings on October 12, winning while whiffing 13 Yankees. Now, working his third start of the Series, this one on just two days' rest, he labored through nine innings, struck out nine batters, and won by two runs, though giving up an un-Gibson-like five runs. When Keane was asked why he let a struggling Gibson go the route, the St. Louis skipper delivered the now-classic line, "I had a commitment to his heart."

Two days after the Series ended, the Yankees fired Berra; a week later they announced they had hired Keane, who had resented Rickey's interference and was willing to leave St. Louis. So, in a bizarre twist, both World Series managers left the clubs they had just guided to a pennant.

Keane, whose entire 31-year baseball career was spent in the Cardinals organization, went into a tailspin. In 1965 his Yankees finished in sixth place, and the following season he was fired just 20 games into the year. Less than a year later, the 55-year-old Keane died of a heart attack.

On May 8, 1966, 57-year-old Busch Stadium saw its final game. The creaky, arthritic facility played host to the Giants, who manhandled the Cardinals 10–5, with Willie Mays hitting the final home run at the park. At the end of the game, Bill Stocksick, a groundskeeper who had set down the original home plate in 1909, unearthed the current plate. The team had it helicoptered to the "new" Busch Memorial Stadium. There, Miss Redbird of 1966, Joan Nolan, and Musial lowered the relic into its new resting place.

In the fall Musial and other ballplayers took a two-week tour of the Vietnam battle zone. The troops seemed most interested in Musial. One wounded soldier gushed, "You're the best." "No," replied Musial, "You are."

Hank Aaron recalled his trip with Musial to visit the soldiers. He said, "Stan and I got to know each other pretty well, and I know how humble he is. I know what kind of person he is—he was a great ballplayer, but he was even a greater man. I think the world of Stan." In fact, Musial was one of Aaron's favorite players as he was growing up in Alabama "because [of] the way he carried himself as a human being." Echoing the sentiments of the soldier in Vietnam, Aaron added, "Stan was a great humanitarian, a great man."

In 1966 the Cardinals finished 12 games off the pace of the pennant-winning Dodgers, managing to win only 83 games. Still, they drew almost 500,000 fans more than they had the previous year, so money wasn't a huge issue as the team began to lay plans for the following season.

The nucleus of a decent team was in place. Before Bob Howsam gave way to Musial as the team's general manager, he had acquired outfielder Roger

Maris on December 8, 1966, for third baseman Charley Smith, who would contribute virtually nothing to the Yankees. Given the opportunity to get a fresh start as the GM of the Reds, Howsam left the Cardinals in January 1967. He was destined for fame in Cincinnati, as he began to put together a team that would soon be known as the Big Red Machine, a dynastic club that would capture four pennants and two world championships.

In St. Louis Musial took over from Howsam and was labeled "the best ballplayer ever to become top dog in a front office," by *Sports Illustrated*. Previously, the only big-name players to become general managers were men such as Hank Greenberg, Eddie Collins, and Joe Cronin. Busch said the decision to give Musial the GM job took "a matter of 15 minutes." After being hired on January 23, Musial, without much time to prepare for his new role, reported to his office in St. Petersburg for spring training at Al Lang Field.

By his own admission, Musial wasn't well versed in the nuances of baseball's regulations dealing with contracts, trades, and other matters he would now have to handle, but he often conferred with Bing Devine, and things worked out well. In fact, when Devine was asked how he felt Musial would do as the GM, he replied, "Name one thing that Musial has ever done wrong."

The team was coming off seventh- and sixth-place finishes, but with players on hand such as Orlando Cepeda, who would go on to win the NL MVP unanimously, the team, which featured a $400,000-plus payroll, then among the most generous ever in baseball, was about to embark on a stupendous season.

Musial explained he had no desire to be the field manager. He felt if he held the job as manager, he would be too demanding of his players. He had no stomach for the "daily diet of winning and losing." As the general manager, said Musial, "You don't have to concern yourself so totally with one loss."

Musial's longtime friend Red Schoendienst was the club's manager. "Red was a great player, and he understood the game," said Groat. "He was around the game, and he could handle people very, very well."

Musial's baseball mind was a fantastic asset to the organization, but when praised, he would merely flash a broad grin and downplay his contributions. Often he joked self-deprecatingly, "I have a darn good job with the Cardinals, but please don't ask me what I do." Some felt that such talk proved that he was never comfortable in management. Others argued Musial was simply being modest and that he did indeed contribute, especially in connection with player development.

Still, Theodore M. O'Leary said in *Sports Illustrated* that placing Musial "in a dark business suit and sober tie, with a sharp pencil in his pocket" was "like making Paul Bunyan vice president of a lumber company."

Speer Ruey played baseball for Donora High School in the late 1960s and attended a tryout for the Cincinnati Reds along with Ken Griffey Sr. and later one run by the Cardinals. About five years after that, and about 16 years after Musial first met Ruey when he was a child, Musial ran into him, asked him how things had worked out, and told him, "I saw your name on a list of prospects out of high school and recognized it." Ruey was taken aback by Musial's sharp memory, which served him well in his front-office role.

It had become evident that in recent years St. Louis had taken on a philosophy that varied greatly from the days of Branch Rickey, who relied, as a rule, upon homegrown players rather than those acquired in trades. Now, under Musial, the Cards returned to depending mainly on players they had developed such as McCarver, Javier, Maxvill, Shannon, Flood, Gibson, Steve Carlton, Bobby Tolan, Ray Washburn, et al.

The defense looked good, and Vernon Law said that even the under-appreciated Maxvill was a great glove who "covered the ground well and turned the double play well."

In addition, playing in a larger home park than the Cards had been accustomed to, they were wise to employ speedy ballplayers to cover ground on defense and to manufacture runs.

Musial and other organizational leaders made decisions to elevate three virtually untested pitchers to the Cardinals: Carlton, with just 77 big-league innings to his credit; Dick Hughes, who had even less experience than Carlton, with just 21 innings; and Ron Willis, who had only pitched three innings in the majors. The additions would pay off well. The 22-year-old Carlton, who would go on to become one of the greatest left-handed pitchers ever, won 14 contests to go with his sparkling 2.98 ERA. Hughes, a 29-year-old rookie, bloomed late with 16 wins, a 2.67 ERA, seventh-best in the league. Willis, also a rookie, chalked up 10 saves, seventh-best in the NL.

Musial also promoted two outfielders—24-year-old Alex Johnson, coming off a year in which he had just 86 big-league at-bats, and 21-year-old Tolan, who had 93 at-bats for the 1966 Cardinals. The club liked the idea of giving them more exposure to the majors, grooming them for what turned out to be bright futures.

Musial and Schoendienst also decided Shannon could handle third-base duties, freeing up right field for the recently obtained Maris. Musial observed Maris hit a single sharply during his first intrasquad contest of the spring. Pleased with what he saw, Musial told the media, "That's what we need. We did not get enough runs last year. It's a long jump...to the pennant, but we're going to work like the devil to go higher. And I think we will."

Essentially, though, Musial played a pat hand. For the most part, the team was healthy and by September had used only 28 men all year long. His only significant roster move was the acquisition of pitcher Jack Lamabe after an injury to Gibson.

The loss of their ace could have been devastating, as he was out of action for most of the second half of the season due to a broken leg, but they prevailed. The gritty Gibson was drilled by a line drive off the bat of Roberto Clemente on July 15 but refused help from the trainer. He even pitched to two batters after his leg was shattered, just before he collapsed on the field. Gibson would return in September, win three games, and help the team cruise into the World Series. In Gibson's first start versus the Pirates after his injury, he fired a pitch over Clemente's head, forcing the Pirates' graceful star to flop unceremoniously into the dirt of the batter's box.

Musial labeled his squad a "tough professional team" that made "very few mistakes." They won 101 times and took the pennant by 10½ games over the Giants. "We knew how to play. Red and I had it easy," concluded Musial. His team drew 2,090,145 fans, a new franchise record.

Gibson was magnificent in the World Series, winning three complete games, posting an ERA of 1.00, and fanning 26 men over 27 innings. On the offensive side, Brock hit and ran wild, batting .414 while stealing a record seven bases. The Cardinals won it in seven games over the Carl Yastrzemski–driven Red Sox. Jimy Williams, with the Cardinals briefly in 1966 and 1967, said, "[Musial] was the general manager one year and [we] were world champions. He left as a champion as a player, and he left as a champion as a general manager."

As a player, Musial had departed the game too soon to reap the big money that came after the reserve clause fell. On the other hand, he became a general manager shortly before enormous new headaches came with that position. For instance, he never had to cope with meddling, powerful agents making outrageous demands on behalf of ballplayers.

Musial's tenure in the majors also preceded such blemishes as the cocaine scandal of the 1980s. On the very day Pete Rose broke Ty Cobb's record for lifetime hits, his Cincinnati teammate, Dave Parker, testified in a federal district court, revealing just how widespread cocaine use was among major-leaguers. It was asserted that Tim Raines used to slide headfirst into bases to avoid shattering his vials of cocaine, which he kept secreted away in his hip pockets. Also, the word *steroids* wasn't even in the sports lexicon during Musial's playing days.

Pulitzer Prize winner David Halberstam was writing about pro basketball in his 1981 book, *The Breaks of the Game*, but what he observed applied to Major League Baseball, too. He pointed out how much sports has changed since the era in which Musial played. Stan's career took place entirely, or largely, in an era before expansion, before free agency, and before gimmicks such as the designated hitter. To purists, those who ran pro sports began—as Halberstam wrote—to sell "the sizzle not the steak."

On December 5, less than a year after he had accepted the job as the Cardinals' general manager, Musial resigned his position. He remains the only general manager of a team that won the Series in his sole season at the helm. Earlier, in June, Musial had grieved the death of his business partner, Biggie Garagnani, and he now realized he would have to step up his role in his business interests. Plus, he said, he didn't like to "work by the clock."

Steve Russell felt that beyond that one-year stint as GM, Musial "never held any positions [with the Cardinals] that amounted to anything. Sure, they had him as a senior consultant or whatever, but if you ever notice it just seemed like he was put out to pasture." Overall, though, Musial did hold the position, nominal or not, of senior vice president for more than 25 seasons.

One author stated, "The fans in St. Louis loved him so much they wanted to stuff him and keep him in the lineup forever." While such an act of taxidermy was impractical, in 1968 the city's baseball writers did the next best thing. They erected a statue of Musial in front of Busch Stadium.

On August 4, under a scorching sun with temperatures reaching 93 degrees during pregame ceremonies, the Cardinals unveiled the 10-foot bronze statue. More than 47,000 spectators turned out to honor the city's favorite player.

The originally suggested title for the statue, which was to have featured Musial leaning on a bat while signing an autograph for a young boy, was "The Boy and the Man...Baseball's Bond." Instead, the statue featured Musial batting. Disappointingly, the artist got, of all things, his stance wrong.

## CHAPTER NINE

# *Kudos*

Managers, fans, players, family, and the media all pay tribute to Musial, a universally loved figure. Superlatives and adjectives with highly positive connotations are liberally sprinkled over Musial like confetti at a ticker-tape parade.

Veteran sportswriter Maury Allen felt there have been only a handful of baseball players who had the glimmering talent and the ineffable charisma that enabled them to "cross that line from playing idol to icon—always honored, recognized, worshipped, and admired." And Angela Labash said of her uncle, "People flock to him like a magnet. He's very popular, and his sincerity is genuine."

Despite his enormous popularity and prowess, Musial remained the type of idol that one does not feel the need to genuflect to. Rather one has the urge to walk up to him and clap him on the back. In fact, even after he owned three MVP Awards, he did not have an unlisted phone number and would take calls from his fans.

In 2007 Charlie Manuel commented, "When he was called 'Stan the Man,' he was called that for a reason, he was one of the best hitters in the game. He was a tremendous, tremendous player, and I think he was outstanding for baseball. I mean, who he was, his character, and as a man, he's a good representative for baseball."

Authors Daniel Okrent and Steve Wulf called Musial, "a gentleman, respected by all, modest in habit and in language, he simply went about his business—and his business was hitting."

Fred Hutchinson, one of Musial's managers, said, "You don't manage him at all. He manages himself."

John Kuenster, longtime editor of the venerable publication *Baseball Digest*, realized Musial had a genuine love of the game because, as Kuenster recalled, Musial "always said the greatest thrill was just putting on a big-league uniform every day, especially for the opener of a new season. I always found him very friendly, cooperative, and he had a great sense of humor."

Vernon Law stated, "Everybody really respected Stan. He wasn't a griper, he didn't give umpires a bad time, he was even-tempered. If you did hit him, he'd just drop the bat and go down to first base. He was kind of a man's man and just an outstanding personality."

Chuck Smith, who attended high school with Joe Montana and still lives in the Mon Valley, once visited and ate with Musial in St. Louis and came away "totally honored to even be around this guy. And all he wanted to do was serve me. There were a couple waitresses there that had no idea who he was, and he treated them like they were queens. [Even after] they found out who he was, he just treated everybody as if he was their servant. He's a servant to the people, and that's quite a tribute to him. He lives his life giving more than he took."

Former teammate Alex Grammas observed, "The thing I liked most about Musial was he was just an easy-going, nice person who was so easy to get along with even with his [enormous] popularity. We were in Brooklyn one time—to show you how he would think—and after the game they had a radio show where they'd get the star of the game and pull him in there [a small room] to ask a few questions on radio. I think they gave you $50 to be on the show, which was pretty good in those days. And I happened to be walking behind Stan back to the clubhouse when this guy was standing in the doorway. He says, 'Would you mind being on the show?' Stan said, 'OK, I'll do it tonight, but from now on get some of the other fellows.' That's the way he was. He wanted to share the wealth."

Although the unpresumptuous Musial would disagree, his giving to others may, in fact, be a case of noblesse oblige. Musial, though, was unmindful of, or at least unaffected by, baseball's caste system—he never flaunted his star status.

Musial's friend, trumpeter Al Hirt said, "You can be a big star. You can be an ordinary Joe, and you're just the same to Stan Musial." Hirt was impressed by Musial's devotion to youngsters and his willingness to sign autographs. "No matter what he's doing, he stops," he said.

Former big-league pitcher Dick Pole summed Musial up as being "a pretty nice guy because every time when I was with San Francisco and we'd go into town, he'd come down and see our clubhouse guy. He's known Mike Murphy for a long time, so I guess that makes him a pretty nice guy." Meaning Musial's good to the little people? "Well, not little people, *people*."

As Bimbo Cecconi of Donora put it, "He makes you feel that you are as important as he is, and he has never changed that attitude."

Musial was equally kind to rookies as he was to veterans he had known for quite some time. When he played first base, if a player singled for his initial big-league hit, he would be greeted by a beaming Musial and a sincere "Congratulations."

Chuck Tanner related the story of the aftermath of his first big-league hit. Upon reaching first base, Tanner heard the friendly Musial say, "Nice hitting. You know, I live near you." Tanner was astonished, "Can you imagine that? He said he lives near me, not that I live near him."

Grammas said, "You would think that a guy who had the fame that he had might be a little snooty at times, but he was the exact opposite of that. I can remember my first day at spring training [in 1954]—I'm going to St. Petersburg to the Cardinals camp, and I'm sitting there, and he walks in, and you know it's quite a feeling to see a guy with the fame that he has and the records he has, and to be such a pleasant and friendly person. From when you first meet him you feel like you've known him all your life. Success just couldn't happen to a nicer guy. And to look up and say, 'I'm on the same team with this guy.' I wondered if I could make it."

Musial had always been known as a great teammate and fan favorite. Warwick said that when he first joined the Cards, Musial immediately greeted him and "took me around introducing me to people on the ballclub. Then he said, 'If there's anything you need, just let me know or let Red Schoendienst know. We'll take care of it. If you have any problems, just let me know.' I don't know that they do that nowadays."

Musial, said Warwick, got to the clubhouse early. "He was always there early, as early as anybody." Nor was he the first one to depart after games. Even when drained, he'd head for his car, then take time to "sign every autograph for kids who were sitting outside."

Musial never forgot his roots, either. Ed Musial stated that Stan lived "halfway across the country," yet he made it a point to trek to Donora frequently for class reunions.

Frances Delsandro, a Musial classmate, said that as a boy, "He was a saint. Oh, he *is* a saint. He always brings a gift for everybody at our reunions, every five years. He gave us an autographed baseball bat, he gave us a bat rack, he even gave us a mouth organ. A lot of people won't come if they hear he's not coming. They ask, 'Is Stan Musial coming?' and if we on the committee say yes, then, 'OK, put me down, I'll be there.' One year he took dollar bills and made rings out of them and gave all of the ladies a ring with his name on it."

Todd Ririe, whose mother Virginia Nadetzky graduated with Stan, said that Musial "attended most, if not all, of their reunions, which they used to have almost every year. And I know that he always played the harmonica and entertained people at the reunions, and I think he also picked up the tabs for a lot of the things. He never wanted to make a big deal about that."

Yet Musial's hitting was so special one got the feeling that prior to each at-bat someone should have reverentially announced, "Behold!" Bob Skinner said that when he played against him, "I always expected him to get a hit—that's how much I respected his hitting. I read a stat one time [that] the most times he went to bat throughout his career without getting a hit was 13 times, or something like that. Anybody who knows anything about hitting, that's just remarkable."

Musial nemesis Warren Spahn remembered, "It seems that every time I walked to the mound, Stan Musial was the batter." While he threw Musial countless pitches, Spahn added, "I don't think he ever hit the ball off the end of the bat or on the handle. Everything was on the barrel!"

Spahn also said that if he had "to draw a picture of Stan at the plate and put a dot at every point where Stan hit the ball off me, the whole strike zone would be painted black. He didn't care what the ball did before it got there, he just put his bat on it when it finally cut across the plate."

Del Ennis stated that Musial would wait for Spahn to glance his way prior to the start of a game in which he was pitching. Then Musial would hold up three fingers, indicating he was about to get three hits off "Spahnie." Spahn would laugh and say, "Yeah?" Soon, said Ennis, "Musial got his three hits."

Bill James wrote of Musial, "He hustled. You look at his career totals of doubles and triples and they'll remind you of something that was accepted while he was active and has been largely forgotten since: Stan Musial was one player who always left the batter's box on a dead run."

In trying to sum up the whole of the man, Roger Kahn called Musial "an American hero" and "a man of limited education, superior intelligence, a guarded manner, a surface conviviality, and a certain aloofness. He knows just who he is."

Sportscaster Bob Costas summarized, "All Musial represents is more than two decades of sustained excellence and complete decency as a human being."

Unfailingly friendly and talented, Musial, a baseball treasure, has truly earned the praise others have lavished on him for decades and continue to lavish upon him today.

## CHAPTER TEN

# The Legacy of the Man— Cooperstown and Beyond

In 1969 Musial gained baseball's greatest honor, induction into the Hall of Fame. While only around 10 percent of the world's population is left-handed, the game of baseball favors lefties, and the Hall of Fame is packed with a disproportionate number of them. Through 2009, 74 position players honored in Cooperstown hit right-handed, eight were switch hitters, while a whopping 59 batted lefty. Musial, certainly one of the greatest left-handed hitters ever, joined baseball's pantheon.

On July 28, 1969, Musial, Roy Campanella, and pitchers Stan Coveleski and Waite Hoyt were formally inducted into the Hall. Musial, his veins now flowing richly with ichor, had attained baseball immortality. The voting results, announced on February 2, revealed Musial had received 317 of the 340 votes cast, good for a scintillating 93.24 percent of the votes, then the sixth-highest total ever.

Ken and Joe Barbao Jr. and their parents drove to Cooperstown for the ceremony. Musial, through his son Dick, had arranged for his old neighbors, the Barbaos, to sit in the second row, directly behind Musial's mother. "One thing that still stands out—it was overcast as the devil, and then as soon as he got up on the podium, the sun came out. There you go—Polish power," laughed Barbao Jr.

Dizzy Dean's widow, Pat, commented on the sun's abrupt appearance, "It figured. The sun always shines on Stan the Man."

Nattily attired in a blue suit and striped tie, his thinning hair the only clue that this trim 48-year-old star was no longer of the age to hoist a bat to home plate at nearby Doubleday Field and leg out a triple, climaxing his three-base hit with a patented hook slide—once a nifty part of his base-running repertoire. He spoke with ease, informally sprinkling "you know" throughout his speech by way of transition.

He told of how his first toy was a baseball and of how his poor family had managed to eke by. His voice cracked as he thanked his mother for being in his corner all his life.

Almost exactly one month before Musial's induction, Cubs outfielder Billy Williams broke a long-standing Musial record, most consecutive games played by a National Leaguer. That record fell, but Musial's reputation as being an iron man of the game—from 1946 to 1956 he missed just 17 games out of 1,689—remained. Joe Cunningham said many a time Musial played while hurt, placing the team above himself.

Another honor came to Musial in 1969 when baseball, celebrating its centennial, ran an election to select the greats of the game. The All-Star Game was being held in Washington, D.C., and President Richard Nixon held a ceremony at the White House one day after a dinner was hosted for the players named to the "Greats" list, one day before the All-Star contest. Two all-time All-Star squads were feted, the "Greatest Living Players" and the "Greatest Players Ever." Musial was slighted, being left off the greatest-ever list, but shared honors with George Sisler as the greatest living first basemen. The first baseman of the all-time list was Gehrig, while the outfielders were Cobb, Ruth, and DiMaggio.

Carl Erskine said a comparison between the lifetime stats of DiMaggio and Musial serves to "bring out the point that I made to a guy who said some years ago when they were both living, 'How could they name DiMaggio the greatest living ballplayer when Ted Williams is still alive and Stan Musial's still alive?' I said, 'I only got one quick answer to that, and that is, if Musial had played in New York, he would be the greatest living ballplayer.'"

Some believe Musial has not received as much credit as he should have because, unlike many stars, Musial didn't demand or crave attention. Hank Aaron stated, "I think that may have some truth to it, and I think Mr. Erskine is absolutely right [regarding Musial being undervalued]. I think he's unappreciated. He won so many batting titles until it was a foregone conclusion that every year Stan Musial was going to win a batting title. The same thing is true of his baseball skills—I think he is certainly underrated."

In addition, Jayson Stark wrote that when Ted Williams died in 2003 *Sports Illustrated* took a survey of 550 active players, asking each one to pick the greatest living player. Alex Rodriguez pulled down more votes than Willie Mays, Nolan Ryan outpolled Hank Aaron, and, amazingly, Musial barely got more votes than Babe Ruth, long dead, and finished eighth in the survey.

McCarver felt Musial was "celebrated" but agreed with Erskine that if Musial had played for a New York team, "he would have reached legendary proportions." George F. Will noted, "The publicity machine is powerful," and the masses believe what they read, and thus rank New York players over men such as Musial.

In 1970 Musial went on safari to Kenya and Nigeria, saying that while he had hunted duck, quail, geese, and deer, he had never gone after big game, so he sought advice from Marlin Perkins of the St. Louis zoo.

When Hank Aaron joined Musial in the 3,000-hit club on May 17, 1970, the perpetually thoughtful Musial made it a point to be on hand. Typical of his concern for others, Musial would often pop up to congratulate his peers who had just set a record or joined an elite group of baseball stars.

Aaron remembered, "It meant an awful lot to me, really. When I got my base hit in Cincinnati and he had taken [time] out of his busy schedule to be part of that was one of the greatest thrills I ever had. A little boy coming from Mobile, Alabama, and listening to Stan Musial on the radio many, many years ago, and here I had the greatest hitter in the world as far as I was concerned come out and congratulate me. That was a great thrill."

Musial also kept busy by playing himself in a two-part episode of *That Girl* starring Marlo Thomas. Musial, once ill at ease speaking, was described as being very calm and at ease in his role.

In spring-training games baseball experimented by using a yellow-tinted baseball. A reporter asked Musial how he'd hit such a ball. He grinned, then displayed his patented sense of humor. "You'd wonder where the yellow went," he said, parodying a TV toothpaste commercial of the day.

When he joined the Society for American Baseball Research, he filled out a questionnaire. Responding to an item asking for the applicant's area of expertise, normally calling for a response such as "ballparks" or "baseball history," he only half-jokingly wrote, "Hitting a baseball."

In 1972 Musial received an honor he would cherish forever. He was the first non-Pole ever to be presented with Poland's Merited Champions Medal, the highest sports award bestowed by the Polish government.

Always on the move, around this time Musial popped up in Hawaii. Author Jim O'Brien stated, "I remember being on a bus one time. I guess it was [while covering] the Major League Baseball owners meeting. Musial was on the bus with his wife. Just to be on the bus with him was special, because he was just such a magnet. He had those eyes that were always sealed shut almost when he smiled. He had two smiles—he'd smile with his eyes and with his lips."

In 1973 Musial began a long stretch on baseball's Veteran Committee, an august group that had the power to select players who had not been elected to the Hall of Fame and thereby grant them the game's ultimate honor.

In February he and Lil traveled to Poland, where he was honored by the Polish Olympic Committee for his work in promoting baseball to the country's youth. A stadium in Kutno, Poland, and a field in Wroclaw were eventually named after him.

Meanwhile, back in Donora, Emma Jene Lelik, who lived a few doors away from Musial's mother, would drop by occasionally to check up on her. "She was a sweet old lady and robust—you could tell that she worked hard all her life. When she spoke of Stan, she always glowed, her face and her eyes.

"If you rubbed her the wrong way or you said something [such as] Stan failed or he lost the game, she would be on the defensive immediately, but I would give her credit for that, protecting her son."

Her health had been failing—at one point she took a spill and had to spend time in Havencrest, a local nursing facility. Donoran Dorothy Kovacik remembered, "She [became] sort of an invalid when she got older."

She died on February 1, 1975, at the age of 78, leaving her son inconsolable.

Despite being grief-stricken, he took the time to write letters to his mother's neighbors who had helped her out in her final years, people such as next-door neighbor Jean Pansino, who said that toward the end of Mrs. Musial's life, after decades of toil, she finally slowed down. "She lagged off and couldn't do too much." Her days of enjoying working with plants and flowers, of bustling around in the kitchen, and of adoring her children came to an end.

During retirement, golf also kept Musial occupied. Barbao Jr. marveled, "He could hit the heck out of a golf ball left-handed. Oh, yeah."

With skin sun-baked over the years and eyes bordered by crow's feet and now relying on spectacles, Musial still looked fit as the 1980s rolled around.

In 1981 he took part in the initial Cracker Jack Old-Timers Classic held in RFK Stadium in Washington, D.C. The game, jokingly nicknamed "the Ben Gay Bowl," also featured such luminaries as Mays and Aaron and a surprise home run by 75-year-old Luke Appling that disappeared 12 rows into the left-field bleachers on the second pitch of the game from 60-year-old Warren Spahn. The pitcher proceeded to chase Appling around the base path, "slapping him good-naturedly with his glove." The game represented the first time an old-timers game was held, not as a sideshow or preliminary but as the exclusive attraction.

In 1985 Musial reminisced during a trip to Pittsburgh, speaking of how he missed the good old days—of dining and chatting with boxer Billy Conn, Pittsburgh Steelers owner Art Rooney, and others. Musial grew nostalgic and said, "It's too bad I didn't play for the Pirates." The Bucs had remained his favorite team, aside from the Cardinals, and when Pittsburgh captured the 1960 World Series, he had made it a point to be in the stands rooting for the Bucs.

Stan and Lil continued to travel and to circulate among an exclusive circle of friends. In 1988 they attended a 20th memorial anniversary of the assassination of Robert Kennedy in Washington, D.C. Laurel Grimes said her aunt and uncle were "close personal friends with the Kennedys, both John and Bobby. He was a close personal friend of Pope John Paul II and went to Poland several times to institute a baseball program there in the country for youths. Stan and Lil are practicing Catholics, Pope John Paul is Polish, and Stan is very proud of his Polish heritage. When the Pope visited St. Louis, one of the reasons he specifically wanted to go there was his friendship with Stan, and St. Louis does have one of the largest Catholic populations."

Grimes observed how busy her aunt and uncle were keeping in touch with friends. "You might say, 'I'm going down to see Tony at the bar.' They're like, 'We're flying to Poland this week' or, 'We're going to Rome for dinner with the Pope.'" Grimes' sister, Susan Naylor, went to a posh event with her aunt and uncle. Naylor was told that a man at their table was in the steel business as a president of a large company to which Naylor, then a crane operator in a Pennsylvania steel mill, replied with a chuckle, "Oh, I'm in the steel business, too."

After Musial's 1988 meeting with the Pope in Rome, Musial was asked what the two had eaten. Musial grinned, "Who knows what I ate? I was eating with the Pope! I didn't know what I was eating."

In 1989, then pushing 70 years of age, Musial, who had suffered from a gastric ulcer in 1983, was diagnosed with prostate cancer. After surgery he dropped 20 pounds but soon rebounded.

He did, however, simplify his business dealings, reducing his holdings to Stan the Man, Inc. which cashed in on the autograph/memorabilia craze.

In 1996 writer Steve Rushin was critical of the memorabilia craze and of mercenary players who sold their autographs: "An ex-Card could always hawk his ex-card on cable TV. So Stan Musial could be seen peddling his signature on a home-shopping channel for $299.95, 'or three monthly payments of $99.98.' Stan the Man with an Installment Plan."

Despite Rushin's rebuke, Musial, once called "an autograph altruist," gave away many more autographs than he sold and retained his enormous popularity.

When Musial made it back to Donora for his 50th high school reunion, he gave classmates an autographed baseball, then joked, "If we all live another 50 years, I'll give you a signed bat."

Early in the career of Ken Griffey Jr., Musial made it a point to meet with the budding star. Griffey Jr. recalled how impressed he was that a man of Musial's standing would do that. "He was nice. He said, 'So you and I come from the same town.' And he talked about us being born on the same day."

Over the years Musial continued to return to Donora for various reasons, including visits to his sister-in-law Anna Palm, who was caring for his small shaggy dog, Dizzy Dean, and dropping in on Dr. William Rongaus about once a year in the nursing home he was living in. Rongaus would crow to visitors, "I delivered Stan Musial, and I delivered Ken Griffey Sr."

On one visit back home in the 1980s, Paul Zolak said Musial experienced sticker shock in a good way. "He was used to paying the prices in St. Louis at big restaurants, and when he got a shot and a beer at the Cro [Croatian] Club in Donora and put down a $10 bill and they gave him eight dollars and 50 cents back in change—he couldn't believe it, a buck and a half for a shot and a beer."

Still, even in one's own backyard, no man is impervious to scrutiny and criticism. By and large, Donorans have lionized Musial, but a few hometown detractors contend he didn't do a lot for the community after he became a full-time St. Louis resident. Robert Jones disagreed, saying, "He wasn't obligated to Donora."

The former mayor of Donora, John Lignelli, also defended Musial, saying he felt the Cardinals star did, in fact, do a great deal for the community, including taking part in ceremonies in town such as the dedication of a baseball field in his honor and signing autographs endlessly. "I think he did [support Donora] because Stan had a rough life himself. He didn't have a silver spoon in his mouth when he was growing up. Then he had a beautiful family and he educated them all quite well. Of course, a lot of people have a different opinion of what they think is 'enough.' Some people, you'll never satisfy. I mean, what do they expect from the guy?"

Earl Gipin, a Ringgold High School art teacher, stated, "He's Donora, through and through, and he'll do anything for this area. He's just a super, super man."

Ron Nagy said that through it all, his uncle Stan was quite proud of his hometown. "Oh, yeah. He always came back, didn't he? He'd come back for his wife's class reunion, and he'd come back for his. Some people said he didn't [return enough]." That, he says, was merely the carping of malcontents and is hardly indicative of most Donorans. Musial himself once mulled, "You never leave your hometown roots."

Nagy continued, "What gets me, people will call [asking for favors], then say, 'Why can't he do this? Why can't he do that?' Well, you can't do something for everybody. They think that, because he has money, every time he walks into Donora he's supposed to drop a check off."

Then, for example, when told Stan can't make a personal appearance, the petitioners get upset and say things such as, "Oh, he doesn't want to come, he doesn't want to do anything for Donora." Nagy added, "They don't realize people have health problems."

Steve Russell stated, "I guess [Donorans] wanted him to live here, that's what it comes down to. He situated himself in St. Louis, he opened up a restaurant there, he conducted his business there. A lot of people feel he turned his back on the Valley. The only thing is they can't justify that rap—he never made any negative comments about the Valley. It's just that he found a new home. It's not turning his back, it's just, 'I have a new home now. Donora's no longer my home.' Maybe that's small-mindedness—he has come back here many times. When he's been honored or when they wanted him for a dedication, he's always responded."

Chuck Smith had heard local bad-mouthing of Musial, too, but after he viewed a media presentation that Stan took part in, shown in lieu of Musial appearing live at a banquet honoring local sports heroes, he dismissed the negativity he had heard. "I'm going to tell you what, after listening to him on his little talk, I actually had a tear in my eye. I just felt that I totally judged this person wrongly. I realized I was a little bit ashamed of myself and of how I thought about him before this media thing.

"You have this [preconception] of somebody from what everybody says, and when you finally get down to meeting him in person, the people who told me that stuff have no credibility with me whatsoever.

"I actually apologized to him and I said, 'I'm telling you right now, anybody I talk to from this day forward and they start bad-mouthing you, I'm going to say, 'That's just not true about him.'

"There are a lot of jealous people out there, and I guess misery likes company. And it's a sad thing. Unfortunately, people listen to whoever's speaking; they'll listen to [and believe] anybody, and there are always these people out there who want to be in the negative. They don't have a clue what they're talking about, they're just spreading rumor and innuendo. I guess that's everywhere."

Nagy also pointed out when one comes from a small town and makes it big, it is inevitable for the celebrity to become deluged with requests from fellow natives. Everybody wants a piece of the star. He also feels that the people who complain about Musial are the ones who "called him and wanted stuff," and felt a sense of entitlement. "They say, 'We're from Donora. We want this. We want that.' But, you know, you [can't please] everybody."

The game of baseball or, more correctly, the business of baseball, in the 1990s was as far removed from the Musial era as modern brain surgery is to phrenology. Steve Rushin wrote of the 1994 players' strike, "As the end of the millennium drew nigh, there was an apocalyptic, last-days-of-the-Roman Empire air about major-league baseball. The fat lady was singing, and she sounded a lot like Roseanne Barr at Jack Murphy Stadium...ballplayers making 57 times the average man's wages plotted to strike," their hands out demanding yet more loot. Further, the impact of television on sports continued to grow, and FOX dished out more than $1 billion for television rights for National Football Conference clashes.

Musial was from a time when players traveled together, including taking bus rides from hotels to ballparks and grueling road trips via train. Such proximity led to a wonderful closeness among players, the antithesis of what many of today's players, here today and gone tomorrow due to the mobility of free agency, experience.

In Musial's older years he would sometimes look back with fondness on his youth. In August 1994 Stan Musial returned to his hometown for the dedication of a youth baseball field named after him at Palmer Park. During his speech, he noted almost wistfully, "I played on this field 60 years ago. It's hard to believe it's been 60 years ago. I'd rather have a bat in my hand than this microphone, because I know what to do with it."

Mulling over his legacy, he told the audience that he wanted the field "to be a symbol and an inspiration to these young ballplayers that someday something like this [his success] might happen to them."

He said, "I've always loved baseball, and it was the only thing I wanted to do as a youngster. It's a great game. I never got bored. Every day was something different and interesting. I hated to retire. The last day I got two hits, and I said to myself, *Why am I retiring?*"

In typical Musial fashion, he signed innumerable autographs and posed for endless pictures long after the ceremony had terminated. He donated $10,000 to the town's baseball association and stated he felt an obligation to his fans.

In 1995 Ross Farmer met Musial in at a Donora Historical Society function. "He was one of the most cordial individuals I ever met, genuinely sincere and humble. Here he is, baseball royalty, sitting, having dinner, talking with old friends like he's just Stan from Donora—and to them, that's all he was. Stan considers himself an extremely lucky individual to have the opportunity to do what he did, but you see somebody who is a world-renowned figure, and he just sat there like one of the guys. Had you not known he was arguably the greatest player in National League history, you would have thought he was an ordinary Joe off the street." In one respect, Musial is precisely that.

Throughout the evening Musial tended to move most of the baseball talk away from himself. Farmer said, "He seemed to be more open with his responses about other players."

In 1999 Musial accepted the Cavalier Cross of the Order of Merit, given to him by the Polish government, their highest honor to a civilian. That same year, the All-Star Game was held in Boston's Fenway Park on July 13. As part of a promotion related to baseball's All-Century baseball team, all of the 54 living players who had been nominated for the team, save Pete Rose, who was banned from baseball, were invited to attend the festivities, and 33 made it there.

Incredibly, Musial had *not* initially been selected for All-Century consideration, finishing 11th among voting for the 10 available outfield spots. A committee that had been appointed to correct oversights added Musial to the list.

As Musial was introduced in Boston, he pantomimed his inimitable swing and doffed his cap to the crowd. Looking dapper as ever, wearing a navy-blue blazer, a powder-blue shirt, and a stylish necktie, he beamed at the fans. Later, Ted Williams was golf-carted onto the field. Fenway Park, noted Bob Costas, had been "transformed into a virtual Field of Dreams."

Prior to the start of the first game of the World Series, the 30 players selected for the final roster of the All-Century Team, an elite squad culled from more than 14,000 20th-century players, marched onto the field. Being on the team was truly a great honor for Musial.

However, a blow to his pride came when he was not selected to the ESPN SportCentury's Fifty Greatest Athletes. Actually, on an extended list, ESPN did rank him 61st. A horse, Secretariat, was even ranked higher (35th ) than Musial. Steve Russell observed, "He was upset about the SportsCentury lords placing him at No. 61, while his superstar contemporaries like Mantle and Williams were [far ahead of him]." New York writer Stan Isaacs, well aware of the heavy Eastern bias in sports, succinctly called Mantle's rank over Musial "ridiculous."

Russell continued, "Of course, on the other side, Stan hasn't helped things to promote his image, either. The FOX Sports network contacted me in 2003 about doing a biography on him, asking for some of my archives on Stan. When they got a hold of Musial, he said he didn't want anything to do with it, and they nixed it. When you have a major television network wanting to do a segment on you and you nix something like that, you're [hindering] future generations [from] knowing about you."

*The Sporting News*, though, saw matters much more clearly than most of the media, ranking rank Musial 10th on its list of the greatest 100 players ever. Of course, the fact that they are based in St. Louis didn't hurt Musial.

Still, an unbiased observer and an unquestioned authority on the art of hitting, Hank Aaron said Musial "has to be right up there. He was a tremendous ballplayer. You can talk about one, two, three, four, five, or six, whatever; Stan has got to be in that category. Anybody that wins as many batting titles as he did, no matter whether he played in a band box, no matter where he played in, it doesn't really make any difference, he was just a terrific hitter. He did the same thing no matter whether he was playing in Busch Stadium or whether he was playing in Milwaukee County Stadium. He was the same kind of ballplayer.

"He wasn't gifted with the great arm, he was gifted with great speed, but he was a great, knowledgeable ballplayer—he could do everything everybody else could do."

By 2002 Musial, walking a bit slower and hearing a touch poorer, commented, "Well, I'm hanging in there. You know, when you get to be 81, every day is a blessing."

On October 1, 2002, Ulice Payne Jr. took over as the CEO and president of the Milwaukee Brewers, making him the first African American to lead a big-league team. Soon he made *Sports Illustrated*'s list of the 101 Most Influential Minorities in Sports, ranked 14th. Payne, the son of a Donora steelworker, vividly remembered his days growing up when everyone in town seemed to work "for the railroad, the coal mine, or the steel mill."

As the date for his first game as the Brewers leader approached, an afternoon road game in St. Louis on March 31, 2003, he received a phone call from Musial's office. Musial apparently had discovered that there was now another Donora native on the baseball scene. "They invited me to have lunch with him on Opening Day. I'll always remember that. He reached out: 'Come to St. Louis—meet me.' The biggest thing was *he called me.* I couldn't believe it! I mean, how did he even know I was president?"

When Payne arrived in St. Louis, he called Musial's office "just to confirm it, because I couldn't believe it. Then I met him at the ballpark for an hour-and-a-half lunch and took pictures." Musial was decked out, fittingly, in his bright cardinal-red blazer.

"I was kind of scared, but he was very warm; he was a small-town guy. He was very proud of Donora and coming from a small town. The Labash store was right next to our [family's] church, and we talked about some well-known Donora Dragon heroes, too. He remembered my family and Arnold Galiffa, and we had a good talk about baseball and what baseball has meant to him. He encouraged me about baseball. He said to be patient and to remember that you've got a lot of guys on the farm.

"He was very proud of the fact that Ken Griffey Sr. had become a major-league player. He would see Senior, who was coaching in the Reds' organization then, from time to time. To have guys from Donora do well in Major League Baseball was important to him.

"I had heard so much about him that I was in awe—also [impressive was] the way they treat him out there in St. Louis; he's a hero. He held court. It was outstanding. Lou Brock was in there, Red Schoendienst showed up. I was in awe by all the people coming by the table, wishing him well.

"He introduced me to a lot of people as they came up to shake Stan the Man's hand. I was very proud that when people would come up to him saying, 'How you doing?' he'd say, 'Let me introduce you to a guy from my hometown.'" Payne stated he would not have taken the initiative to make the first move because he saw Musial as "somebody you honor and respect. I wouldn't have called Stan Musial—he's a Hall of Famer you hope one day to meet, but I never would have called.

"By the time I got back to Milwaukee—boom—I get a bat [in the mail] that was signed by him, and I had a bat rack put up in my office. I called my mother, 'Hey, Ma, you won't believe this.' I'll never forget that afternoon [spent with Musial]." Such is the impact of Musial on those fortunate enough to spend time with him.

By this time period, Stan had outlived his siblings and remained fairly active, all things considered. "He's slowed down in recent years," said niece Laurel Grimes in 2008. "I mean, even about four years ago when my Aunt Helen died, he came in. He had some trouble getting a flight, but he came in, way late in the evening of the viewing, but he made it—he was bound and determined. My Aunt Lil couldn't come in, but he did." Musial, with a strong sense of family, paid his respects in what, to date, was his last trip back to his hometown.

Musial also remained a consummate showman. Martha Muniz, whose aunt married Ed Musial, recalled Stan coming to visit family. "He was always the entertainer; he would sing for everybody, and he loved little magic tricks. He would make rings out of dollar bills and hand them out to people." He also loved to regale people with baseball stories, laughing at his own punch lines.

"I think," Grimes added, "his athleticism all these years probably has helped a good deal to keep him as young as he has been."

In August 2004 Michael J. Kelley, originally from Richeyville, a town not far from Donora, made a road trip, a sort of pilgrimage to the mecca of Musial, and noted, "He has some health issues—he can't get around as much as he'd like to—but he looked very, very good for his age and he was still going strong. I got a warm feeling, knowing that I got to meet such a great person—morals, values, and so forth."

Kelley jokingly told Musial he should have brought him some Stoney's beer, which was manufactured by the Jones Brewing Company (once owned by actress Shirley Jones' grandfather) in Smithton, Pennsylvania, a town near Donora. Musial smiled, "I would have liked that." Kelley's father, Michael E. Kelley, harkening back to the era Musial grew up in, said local "coal miners and steel mill workers were practically weaned on Stoney's beer. Those men worked hard, they played hard, and they drank hard."

Linda Ruth Tosetti is the granddaughter of Babe Ruth and, over the years, she and her husband Andy have become fast friends with the Musials. The two families first met during their annual visits to Cooperstown for the induction ceremonies, an event Musial seldom missed. She related, "We would all reconnect as a baseball family. I was told once, probably by

Lil, that it was all about 90 percent family reunion, 10 percent baseball then.

"Stan and Lil were very good to [my husband] Andy and me when we started going back to the Hall of Fame inductions without my mom. I was really nervous, but Lil and Stan took us under their wings.

"The first time I ever saw them, my mother Dorothy and I were waiting for the elevator in the lobby at the Otesaga Hotel during the 1972 inductions. We heard singing coming from below as we waited. When the doors opened, there was Lil and Stan singing! Mom said hello and laughed and said to them that we would take the next elevator. When the doors closed I asked who they were. My mom just laughed again and said it was Lil and Stan Musial, having a good time. I'll never forget that.

"They were known as the First Family of the Hall of Fame then. They hosted the big parties every night after the official things were done. Stan would have three musicians come into the Hawkeye Lounge at the Otesaga [Hotel], and he would play the harmonica. Everyone would look forward to it and have so much fun laughing. Lil and Stan were the Masters of Ceremony."

Sportswriter Maury Allen said that one of the things he relished during the annual Hall of Fame inductions weekend is seeing "Musial in action." When he is introduced to a crowd, he invariably "steps forward, bends deep in his famous batting stance, and takes a big swing at an imaginary baseball. Then he laughs."

Musial was still hardy enough to entertain frequent visitors to his office, including friends and supplicants from the Mon Valley. The first greeting they heard was the doorbell chimes playing "Take Me Out to the Ballgame."

Former Ringgold High School football coach Joe Ravasio said the first time he met Musial, in 2004, he felt "like a little kid at Kennywood [a popular amusement park in the Pittsburgh area]." He found Musial to have, even in his declining years, a captivating personality and "a passion and an immense love for the game of baseball, but he wanted to share his knowledge, his excitement of the game with you as a human being. I will always have a special place in my heart for him." Musial came across "like a father figure. He is very endearing.

"You feel that you're in the presence of great humility when you're around him. You hope someday that another young boy has the same dream that Stan Musial had and will follow through on that dream of becoming a great baseball player."

Ravasio smiled, "When we were getting ready to leave, he said, 'Nobody's ever allowed to leave til…,' and he pulls out his harmonica, and we all sang 'Take Me Out to the Ballgame' as he played it."

Musial showed up for the unveiling of the new Busch Stadium (where his statue had been moved) on April 10, 2006, but, handing his cane to Lou Brock, he required additional assistance and walked out onto the field with his arms linked with Schoendienst and Brock for support. He managed to navigate with short, shuffling steps, a sad picture for fans who remembered his greyhound days. This year also marked the final time Musial made an appearance in the Cardinals' spring-training camp.

Like the "germophobic" comedian Howie Mandel, Musial, said Chuck Smith, "[usually] doesn't shake hands, he touches fists," a fist bump à la ballplayers greeting each other in the dugout after a home run. "The reason for it, he shakes so many hands he said he was getting ill from it, so he punches your fist, kind of like giving you five, like the kids do. But he does it with an attitude, like he's happy to do it. He gave me a pop [a greeting with some authority]."

Donora schools had merged with those of Monongahela in late 1969, forming the Ringgold School District. By autumn 2006, Stan and Lil's health issues prohibited him from attending a special Ringgold Hall of Fame weekend. Their niece, Laurel Grimes, stated Stan "doesn't like to leave her alone. He's devoted to her." The September 1, 2006, ceremonies honored NFL kicker Fred Cox, Hall of Fame quarterback Joe Montana, Ken Griffey Sr., and Musial, the first two graduates from Monongahela High, the latter from Donora High.

"It's obvious why he didn't show up," stated Smith. "I wish we would have done something like we're doing now 20 years ago." Musial also did not make the trip in deference to Lil, telling Smith, "She has not been well." Still, said Smith that year, Musial "is sharp as a button."

The acrimonious Musial-Garagiola feud, dormant for years, resurfaced in 2006. It came about as a result of a disagreement concerning the bowling alley, Redbird Lanes. Garagiola and his wife Audrie owned one-third interest in the corporation. In April 1986 they filed suit against Musial and three others, claiming, along with other matters, Musial had approved a business arrangement without discussing it with them. The issue was settled without a trial, but Musial could neither forget the matter nor forgive his former friend. Garagiola had committed an unthinkable act, making Musial look bad to his public.

Nor could Musial forget Garagiola's saying he was not a nice person after the lawsuit had been settled. Ed Musial, well aware his uncle had perpetually received positive media coverage, said, "He was probably too nice of a guy for anybody to [rip]. The only one I know [who had an issue with Stan] was Joe Garagiola. It was…an ongoing disagreement that's lingered all these years. That's the only time I've ever, ever, heard anybody say anything about somebody not liking him, because I think everybody liked him."

Musial must have seen Garagiola as an ingrate. As a teammate of Garagiola, Musial, always bombarded with requests to speak, told Garagiola to come along with him, and they would split the speaker's fee. Laurel Grimes observed, "He helped Joe Garagiola get going with his broadcasting career," putting in a good word for him. Thus, Musial had, on numerous occasions, helped out Garagiola.

Two decades later, in 2006, Cardinals officials wanted Musial to toss out the ceremonial first pitch to Garagiola before the start of the third game of the World Series. On the morning of Game 3, when Musial first learned the particulars of those plans, he immediately backed out. Instead, Musial made the opening lob prior to Game 5. In a 2009 interview Solly Hemus noted, "He's still, I think, hostile about [Garagiola]."

Once again Musial was snubbed when FOX television neglected to broadcast his throwing out of the first pitch. Musial, more so than any other living baseball legend, seems virtually ignored by today's media.

Musial kept in touch with his Cardinals roots throughout the years, almost invariably in spring training. In a 2007 interview Cardinals coach Milt Thompson said he had just met Musial at the beginning of the season when Stan "would come around. You could see that he was a very loose and relaxed individual, and he loved the game."

However, Musial was decidedly slowing down. Unlike the year before, when he visited the team's spring-training camp, this year he skipped that trip although he did attend the home opener in St. Louis.

Donora native Dave Sarkus and Mon Valley businessman Chuck Smith visited St. Louis in 2007. They contacted the avuncular Musial, who met them in their hotel's restaurant. Smith said they would have gone to him, but even at the age of 86, the thoughtful Musial "made it more convenient for us." Sarkus recounted, "He has a hand on me and he's walking through the lobby. He says, 'I don't get around too good anymore.' I said, 'Oh, you do fine, Mr. Musial.' He said, 'No, I think I hit too many triples.'" Musial had always considered the triple to be the game's most exciting play, a race between man and ball that unfolded over several suspenseful moments, as opposed to the home run, over in an instant. Now, sadly, he required some assistance in walking.

Smith noted, "He's getting around okay, but he walks with a cane. His grandson helps him with his balance a little bit, and it was obvious he's a man who is aging." Often, though, he proudly refused to use a walker or cane and would instead lean on the shoulder of a close friend or relative.

Sarkus and Smith petitioned Musial to donate some memorabilia to be placed in a display case at the old Donora High School building, now used as an elementary center. Officials hoped children seeing the display would become inspired. When Smith thanked Musial for cooperating, he replied, "No, don't thank me, I want to thank you and your group, all the guys for doing all that you're doing for the children in the community. You guys are the ones who are the unsung heroes; I'm just a guy that played baseball." He added, "I'm 1,000 percent with you." Then he said with a chuckle, "But don't drag your feet because I'm getting old."

In May nephew Ron Nagy noted, "Right now he's not in that great a shape. He doesn't drive anymore. He doesn't do much traveling." Lil was in a wheelchair, due to heart problems and arthritis but, said one relative, "They're both very sharp mentally."

Musial's health was such that although he had been an annual fixture at Cooperstown during induction weekends seemingly forever, he did not make it in 2007. Still, he continued to go to his office at Stan the Man, Inc., arriving in the morning almost every weekday to sign memorabilia for an hour or so. The company offers items from bats to photos to harmonicas with his signature. By 2009 a signed baseball went for $100.

He spent part of his 87th birthday with a small circle of friends gathered at Beffa's restaurant. They sang "For He's a Jolly Good Fellow," and Musial even joined in while joking that the song had no apparent ending, with his friends finishing one verse then going right back to the top. During the afternoon celebration he was interrupted by a phone call from Jerry Reinsdorf, owner of the Chicago White Sox. Musial played "Happy Birthday" on his harmonica, joked, did a few tricks—including hanging a spoon off his nose—then walked out of the restaurant holding on to the proffered crooked elbow of his grandson.

On May 18, 2008, the Cardinals held "Stan the Man" day at Busch Stadium. A St. Louis street was renamed Stan Musial Drive alongside Musial Plaza, where his statue now stands. To date, this was one of his final major appearances.

In a July 2008 *Baseball Digest* interview, Musial stated he still usually manages to go to the Cardinals' Opening Day games but, due to his condition, must watch the rest of the games on television. "That's because I can't walk," he said. According to the magazine's editor, John Kuenster, Musial then joked about his old age, "reflecting his customary light-hearted approach to life," and noted that Musial maintained his "usual upbeat frame of mind." He quoted a poetic, light-hearted Musial as reciting, "You're not old when your hair turns gray/ You're not old when your teeth decay/ You're only old if you're on a long, long street/ and your mind has a date your body can't meet."

In April 2009 Musial's brother-in-law said Stan's health had gone "downhill the last two years" but said he and Lil were "going for 100 [years of age]." Lil continued to have heart problems and a nerve condition known as neuropathy. Musial once more attended Opening Day. Among all of the Cardinals greats on hand, he was introduced last. He rode around the warning track while the PA system played the theme song from the great baseball movie *The Natural*. Then, with his old roomie of 10 seasons, Red Schoendienst, he helped out with the duties of throwing out the season's ceremonial first pitch.

Their health prohibited them from traveling to Pennsylvania for a June WPIAL (Western Pennsylvania Interscholastic Athletic League) Hall of Fame induction. Joe Collins, the Hall of Fame chairman, said that the first class of inductees—selected for their accomplishments in high school play in the WPIAL—came in 2007 and that "Stan Musial's name had been up each of the three years. We, quite frankly, would have liked to have had him in attendance. We were holding out on that, but the fact is that's probably not going to be possible." Instead, Stan's nephew Ed accepted the award of his behalf.

Still, Musial continued to show up at his office to sign memorabilia for a couple of hours on most weekday mornings, and he also continued to enjoy the camaraderie of close friends, often dining with them and swapping stories.

Shortly before the All-Star break, St. Louis Cardinals star first baseman Albert Pujols enjoyed his first lengthy discussion with Musial, who was approaching his 70th wedding anniversary and his 89th birthday. A standout hitter himself, Pujols called it a great opportunity to pick the baseball brain of Musial, so they spoke of the art of hitting (and more) with both men stating that during their first trip to the plate in each game they liked to go deep in the count. "I didn't like to swing at the first pitch," said Musial, still an ardent student of the game. "I liked to see what the pitcher was throwing."

Pujols said he was shocked at the relatively low salaries Musial pulled down, a total of about $1,250,000 over nearly a quarter of a decade of baseball excellence, for an average of about $57,000 earned per season. Pujols was in the sixth year of a seven-year contract calling for $100 million.

A day before the 2009 All-Star Game, hosted by the Cardinals, Pujols, a star who Musial called the best Cardinal he has seen since he retired, spoke of his nickname, the Spanish phrase for "the man." During the Home Run Derby he told ESPN, "They call me 'El Hombre' here which I get mad about. You can call me 'Winnie the Pooh,' 'King Arthur,' whatever you want, but that's about the only name that I don't like, and it's because I feel that Stan is 'the Man,' and you should respect that."

Commissioner Bud Selig called Musial "a living legend" and "an American icon" who "represents the Cardinal tradition in an absolutely magnificent way." It was his hope, reported the *Palm Beach Post*, that the 2009 All-Star Game would "celebrate Musial's accomplishments much the way the 1999 classic in Boston celebrated Ted Williams."

The 80th All-Star Game was held on July 14, and 46,760 fans watched as Musial was driven onto the field from behind a gate down the right-field line just prior to the first pitch of the evening. Musial soaked up the nearly thunderous applause as he waved a baseball at the crowd in tiny throwing motions, a gesture not unlike the royal wave associated with the Queen of England.

The golf cart slowly made its way along the dirt path by the NL dugout on the first-base side of the field and stopped on the grass not far from home plate. There he was joined by President Obama, who chatted with him briefly. Musial then handed the baseball to the president, who threw it to Pujols as the ceremonial first pitch of the game. After Musial had given up the ball, his golf cart silently slid into reverse, and like the all-too-short focus given to Musial, faded off the television screen and into the background, quite unceremoniously.

Moments later, after the president returned to Musial to bid him a farewell, Musial just sat in the cart, as Bernie Miklasz of the *St. Louis Post-Dispatch* put it, "with nothing really happening around him. The Man was sitting there, all alone." Unlike the mob scene in Boston, the players did not engulf Musial. Kuenster said, "The one person who I noticed that did go out to the car that [Stan] drove in was Joe Torre, and he talked to him for some time and then patted him on the shoulder several times, but that was the only person [who approached him]." Only Torre, stated Miklasz, "seemed to understand what was required here."

The actual television coverage of Musial ran under two minutes. When the FOX network returned from a commercial break to open the bottom half of the second inning, a shot of the Clydesdales trotting around the field seemed to get almost more air time than Musial.

Ann Rubin reported that a host of Musial fans were upset over his treatment and that sources had told News Channel 5 in St. Louis that his "family was disappointed" as well, that "before the presidential pitch was announced, they'd been counting on a more elaborate display."

Hank Aaron also felt that Musial didn't receive enough attention. "I didn't think about that until the next day, and I was telling my wife I thought that [with] the All-Star Game being played in Stan's hometown [and] I don't know when it's going to ever get back there again or will Stan be alive to see it, but I think that Major League Baseball could have done a little bit more to show their appreciation for a man that played the game the way it's supposed to have been played." Knowing Musial, he added, "I'm sure Stan never said anything," because that simply was never his style.

Rubin also stated that a baseball spokesman said that because Obama was on the field "there was less room for spontaneity from the players," but "the tribute went off exactly as scripted." The spokesman justified the ceremonies, saying that there "isn't a bigger tribute than handing a ball to the president." Finally a spokesman, wrote Rubin, "said another factor in their planning was Musial's comfort. He said they wanted to make sure they didn't place any undue stress on him."

Kuenster added, "He can't walk [so] he was there very briefly, and they drove him right back out. He didn't stay around. He certainly received a tremendous ovation. I don't know how much more you could honor him. It was the fans who really showed their appreciation. And his physical condition qualified that to some extent—you know he couldn't get up and stand around and have pictures taken of him—that was part of it. I'm quite sure it's his health—he couldn't handle that too well, so I understand that."

Still, Miklasz wrote that just as the Ken Burns documentary *Baseball* left Musial "largely overlooked," the pregame celebration of Musial was lacking, that he was "an afterthought." Sadly, it reaffirmed the fact that he has "never quite received the accolades he has deserved through many years of graceful, ambassadorial retirement."

Miklasz noted that after repeated snubs, such as the time Musial nearly wasn't on the All-Century team, he felt another such slight would not happen, "not on this grand occasion, not in St. Louis, not in Stan's town. But it did.

"Man, oh, Man.

"You deserved better."

Perhaps such oversights happen to a guy who is too nice to make a fuss over himself. The meek may inherit the Earth, but they do not reap the respect they often deserve.

\* \* \*

One classmate of Musial's, Minor Hawk, went on to become an evangelist. At one of their reunions, Hawk spoke of how he had "become a Christian and a radio preacher for 53 years. I was saved, born again." When it was Musial's turn to speak, he commented, "I've done a lot of things, but I'd give anything if I could say what Minor Hawk has just told you." Hawk explained that Musial wasn't saying he wasn't a good Christian but was pointing out how he found Hawk's calling and dedication to be laudatory. "He was very devout and very humble. He was a real man," stated Hawk. "They don't make them like that anymore."

Joe Ravasio philosophized that it would be great "if everybody lived the life [that Stan has] and loved what they did." Like a modern Midas but without his flaw and without tragic consequences, Musial's ebullient ways, talents, and his business "touch" have led to a solid-gold life.

Certainly there are no phoenix metaphors required for Musial. He arose, not from ashes, but from the soot spit out from United State Steel Mill smokestacks. Unlike a phoenix, he ascended frequently and with longevity, never sporadically. His bat spewing fire like a Donora Dragon, he blazed his way to the majors. From there, he continued to fly high, to prosper, and to savor life.

Musial once said he was appreciative of what baseball had given him "in recognition, records, thrills, money, and tons of memories." His fans would counter that thanks were due to Musial for giving them and the game of baseball so many golden, magical memories.

During an interview in 2008, former teammate Bill Virdon stated, "I'm sorry that Stan is not doing well right now. His health is not real good, but he's had a good, long life, and it's been a pleasant life. And it's sure been good for a lot of people."

Musial has been canonized in St. Louis and loved everywhere. Virdon was right, but he understated it: Musial, the perfect knight, has had a journey through life that has been not a good one, but a great one.

All of Musial's life, he has heeded Rudyard Kipling's words: "If you can fill the unforgiving minute with sixty seconds' worth of distance run, yours is the earth and everything that's in it, and—which is more—you'll be a Man, my son!" In this case, Stan the Man.

# Appendix

# *Records, Stats, and Feats*

In a sport in which success is frequently as ephemeral as the life expectancy of an ice cube under an August sun, Musial shone brightly for several decades. He is a statistics lover's delight.

Take a legion of superb major-leaguers, whittle that group down to an elite battalion of ballplayers, and Musial *still* stands out. His career was, for the most part, a one-way funicular ride, a steady ascension to the top with very few bumps along the way. When Musial retired, he held 17 big-league records as well as 29 NL bests and nine All-Star Game records. In an era when revered records such as the single-season and the career home-run marks have tumbled like dominoes, many of Musial's feats remain hallowed.

Even now, nearly 50 years and who knows how many chemically enhanced players after Musial's retirement, he still ranks among the upper echelon in numerous departments. Rounded off, approximately 20,000 men have played in the majors, and only four of them, all giants of the game, finished among the top 20 for homers, ribbies, and batting average: Ruth, Gehrig, Williams, and Musial.

Musial's lifetime statistics, divided up to determine his average numbers based on a 162-game schedule, are monumental. He was good for 194 hits each season. Further, he averaged 104 runs and runs driven in per year—for his career, he scored almost exactly as many times as he drove in a run, 1,949 runs to 1,951 RBIs. He amassed 100 RBIs 10 times and scored 100 in 11 consecutive seasons.

He led the NL in doubles a record eight times, in extra-base hits a record seven times, and six times he topped the league in hits, slugging, on-base percentage, and total bases. He led in triples and runs five times and twice for RBIs. In addition, he reached the 200-hit plateau on six occasions. Only Aaron, Mays, and Musial (his 6,134 total bases still stand second-best lifetime) racked up more than 6,000 total bases. Musial's on-base percentage stood 84 points above the average hitter of his era, and his slugging percentage (.559) a lofty 151 points above the norm of his time period. He was on base 5,282 times, sixth-best ever. Lifetime, he hit .323 or better in every month of the season. He reached double figures for homers in each and every one of his full seasons, and he even tied the record for the most game-ending home runs, 12.

It's difficult to believe that Musial is somehow underappreciated when one considers this litany of stats: just Aaron and a suspiciously pumped-up Barry Bonds compiled more extra-base hits; only Tris Speaker and Rose hit more doubles; he finished among the league's top five hitters based on batting average a record 17 times, and his lifetime batting average of .331 was so high that since Musial's final day, only one man has ever retired with a better average, Tony Gwynn (.338). Musial hit .310 or better over a stretch of 16 straight seasons, and just two men, Speaker and Cobb, hit .300-plus more times than Musial (17). He hit .326 on the road and .336 at home, even though the mound at Sportsman's Park was 14 inches high, four more than today's standard height.

Just three men—Cobb, Gwynn, and Honus Wagner—won more batting crowns than Musial. His 1,951 RBIs trail just four modern-era players, and a mere seven scored more runs. Musial also trails only Rose, Cobb, and Aaron on the all-time hit list.

Amazingly, Musial struck out fewer than half as many times as he walked (1,599 walks to 696 strikeouts). His strikeout total for 22 years is less than Williams' even though he played three years more than Williams. During an average season, Musial would lift 25 homers and fan only 37 times, an utterly jaw-dropping ratio.

He was a perennial contender for the MVP trophy, winning it three times and finishing second in 1949, 1950, 1951, and 1957. He finished in the top five for MVP voting nine times and in the top 10 on 14 occasions, the most ever. Of his 20 full seasons, defined by having played in more than 115 games, 18 times he was in the top 20 MVP vote getters and on 16 of those occasions he was in the top dozen. What's more, *every* year he had 375-plus at-bats he was in the top 12 except his only 20th-place finish in 1947.

As Bill James noted, there is a tendency for MVP voters to not award that trophy to players more than three times "because the writers don't want to give the award to the same guy every year." James believes Musial was cheated of an MVP in 1952 when Hank Sauer, playing for the .500, fifth-place Cubs (19 ½ games behind Brooklyn), won it. Baseball Reference's website lists Musial as having led the league in 12 offensive categories; Sauer led in two.

Upon his retirement, no player spent more seasons or had more hits while playing for just one team than Musial. Because he averaged more than one hit per game played over his 3,026-game career, if he took an 0-for-4 one day, he knew that by the immutable law of averages that he'd spring back with a 2-for-4 showing. Pirates pitcher Tom Cheney stated his 1960 Pirates team "hoped he got two or three hits in games before [we] faced them because they knew if he'd been shut out, he'd break loose against them."

When it came to naming the greatest hitters he ever saw when he covered the baseball beat on a daily basis, veteran sportswriter John Kuenster said he'd have to hedge a bit and call it a tie between Ted Williams and Musial. "They were two different types of hitters, really. I saw Pete Rose a lot, but Musial had better power."

In the one statistic players insist is the only one that counts, winning, Musial stands tall. His teams won 1,683 times and lost 1,343 times for a win-loss percentage of .556. Not as impressive as Babe Ruth (.605) or Mickey Mantle (.590), but among the best and certainly better than Willie Mays (.546) and Ty Cobb (.541) and a light year better than Rogers Hornsby (.499).

In short, if Musial's career had a theme song, it would have to have been a majestic one, a tune which also conveyed his inexorable march toward greatness—perhaps "Pomp and Circumstance."

# About the Author

Wayne Stewart was born and raised in Donora, Pennsylvania, a town that has produced a handful of big-league baseball players, including Stan Musial and Ken Griffey Sr. and Jr. In fact, Stewart was on the same Donora High School baseball team as Griffey Sr. as a good-glove, no-stick bench player. Stewart now lives in Lorain, Ohio, with his wife Nancy (Panich). They have two sons, Sean and Scott, and one grandchild, Nathan.

Stewart has covered the sports world since 1978 and has written over 500 articles for publications such as *Baseball Digest, USA Today/Baseball Weekly, Boys' Life,* and Beckett Publications. Furthermore, Stewart has appeared as a baseball expert/historian on Cleveland's FOX 8 and on an ESPN Classic television show about Bob Feller. This is his 25th book to date.

# Sources

## Books

Alexander, Charles C. *Our Game*. New York: Henry Holt and Company, Inc., 1991.

Allen, Lee. *Cooperstown Corner*. Cleveland: SABR, 1989.

Allen, Maury. *All Roads Lead to October*. New York: St. Martin's Press, 2000.

———. *You Could Look It Up*. New York: Times Books, 1979.

Barber, Red. *1947—When All Hell Broke Loose in Baseball*. Garden City, NY: Doubleday and Company, Inc., 1982.

Black, Joe. *Ain't Nobody Better Than You: An Autobiography of Joe Black*. Scottsdale, AZ: Ironwood Lithographers, 1983.

Broeg, Bob. *Bob Broeg's Redbirds A Century of Cardinals' Baseball*. St. Louis: River City Publishers Limited, 1981.

Bryson, Bill. *Made in America*. New York: Perennial, 2001.

Bucek, Jeanine, editorial director. *The Baseball Encyclopedia,* Tenth Edition. New York: Macmillan, 1996.

Campanella, Roy. *It's Good to Be Alive*. Lincoln, NE: University of Nebraska Press, 1995.

Carter, Craig, editor. *World Series Records*. St. Louis: The Sporting News, 1979.

Chalberg, John C. *Rickey and Robinson*. Wheeling, IL: Harlan Davidson, Inc., 2000.

Chieger, Bob. *Voices of Baseball: Quotations on the Summer Game*. New York: Atheneum, 1983.

DeVito, Carlo, compiler. *The Ultimate Dictionary of Sports Quotations.* New York: Facts on File, 2001.

———. *Yogi The Life and Times of an American Original.* Chicago: Triumph Books, 2008.

Dickson, Paul. *Baseball's Greatest Quotations.* New York: HarperPerennial, 1992.

Durocher, Leo with Ed Linn *Nice Guys Finish Last.* New York: Simon & Schuster, 1975.

Durso, Joseph. *Baseball and the American Dream.* St. Louis: The Sporting News Publishing Co., 1986.

Eig, Jonathan. *Opening Day.* New York: Simon & Schuster, 2007.

Ezra, David. *Asterisk.* Chicago: Triumph Books, 2008.

Freeman, Dr. Criswell, compiler and editor. *The Wisdom of Old-Time Baseball.* Nashville, TN: Walnut Grove Press, 1996.

Freese, Mel R. *The Glory Years of the St. Louis Cardinals.* St. Louis: Palmerston & Reed Publishing Company, 1999.

———. *The St. Louis Cardinals in the 1940s.* Jefferson, NC: McFarland & Company, Inc., 2007.

Garagiola, Joe. *It's Anybody's Ballgame.* Chicago: Contemporary Books, 1988.

Gershman, Michael. *Diamond: The Evolution of the Ballpark.* New York: Houghton Mifflin Company, 1993.

Getz, Mike. *Baseball's 3000-Hit Men.* Brooklyn, NY: Gemmeg Press, 1982.

Giglio, James, N. *Musial: From Stash to Stan the Man.* Columbia, MO: University of Missouri Press, 2001.

Golenbock, Peter. *The Spirit of St. Louis.* New York: Avon Books, 2000.

———. *Wrigleyville.* New York: St. Martin's Press, 1996.

Goodman, Irv. *Stan the Man Musial.* New York: Bartholomew House, Inc., 1961.

Grabowski, John. *Stan Musial.* New York: Chelsea House Publishers, 1993.

Grossinger, Richard, and Kevin Kerrane, editors. *Into the Temple of Baseball.* Berkeley, CA: Celestial Arts, 1990.

Halberstam, David. *The Breaks of the Game.* New York: Knopf, 1981.

———. *Summer of '49.* New York: Avon Books, 1989.

Heine, Marc. *Poland.* New York: Hippocrene, 1987.

Helya, John. *Lords of the Realm.* New York: Villard Books, 1994.

Herman, Bruce. *St. Louis Cardinals Yesterday and Today*. Lincolnwood, IL: West Side Publishing, 2008.

Higbe, Kirby, with Martin Quigley. *The High Hard One*. New York: Viking Press, 1967.

Hollander, Zander, editor. *Great American Athletes of the 20th Century*. New York: Random House, 1966.

Hoppel, Joe, coeditor-writer. *Baseball: A Doubleheader Collection of Facts, Feats, and Firsts*. New York: Galahad Books, 1994.

Jacobson, Steve. Carrying Jackie's Torch. Chicago: Lawrence Hill Books, 2007.

James, Bill. *The New Bill James Historical Baseball Abstract*. New York: Free Press, 2001.

Kahn, Roger. *Beyond the Boys of Summer*. New York: McGraw-Hill, 2005.

———. *The Era 1947–1957*. New York: Ticknor & Fields 1993.

———. *Memories of Summer*. New York: Hyperion, 1997.

———. *A Season in the* Sun. New York: Harper & Row, 1977.

Kiner, Ralph. *Baseball Forever*. Chicago: Triumph Books, 2004.

King, Larry. *Why I Love Baseball*. Beverly Hills, CA: New Millennium Press, 2004.

Krantz, Les. *Reel Baseball*. New York: Doubleday, 2006.

Kuenster, John, ed. *The Best of Baseball Digest*. Chicago: Ivan Dee, 2006.

Lansche, Jerry. *Stan "The Man" Musial: Born to Be a Ballplayer*. Dallas: Taylor Publishing Company, 1994.

Lowry, Philip J. *Green Cathedrals*. Cooperstown, NY: SABR, 1986.

Magee, David, and Philip Shirley. *Sweet Spot*. Chicago: Triumph Books, 2009.

Maraniss, David. *Clemente*. New York: Simon & Schuster, 2006.

Mazer, Bill, with Stan and Shirley Fischler. *Bill Mazer's Amazin' Baseball Book*. New York: Zebra Books, 1990.

McCarver, Tim edited with Jim Moskovitz and Danny Peary. *Tim McCarver's DiamondGems*. New York; McGraw-Hill, 2008.

McCarver, Tim, and Danny Peary. *Tim McCarver's Baseball for Brain Surgeons and Other Fans*. New York: Villard Books, 1998.

McCarver, Tim, with Phil Pepe. *Few and Chosen*. Chicago: Triumph Books, 2003.

McCarver, Tim, with Ray Robinson. *Oh, Baby, I Love It*. New York: Villard Books, 1987.

Mead, William B. *Even the Browns*. Chicago: Contemporary Books, Inc., 1978.

Michener, James. *Sports in America*. New York: Random House, 1976.

Morris, Peter. *A Game of Inches*. Chicago: Ivan R. Dee, 2006.

Musial, Stan, and Bob Broeg. *The Man Stan: Musial, Then and Now*. St. Louis: The Bethany Press, 1977.

Nash, Bruce, and Allan Zullo. *The Baseball Hall of Shame 2*. New York: Pocket Books, 1986.

Nelson, Kevin. *The Greatest Stories Ever Told About Baseball*. New York: Perigee Books, New York, 1986.

Oakley, J. Ronald. *Baseball's Last Golden Age, 1946-1960*. Jefferson, NC: McFarland & Company, Inc., 1994.

Obojski, Robert, and Wayne Stewart. *Out-of-Left-Field Baseball Trivia*. New York: Sterling, 2004.

Okrent, Daniel, and Steve Wulf. *Baseball Anecdotes*. New York: Perennial Library, 1989.

Peary, Danny, ed. *We Played the Game*. New York: Black Dog & Levanthal Publishers, Inc., 1994.

Phillips, John. *The Cardinals vs. the Red Sox: The World Series of 1946*. Perry, GA: Capital Publishing Company, 1997.

Reichler, Joseph. *30 Years of Baseball's Great Moments*. New York: Crown Publishers, Inc., 1974.

Ribowsky, Mark. *The Complete History of the Home Run*. New York: Citadel Press, 2003.

———. *Don't Look Back*. New York: Simon & Schuster, 1994.

Ritter, Lawrence S. *The Story of Baseball*. New York: William Morrow and Company, 1983.

Ritter, Lawrence S. and Donald Honig. *The Image of Their Greatness*. 3rd ed. New York: Crown Publishers, Inc., 1992.

Roberts, Russell. *Ellis Island*.

Robinson, Ray. *Stan Musial: Baseball's Durable "Man."* New York: G. P. Putnam's Sons, 1963.

Robinson, Ray, and Christopher Jennison. *Greats of the Game*. New York: Harry N. Abrams, Inc., 2005.

Rockwell, Bart. *World's Strangest Baseball Stories*. Watermill Press, 1993.

Rubin, Louis D. Jr. *The Quotable Baseball Fanatic*. New York: The Lyons Press, 2000.

Rushin, Steve. "The Selling of Sports" from *The Best of Sports Illustrated*. New York: Sports Illustrated, 1996.

Rust, Arthur Jr. *Legends*. New York: McGraw-Hill, 1989.

Smith, Red. "The Bending Branch" from *Sports Illustrated Baseball*. New York: Crescent Books, 1997.

———. *Red Smith on Baseball*. Chicago: Ivan R. Dee, 2000.

Smith, Ron. *The Sporting News Selects Baseball's Greatest Players*. St. Louis: The Sporting News Publishing Co., 1998.

Snyder, Brad. *A Well-Paid Slave*. New York: Viking, 2006.

Solomon, Burt. *The Baseball Timeline*. New York: DK Publishing, Inc., 2001.

Stark, Jayson. *Stark Truth*. Chicago: Triumph Books, 2007.

Stewart, Wayne. *Fathers, Sons, and Baseball*. Guilford, CT: The Lyons Press, 2002.

———. *Hitting Secrets of the Pros*. New York: McGraw-Hill, 2004.

———. *Pitching Secrets of the Pros*. New York: McGraw-Hill, 2004.

Stump, Al. *Cobb: A Biography*. Chapel Hill NC: Algonquin Books of Chapel Hill, 1996.

Sullivan, George. *Sluggers*. New York: Atheneum, 1991.

Vincent, David W, editor. *Home Runs in the Old Ballparks*. Cleveland: The Society for American Baseball Research, 1995.

Vincent, Fay. *The Last Commissioner*. New York: Simon & Schuster, 2002.

———. *We Would Have Played For Nothing*. New York: Simon & Schuster, 2008.

Vricella, Mario. *The St. Louis Cardinals—the First Century*. New York: Vantage Press, 1992.

Ward, Geoffrey, C. and Ken Burns. *Baseball: An Illustrated History*. New York: Alfred A. Knopf, 1994.

Will, George F. *Men at Work*. New York: Macmillan Publishing Company, 1990

## Booklets

Clark, John P. *Donora Diamond Jubilee, 1901–1976*. Borough of Donora, Donora Chamber of Commerce. Locally printed, 1976.

Clark, John P., and Ruth Ann Yatsko. *Donora Centennial, 1901–2001*. Monessen, PA: The Valley Independent, 2001.

Jozwiak, Dorothy. *Golden Jubilee of the Church of St. Hyacinth*. Monessen, PA: Kovach Printers, 1959.

Karcher, Clara. *Polish Immigrants Build Legacy of Church.*

Raitano, Barbara A., General Manager. *The Last 100 Years.* Monessen, PA: *The Valley Independent*, 1999.

## Films and Video

Ashley, Thomas J. *The Legend of Stan The Man Musial.* TMM, Inc., New York, 1990.

Belinfante, Geoff. *The History of Baseball.* MLB Productions, 1987.

Burns, Ken. *Baseball.* Washington, DC, WETA-TV, Florentine Films, 1994.

Gavant, David. *All Century Team.* MLB Productions, 2000.

Greenberg, Ross. *When It Was a Game 3.* HBO Video, 2000.

HBO. *Costas Now.* HBO Production, 2007.

Moskovitz, Jim. *The Tim McCarver Show.* JMJ Films Production, c. 2008 (episode with Robin Roberts)

Phoenix Communications Group. *St. Louis Cardinals Vintage World Series Film.* Major League Baseball Properties, Inc., 1993.

Rotfeld, Berl. *Stan Musial…"The Man."* Legends Enterprises, Inc., 2000.

Samels, Mark. *American Experience* "Roberto Clemente" WGBH Educational Foundation, 2008.

Scherr, Mitchell. *100 Years of the World Series.* MLB Productions, 2003.

Schwartz, Larry. *SportsCentury* (Musial biography). ESPN, Inc., 2001.

Tollin, Michael. *Hank Aaron Chasing the Dream.* TBS Productions, Inc., 1995.

Verna, Tony. *Great Sports Legends.* A Sports Legends Inc. Production, 1973.

WQED-TV. *The Polish-Americans.* Pittsburgh.

## Newspapers

*Brooklyn Eagle*

*Chicago Daily Tribune*

*Cleveland Plain Dealer*

*Daily News*

*The Evening Genius*

*The Herald-American*

*New York Post*

*New York Times*

*The Pittsburgh Post-Gazette*

*The Pittsburgh Press*
*Pittsburgh Tribune-Review*
*Sunday News*
*The Valley Independent*

## Magazines

Bodley, Hal. "Cards Draw Comparisons to 1942 World Champs." *USA Today* (October 15, 2004).

Breslin, Jimmy. "The Town That Spawns Athletes." *Saturday Evening Post* (October 15, 1955).

Busch, August A., as told to Milton Gross. "Baseball's Got Me." *Saturday Evening Post* (May 18, 1957).

Cohane, Tim. "Changing Days of Stan Musial." *Look* (April 7, 1964).

Cutter, Bob. "The Stan Musial Story." [no other data available]

Davids, L. Robert. *Baseball Research Journal 1983* ed. Material taken from "Baseball Cartoon Memories" by Robert Cole

Goold , Derrick. "Still 'the Man.'" *Baseball Digest* (July 2007).

Heinz, W. C. "And Now There Are Eight." *Life* (May 26, 1958).

———. "Stan Musial's Last Day." *Life* (October 11, 1963).

Kreuz, Jim. "How Mantle and Musial Fared as High School Athletes." *Baseball Digest* (December, 1994).

Kuenster, John. "Stan The Man Has Never Lost His Love of The Game." *Baseball Digest* (July 2008).

Leggett, William. "Stanley, the General Manager." *Sports Illustrated* (March 20, 1967).

Nelson, Scott. "Individual Records by Decades." From *The Baseball Research Journal, Number 29.* Edited by Mark Alvarez Cleveland: SABR, 2000.

Paxton, Harry T. "A Visit With Stan Musial." *Saturday Evening Post* (April 19, 1958).

Schlossberg, Dan. "Stan Musial." *Baseball Digest* (December 2001).

Shane, Ted. "Veeck—The Barnum of Baseball." *Baseball Magazine* (April 1952).

Stockton, J. Roy. "Rookie of the Year." *Saturday Evening Post* (September 12, 1942).

Warburton, Paul. "Stan Musial." From *The Baseball Research Journal*, 30. Cleveland: The Society for American Baseball Research, 2001.

No author listed. "Brooklyn Saw the Day Stan Became 'The Man.'" *USA Today Sports Weekly* June 17–23, 2009.

No author listed. "Old Pros Take on Trimming." *Life* March 21, 1960.

No author listed. "That Man." *Time* (September 5, 1949)

## Websites

http://www.americanchronicle.com/articles/yb/132977193

http://stlcardinals.scout.com

www.baseball-almanac.com

www.baseballhalloffame.org

www.baseballreference.com

www.bioproj.sabr.org

www.crackerjack.com

www.jsonline.com

www.ksdk.com/news/local/story.aspx?storyid=180264

www.mysticgames.com

www.nwanews.com/adg/Sports/264233/

www.palmbeachpost.com/marlins/content/sports/epaper/2009/07/13/
0713musial.html

www.sportingnews.com

www.sportsillustrated.cnn.com

www.stltoday.com

www.thebaseballpage.com

www.time.com

www.travel-watch.com

www.wpial.com

## Other Sources

*Fourteenth Census of the United States: 1920—Population*, Department of
Commerce

Microsoft Encarta96 Encyclopedia

*The Oradon*, Volume Seven, 1930. Senior Class of Donora High School,
1930 Donora, PA.

*Varsity Dragon*. June 1938. Senior Class, Donora Senior High School:
Donora, PA.